Programming
Microprocessors

Programming Microprocessors

By M. W. Mcmurran

TAB BOOKS
Blue Ridge Summit, Pa. 17214

FIRST EDITION

FIRST PRINTING—MARCH 1977

Copyright © 1977 by TAB BOOKS

Printed in the United States
of America

Library of Congress Cataloging in Publication Data

McMurran, Marshall
    Programming Microprocessors

    Bibliography: p.
    Includes index.
    1. Microprocessors-Programming.   I. Title.
QA76. 6. M326   001. 6'42   77-3736
ISBN 0-8306-7985-5
ISBN 0-8306-6985-X pbk.

ACKNOWLEDGMENTS

I wish to thank the engineers and management of Rockwell International Electronics Operations, who provided valuable source information, and in particular, colleagues from the Microelectronic Device Division, who prepared the programs from which some of the AMP examples were adapted. I wish also to acknowledge the use of literature from Motorola and Intel Corporations, which was taken as source data for the discussions of the M6800, MP/L, and the 8080. And I thank Shirley Pairish, Ihla Crowley, and Jane Hornback for their invaluable aid in preparing the manuscript.

1969085

Contents

Bibliography   243

Appendices

Index   275

Introduction

It is the intent of this book to impart a basic understanding of microprocessor configurations and functions, and to describe the requirements and techniques of microprocessor programming in sufficient detail that any user may, in conjunction with the literature for a specific microprocessor, define a useful system and prepare working programs with little difficulty.

Emphasis has been placed here on describing the interaction of the hardware and software systems, the fundamentals of processor arithmetic, and numerical conversions both to and from readable decimal numbers and their equivalent machine representations. Also discussed in some detail are scaling techniques for magnitude control of fixed-point processor data, the basics of floating-point arithmetic, and the efficient use of instruction and data storage. Such important elements are often under-emphasized today by programmers and programming instructors who have come to depend upon powerful compilers using near-English or near-algebraic programming languages. But many would-be programmers do not have unlimited access to a large-scale computer system with almost unlimited memory. Though such compilers can and often do play an important role in later stages of microprocessor programming and system design, it is the purpose of this book to bridge the gap between the elementary microprocessor programming techniques and the more sophisticated techniques that are becoming available. A good understanding of a microprocessor's features and limitations, as well as established programming techniques, will make it much easier to write simple programs and to make best use of advanced computer-oriented programming systems.

The evolution of microprocessors and programming techniques goes back over many years, and it might prove helpful to gain a brief overview to place things in the proper perspective. Digital computational hardware has been in use since the days of the clever Chinese mathematicians who used simple beads as memory devices, although in fact all arithmetic operations were done in the head of the operator. Actually, the first successful attempt to mechanize arithmetic processes was made by Charles Babbage, who, in 1830, designed and built a "calculating engine" to compute artillery tables. This "engine" consisted of sets of gears and counters that approximated the generation of table entries by use of finite differences. The earliest *electronic* digital computer, the ENIAC, was developed in 1945 by Eckert and Mauckley at the Moore School of Engineering. This machine consisted of an arithmetic center and a memory that stored information in flip-flop bistable registers for rapid retrieval and use by the arithmetic and control portion. This was not a stored-program machine, however. The first truly general-purpose machine, called the EDSAC, was built by a group headed by M. V. Wilkes at Cambridge University in England. The Wilkes team was the first to use assemblers and subroutine libraries, as well as making other contributions to programming techniques and procedures.

The development of other digital computers came rapidly and can be thought of as occurring in four "rounds." The first round included the development of large and very expensive scientific and business computer systems such as the IBM 700 series, Univac 1103, etc. The second round included medium- or small-scale machines that were intended for use by scientific and engineering organizations; these sold in the price range of $50,000 to $100,000. The third round resulted from engineering efforts directed toward increasing inherent reliability, reducing size, and providing "building blocks" or modules that could be purchased separately and combined to form a single system.

Coincident with the latter part of the first round was the development of compilation programs to ease the programming burden. And by the mid 1960s, the old 256-word cathode-ray-tube memory in the Bureau of Standards' Western Automatic Computer (SWAC), an impressive machine built in the early 1950s, gave way to a 128,000-word high-speed core memory.

The fourth round was driven by the ability of industry to provide small, reliable, and inexpensive semiconductor devices, each containing thousands of transistors and diodes (so-called large scale integration, or LSI). This then paved the way for the powerful but small minicomputers.

The microprocessor (or microcomputer) is a very recent configuration based on the organization of the minicomputer, but using only LSI for memory and logic electronics. A minimally configured microprocessor system consists of a power source, a central processing unit, two memories and an input/output mechanism with interfacing electronics. Either the central processor or a memory device with well over 1000 storage elements can be contained on one silicon chip approximately 0.2 inch square.

The technology permitting this high circuit density was initially spurred on by the requirements of military and space programs during the 1960s, and has grown phenomenally in the last five years. With the broadening production base, primarily in the United States and the Far East, the unit cost of a useful set of microcomputer devices had dropped from around $1500 in 1972 to approximately $150 for equivalent computational capability by late 1975. Even more recently, several central processor units have dropped in price from $60 to $20 each for small quantities. The result of this kind of price erosion is that the computational power derived from a roomful of hardware in the 1950s is now available to a user on a few silicon chips for about $100, with several complete single-chip microprocessor systems already beginning to reach the marketplace.

The result of this relatively inexpensive computational tool is a tremendously expanding interest in designing and programming microprocessor systems for an unbelievably wide variety of applications. And, of course, experimenters and hobbyists have quickly welcomed the microprocessor as yet another sophisticated toy evolving from our technological society. But whether a mere curiosity or an important component in an industrial system, the microprocessor has found solid footing in today's world, and both the serious-minded experimenter and the modern engineer need to know the essential architectural characteristics and programming techniques of these microprocessors in order to achieve the computational functions they desire.

M. W. McMurran

Chapter 1
Basic Microprocessor Organization and Functions

The systems described here are called *microcomputers* about as often as they are called *microprocessors*. Traditionally, the term *microprocessor* was reserved to describe the *central processing unit* (CPU), which contains various registers used to store and manipulate numbers and instructions, thereby performing arithmetic and logic operations. Present usage, however, tends toward calling an entire assembly of devices a microprocessor since the CPU cannot by itself do useful work. Thus the CPU is considered just a part of a larger microprocessor system.

Microprocessors are assembled from a wide variety of integrated circuit (IC) building blocks and so can assume an even wider variety of useful configurations. This variety, however, does not lend itself to an introductory discussion of microprocessors, so it is desirable to first select a representative system as the basis of discussion. Variations of this basic system, as they occur in real systems, will then be treated as modifications of the central theme.

The basic system we will use is based on the Rockwell PPS-4 system. We will call this configuration *AMP*—standing for *A Micro-Processor*. The AMP system illustrated in Fig. 1-1 is made up of a central processor unit (CPU) that is a large-scale integration (LSI) device performing the arithmetic and logic functions, a metal-oxide semiconductor (MOS)

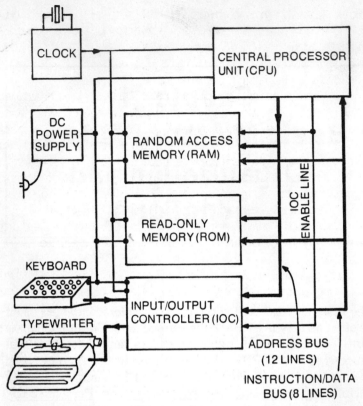

Fig. 1-1. AMP organization and data flow.

read-only memory (ROM) used for permanently storing programs and data, a MOS random-access memory (RAM) used as a "scratchpad" memory for temporarily storing modified instructions and results from calculations, and an input/output controller (IOC) used to direct and format data traveling between the CPU and the outside world.

The processor also needs an appropriate power supply, so the AMP will use +5 and −12 DC supplies. A crystal-controlled clock provides the basic timing source and completes the electrical components. The basic clock rate is 200 kHz and is separated into four phases for control of the internal MOS logic. For input/output the AMP uses a keyboard and a simple pointer.

Data flow in this system is via two information channels, or *buses*. This configuration requires individual devices to be smart enough to talk only during proper time slots. Since the clock signals are common to all devices, system synchronization is relatively easy to achieve. We will consider all devices to be PMOS (P-channel MOS), though other options would be NMOS, CMOS, or I^2L. A description of these various technologies is given in Chapter 13.

The microprocessor obeys a set of operating rules similar to those of any stored-program digital computer. Processor functions are determined by the CPU under control of a set of instruction patterns, most of which are permanently stored in the ROM. These patterns are decoded by the CPU, resulting in the execution of an operation belonging to one of the following instruction classes or groups, which include some examples of the instruction types and characteristics of each group.

Arithmetic and Logic Instructions. Examples: Add two binary numbers. Logically combine two binary numbers (see Chapter 3).

Data Transfer Instructions. Examples: Load data from memory into an internal CPU register. Store data from an internal CPU register into memory. Exchange data between two registers. Load data from instruction memory (ROM) into a CPU register. (These instructions are termed *immediates*.)

Control Transfer Instructions. Examples: Take next instruction out of normal sequence if content of selected register is less than zero. Skip one instruction if a particular bit equals one.

Input/Output Instructions. These instructions are strongly dependent upon the type of processor used. Examples: Load *n* bits (binary digits) from an external device into a CPU register, or directly into memory. Read single-bit input lines and transfer the data into a CPU register. Transfer *n* bits of output data with the appropriate timing control to an external device.

The various permitted or recognized instructions that a microprocessor will accept is referred to as the *instruction set*. The PPS instruction set, which is the basis for the AMP instructions, is quite flexible and often complex. For example, the execution of some of these instructions will cause as many as four independent operations to be performed simultaneously.

To reduce the work of decoding the bit patterns that represent these instructions, the CPU will normally first determine the class, and then the specific instruction type within the class. As a result, the bit patterns defining instructions within classes generally have something in common. In addition to the instruction groups introduced here, microprocessors more sophisticated than the AMP have instructions that further extend the processor's capability. Notable are:

Shift Instructions. Most microprocessors have the capability of shifting the binary contents of a register, usually the accumulator, either right a fixed number of spaces or left a fixed or variable number of spaces to provide for the arithmetic operations discussed in Chapters 5 and 6. The simple instruction list chosen for the AMP contains only a right shift command, and this makes programming the AMP a bit more involved than programming some other processors.

Stacking Instructions. A stack is a series of registers connected together so that data enters and leaves through only the first, or top, register. Stacks are generally used for storing reference addresses, usually the next address of an instruction occuring before the microprocessor was interrupted for some reason. Stacking instructions are usually of two types: *push* instructions store a new address on the top of the stack, pushing any other addresses deeper into the stack registers, while *pop* instructions raise the addresses in the stack registers to expose the next in order at the top. This procedure permits the orderly storing and removal of address data, and it is discussed further in Chapters 11 and 12.

Multiplication and Division. These functions are now being built into microprocessor hardware as new processors are introduced, thus significantly adding to the effective speed of these machines. Multiplication and division operations are performed by automatically creating strings of instructions (subroutines). Each time the function is needed, control is transferred to these subroutines. Multiplication is then mechanized by a controlled set of successive additions, and division by a controlled set of subtractions. This permits 20 to 100 instructions to be automatically executed for each multiply or divide instruction, depending upon the precision needed and the idiosyncrasies of the processor used. The resulting trade-off penalty in the excecution time of this method when compared with a separate hardware mechanization is often quite severe, but of course the approach is simpler and cheaper.

MICROPROCESSOR CONFIGURATION

The microprocessor consists of many components whose functions differ to perform specific tasks. Because the CPU is the heart of any microprocessor system, we will first examine the CPU and its internal elements in some detail. This will be followed by a discussion of the remaining major components of the microprocessor system.

The CPU. The AMP CPU contains registers whose contents determine the storage locations of the next instruction to be executed. When a specific address register is accessed, the CPU places that address on the address bus, and the ROM connected to that bus is commanded to fetch the instruction in memory stored at that address. This instruction is returned to the CPU over the instruction/data bus. The CPU then decodes the instruction to extract the functional data and if necessary determines the location of the *operand*—the data to be worked on. The CPU causes the operand (if any) to be read from the particular ROM or RAM where it is stored, executes the operation indicated by the instruction, and determines the address of the next instruction. Figure 1-2 indicates the various CPU functional elements and shows the direction of data flow with arrowheads.

Program (P) and Data Address (B) Registers. These registers hold the addresses of the program instruction to be executed and the data to be extracted from memory. The address pattern in P is placed on the address bus and transmitted to the ROM. The ROM responds by placing the encoded instruction (or data in the case of *immediate* instructions) on the lines of the instruction/data bus. The contents of the P register is normally incremented by one each cycle, providing for stepping through the program sequence. But this sequence can be broken by executing a *branch* command or by unconditionally breaking off the sequence. In these cases we override the address incrementation by executing special instructions designed for this purpose. The B register supplies address control to direct data transfer between the CPU and the RAM. The content of B is modified under program control and is set to zero on application of power.

Clock Decode. This section interprets the basic clock signals and distributes them to the CPU registers, providing proper timing and synchronization.

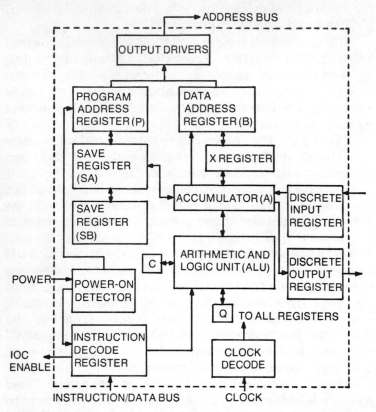

Fig. 1-2. AMP central processor (CPU) block diagram and data flow.

Save Registers (SA and SB). While program control is temporarily passed to a subroutine (see Chapter 4), these special registers provide memory for holding the return instruction address. The SA register also communicates with the accumulator to provide for more than two levels of subroutine control.

ALU and Accumulator (A). Together these units perform all arithmetic and logic functions. The accumulator in the AMP is 8 bits long, and this defines the basic length of the data *word* or *byte* that a the microprocessor handles.

X Register. This 8-bit register can communicate with both the B register and the accumulator, providing intermediate storage for arithmetic and data information.

Carry (C) Register. This register is 1 bit long. It contains the final carry resulting from an addition operation and enables the processor to work on data in integral multiples of 8 bits (with a bit of extra effort). The information held in C may also be used in branching operation.

Q Register. This is also a 1-bit register. It holds the state of the carry after the first 4 bits have been processed, permitting the addition and subtraction of numbers in a binary-coded-decimal format (see Chapters 2 and 4).

Instruction Decode Register. This register makes sense out of the instruction bit patterns, according to the predetermined logic of the CPU. (We will discuss this in some detail in Chapter 4.) The complete AMP instruction set description and timing can be found in Appendix E.

IOC Enable Signal. This provides control to the IOC device for input/output data transfers, and advises the RAM when an input/output operation is about to occur so it is prepared to respond.

Discrete Input and Output Registers. These are each 4 bits long. The output register is under program control and provides commands to the IOC, causing it to accept keyboard inputs or to take data from the instruction/data bus and send it to the printer. The discrete input register, when sampled by the program, may be used as an indicator of "printer ready" or "data available" from the IOC.

Output Drivers. These perform signal amplification and conditioning for information to be sent off-chip because of the added loads imposed by chip-to-chip communication.

Power-On Detector. This provides for starting a desired computational sequence when power is applied to the CPU. The discrete registers are set to all zeros (off). The CPU is placed into the *halt* mode by setting the content of the instruction decode register to a halt or no-operation configuration. The program address register is set to all zeros, to prepare for reading the first instruction from location 000 of ROM-0.

THE ROMS

The AMP has two ROMs (ROM-1 and ROM-2) into which information has been permanently written, but from which information can be read many times. ROMs are used to hold program instructions and data that need never be changed. Normally about 95% of the instruction memory in large computers falls into this category, but not all, because of the necessity to alter programs. However, *all* AMP instructions will be taken from ROMs since the penalty for this is small if given a reasonable capability for address modification. The fraction of ROM data storage needed is quite dependent upon the program structure, but is generally about 10% of the total data requirement. Some microprocessors permit the addition of RAMs for program storage, but we will consider this to be merely an embellishment of the basic AMP system.

The primary reason for using a ROM instead of a RAM is one of compactness, with a secondary advantage of data integrity, since the ROM configuration is established by the use of one or more unique masks during the device processing. Once fabricated and tested, the probability of errors emanating from the ROM is quite small. ROMs suffer no permanent upset from all but the most severe power transients.

The programmer must be very sure of the accuracy of his program before committing the code to mask fabrication, which is a moderately expensive step. To aid him in program checkout, other memory types are made available by the manufacturer, which are functionally interchangeable with a ROM but the information stored can be altered. Most readers will probably find that one of the alterable memories will serve their purposes quite adequately, so they may never use a

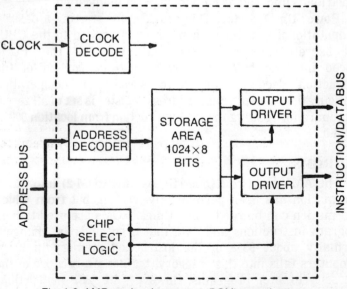

Fig. 1-3. AMP read-only memory (ROM) organization.

ROM. These are called PROMs (Programmable ROMs) and are electrically programmable. Some popular PROMs are erasable (all locations set to zero) by exposure to ultraviolet light.

The AMP ROM functional configuration can be seen in Fig. 1-3. The ROM is an 8192-bit unit organized in 1024 8-bit groups. The selected ROM must respond to an inquiry from the CPU only during specific time slots. This timing control is accomplished by the *clock decode* block, which identifies the proper time, using the common clocking signal as reference. Since fixed information is stored in the ROM (coefficients for evaluating trigonometric functions, addressing and book-keeping constants, scale factors, etc.), the data flow must be handled in a manner to prevent confusing the numerical information from program instruction. This is accomplished by identifying a class of data transfer instructions that cause the ROM byte immediately following the instruction code to be steered to the accumulator.

ROM addressing is accomplished first by the chip select, which determines when a particular ROM is being asked to supply data. (In the AMP there are only two ROMs, but for most real processors, several ROMs are likely to be used, requiring each to be able to identify when it is spoken to.) Once having selected the proper ROM, the particular 8-bit group desired must be identified. The address of this group is transmitted from the CPU to the ROM and is put into the form of X-Y coordinates by the address decoder. It is by determining this intersection that the ROM selects the addressed information.

The storage area contains a pattern of 8192 1's and 0's in an orderly format that simplifies reading the proper 8-bit groups when selected. Because signals that are used to control and transfer data within the ROM chip are not normally adequate to provide reliable transmission between chips, output drivers are provided.

The RAM

While it is proper to consider the RAM a true random-access memory, the ROM is also random access insofar as reading is concerned. It is a bit of a misnomer to distinguish the two memory configurations in this fashion, but the acronyms have stuck and are unlikely to change. The AMP

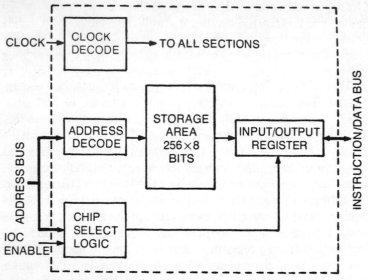

Fig. 1-4. AMP random-access memory (RAM) organization.

RAM contains 2048 bits of storage organized in 256 8-bit groups. When commanded, information is transferred to the CPU accumulator in one clock phase time. This is accomplished by the RAM placing the 8-bit content of the addressed location in the RAM output registers, which in turn place the data in parallel on the 8 lines of the instruction data bus.

The functional configuration of the RAM is equivalent to that of the ROM. The similarities can be seen from examining Fig. 1-3 and 1-4. Differences lie in the storage area, in the clock decode, and the input/output register which, unlike the ROM, must handle incoming data as well as outgoing.

The RAM storage area is not as densely packed as that of a ROM, and this results because of the larger number of transistors required to construct each memory cell in the RAM. For equal amounts of memory storage, a RAM needs about four times as much chip area as a ROM.

Clocking is also somewhat different. The RAM must receive and supply data during a different time slot than the ROM, so the RAM clock decoder looks for different clock phasing.

Clock

The AMP clock, also called the clock generator (see Fig. 1-5), provides two synchronous wave forms (A Clock and $\overline{B}$

Clock) which control the timing of the microprocessor. The device has an internal oscillator stabilized by a 3.6 MHz quartz crystal. The crystal frequency is divided by 18 in the count-down controller to obtain the basic 200 kHz clock frequency. Drivers are provided as in the other devices to amplify clock signal levels, assuring reliable system performance.

Input/Output Controller (IOC)

The AMP IOC (Fig. 1-6), provides 8 static (discrete) outputs and accepts 8 inputs. It controls the data exchange with the peripheral keyboard and teletypewriter mechanisms. The IOC interprets an operation code supplied by the ROM under control of the CPU, to control data flow to and from the input receiver, output register and the CPU accumulator. Output drivers are used to provide proper amplification. Once set, data remains on the output lines until altered, and remains in the input receiver until transferred, thus capturing the latest keyboard inputs. Data is transferred either by copying the content of the CPU accumulator into the output register for ultimate destination to the teletypewriter, or transmission of the contents of the input receiver into the accumulator. Information transfers are initiated by the CPU using the IOC enable signal from the CPU instruction decode register. If the decoded instruction is other than an input/output instruction, data memory (RAM) is selected and the IOC enable is not turned on.

These packaged MOS devices comprising the AMP are interconnected by means of a printed circuit board containing

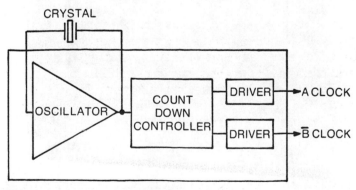

Fig. 1-5. AMP clock block diagram.

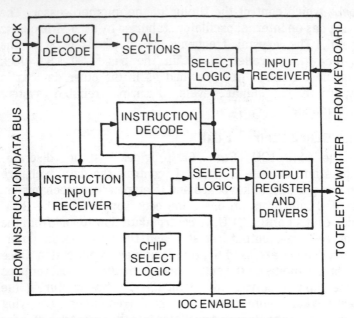

Fig. 1-6. AMP input/output controller (IOC) block diagram.

the necessary electrical paths formed from etched copper conductors. Figure 1-7 is a photograph of a Rockwell system assembled on a printed board.

Fig. 1-7. Microprocessor ALU assembly on two-sided printed circuit board. (Courtesy Rockwell International)

Summary

The AMP System is not complex. It is illustrative of the simpler microprocessor configurations. Because of the distributed and cooperative nature of the bus-oriented organizations, data flow may at first appear loosely structured, with many devices talking on the same "party line." But the CPU is the traffic director; the synchronized timing insures that the messages requested or transmitted by the CPU are on the buses at exactly the proper time to be handled by the proper devices. Next we turn out attention to the language of digital equipment—the binary and associated number systems.

Chapter 2
Number Systems

The decimal number system is considered by nearly all people to be natural and easy to use. Further, it allows for the implementation of an orderly set of arithmetic rules. The decimal system is undoubtedly a consequence of our having five fingers on each hand, which permitted our ancestors, as well as most of us when we were children, to count to five, twice, before we ran out of fingers and had to do something more advanced to count higher. That "something" involved the development of a set of rules that let us mark the number of times that we had exceeded the counting capacity of ten fingers, while not increasing the number of digits or "admissible marks" used so that the same arithmetic could be used throughout the system. The Romans did not recognize the utility of a *positional system* until it was too late, and they were tied to their cumbersome Roman numerals. The decimal system has served us well, at least until digital computers made the scene.

The language of microprocessors is the language of switches. A properly operating switch is either open or closed. A properly operating MOS gate is either conducting or not conducting. This style of operation allows only two stable states. A stable *on* state is normally designated by a *1* and stable *off* stage by a *0*. *Stable* is used here to mean that the switch is indeed fully open or closed, or the gate is either fully turned on or off. If we try to sample the state during a

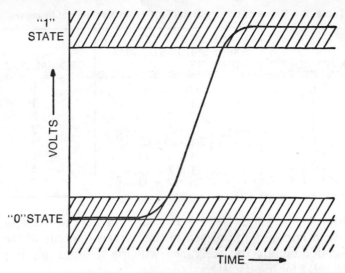

Fig. 2-1. Zero-to-one transition waveform.

transition period, we cannot reliably determine the state the element is in. In the case of MOS or other semiconductor switches, the transition from a 0 to a 1 will probably look like Fig. 2-1. We will consider only those cases where the existence of the proper state has been fully established.

BINARY INTEGERS

We are now faced with the problem of using these bistable, or *binary*, states as vehicles for computations that we can relate to our familiar decimal system. Because we have available in the binary system only the symbols 0 and 1, and desire a positional notation structure, we count as we would in decimal, but can use only the 0 or 1 before we exhaust the symbol set; we must create new digit positions (columns) to continue counting. The value of a 1 in the new higher order column is then 2 times the value of a 1 in the old.

Table 2-1 indicates the binary counting sequence and the equivalence of binary and decimal integers. The right-most binary integer is multiplied by 2^0 or 1; the next 2^1 or 2; the next by 2^2 or 4, and so on. These numbers are then added to obtain the decimal equivalent. As an example, the binary number 1001101 can be expressed as

$$(1 \times 2^6) + (0 \times 2^5) + (0 \times 2^4) +$$
$$(1 \times 2^3) + (1 \times 2^2) + (0 \times 2^1) + (1 \times 2^0)$$

Table. 2-1. Value of Binary Digits Expressed as Decimal Numbers

BINARY COUNT	VALUE OF BINARY DIGITS EXPRESSED AS DECIMAL NUMBERS	DECIMAL COUNT
0	(0)	0
1	(1)	1
10	(2 + 0)	2
11	(2 + 1)	3
100	(4 + 0 + 0)	4
101	(4 + 0 + 1)	5
110	(4 + 2 + 0)	6
111	(4 + 2 + 1)	7

or $64 + 0 + 0 + 8 + 4 + 0 + 1 = 75_{10}$. (In order to distinguish between numbers expressed in the various systems where a misunderstanding is likely, we will use a subscript, 10 for decimal, 2 for binary, etc.)

BINARY ARITHMETIC

Binary addition (Table 2-2) is quite simple. A complete table of binary summation performed bit-by-bit is also shown in Table 2-3, which includes all possible combinations of addend, augend, and carry. The state of the carry determines any addition to be made into the next higher-order column. Table 2-3 can be simplified by observing that the order of addition is commutative, that is $0 + 1 = 1 + 0$, and as a consequence, only four entries are needed to generate all unique sum and carry combinations.

Adding two binary numbers is illustrated by the following example:

$$
\begin{array}{r}
100010000 \rbrace \text{carry digit (initially 0)} \\
204_{10} = 11001100_2 \\
+\ \underline{170_{10}} = +\underline{10101010_2} \\
374_{10} = 101110110_2
\end{array}
$$

Table 2-2. Binary Addition Table

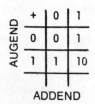

	+	0	1
AUGEND	0	0	1
	1	1	10

ADDEND

28

Table 2-3. Two-Argument Binary Summation

AUGEND	ADDEND	CARRY	NEW CARRY	SUM DIGIT
0	0	0	0	0
0	1	0	0	1
1	0	0	0	1
1	1	0	1	0
0	0	1	0	1
0	1	1	1	0
1	0	1	1	0
1	1	1	1	1

Note that each digit multiplies the appropriate power of 2.

$$2^8 \quad 2^7 \quad 2^6 \quad 2^5 \quad 2^4 \quad 2^3 \quad 2^2 \quad 2^1 \quad 2^0$$
$$1 \quad 0 \quad 1 \quad 1 \quad 1 \quad 0 \quad 1 \quad 1 \quad 0$$

or,

$$256 \quad 128 \quad 64 \quad 32 \quad 16 \quad 8 \quad 4 \quad 2 \quad 1$$
$$1 \quad 0 \quad 1 \quad 1 \quad 1 \quad 0 \quad 1 \quad 1 \quad 0$$

The result expressed in decimal is

$$256 + 64 + 32 + 16 + 4 + 2 = 374_{10}$$

COMPLEMENTATION

Direct binary subtraction could be performed in the same way as decimal subtraction, but no processor does subtraction in this fashion. The problem is that you would not only have to mechanize the subtraction process, you would also be faced with the fact that you cannot depend upon a "borrow" digit being conveniently available in the position immediately to the left of the one in which the subtraction is taking place. This complicates the processor hardware design unnecessarily. For example, consider the problem:

$$
\begin{array}{rcr}
10010001_2 & = & 145_{10} \\
- \quad 1111111_2 & = & - \ 127_{10} \\
\hline
00010010_2 & = & 18_{10}
\end{array}
$$

To solve this problem directly, you perform the first digit subtraction easily. But then you are required to generate a borrow to operate on the second digit from the right. You have to search left three digits to find a 1, change that 1 to a 0, all the intervening 0's to 1's, perform the subtraction, and add 1 into the result (to correct for the difference between 1000 and 0111).

This is not the orderly process we would like to mechanize. Instead, negative numbers are expressed in *complementary* form, and arithmetic is performed on these complements. Complementary arithmetic may be used to perform subtractions in any number system.

Returning to the decimal system, we can define a 9's complement as the result of subtracting the number in question from all 9's. For example, the 9's complement of 3756 is 6243:

$$\begin{array}{r} 9999 \\ - \ 3756 \\ \hline 6243 \end{array}$$

If we wish to subtract 3756 from 7682, it can *almost* be done by adding the 9's complement of 3756 to 7682:

$$\begin{array}{r} 7682 \\ + \ 6243 \\ \hline 13925 \end{array}$$

Among other things, you will note that the answer 1395 is too large, so another step is required to bring us closer to the correct answer. The complement was obtained by adding 9999 to −3756, so we first correct this situation by subtracting 10,000, which effectively removes the left-most digit:

$$\begin{array}{r} 13,925 \\ - \ 10,000 \\ \hline 3,925 \end{array}$$

(The left-most 1 resulting from the final carry in the addition operation could have been blocked in the processor to obtain the same result.) We must now make one last correction by adding 1 to 3925 (since $10,000 - 9999 = 1$), giving the correct result of 3926. The process can be made a bit simpler by defining a *10's complement* as being the 9's complement plus 1, thus removing the need to add in a final 1 to obtain the correct result, but slightly complicating the complementation process.

Binary Complements

The use of complementary arithmetic to perform decimal subtraction is of little real value since it saves no work. However, in the binary system, real savings are achieved. The binary complementation process is identical to that used in the decimal system. We may define a *1's complement* and a *2's complement* as follows:

To determine the 1's complement, the number is subtracted from all 1's. This subtraction amounts to nothing more than exchanging the 0's for 1's and the 1's for 0's in the number in question. For example, the 1's complement of 101101101001_2 is 010010010110_2 .

The 2's complement is equal to the 1's complement plus 1, and it is normally formed by the following process: First, examine the least significant digit; if it is a 0, copy it and all contiguous zeros until the first 1 is found. Copy this first 1 also. Invert all other digits as in 1's complementation. For example, the 2's complement of 110110101000 is 001001011000.

Virtually all processors use 2's complement arithmetic. Negative numbers are identified by a 1 in the most significant, or sign bit position, and are stored in 2's complement form. A -45_{10} may be stored in the AMP's 8-bit data word as

$$\boxed{1\ |\ 1\ \ 0\ \ 1\ \ 0\ \ 0\ \ 1\ \ 1} = -45_{10}$$

sign bit ⌐   ⌐numerical bits ⌐

The addition of $+75_{10}$ to -45_{10} is performed as follows:

combined by addition
$$\boxed{0\ |\ 1\ \ 0\ \ 0\ \ 1\ \ 0\ \ 1\ \ 1} = +75_{10}$$
$+$
$$\boxed{1\ |\ 1\ \ 0\ \ 1\ \ 0\ \ 0\ \ 1\ \ 1} = -45_{10}\ \text{(complementary form)}$$
$=$
$$\boxed{0\ |\ 0\ \ 0\ \ 1\ \ 1\ \ 1\ \ 1\ \ 0} = +30_{10}\ \text{(0 in the sign bit is a plus)}$$
carry (1)

Note that the final carry falls off the left-hand end of the register, thus correcting for the addition performed in creating the 2's complement. Note also that arithmetic is performed on the sign bit exactly as on the data bits.

The addition of -10_{10} and -45_{10} looks like:

$$\boxed{1\ |\ 1\ \ 1\ \ 1\ \ 0\ \ 1\ \ 0\ \ 1} = -11_{10}$$
$+$
$$\boxed{1\ |\ 1\ \ 0\ \ 1\ \ 0\ \ 0\ \ 1\ \ 1} = -45_{10}$$
$=$
$$\boxed{1\ |\ 1\ \ 0\ \ 0\ \ 1\ \ 0\ \ 0\ \ 0} = -56_{10}$$
1

all in complementary form

To check the result we can complement our representation for -56 to obtain the result in a readable absolute-value form. (Note that if the complementation operation is done twice, or an even number of times, we will have our original number back.)

−56 in 2's complement form $\boxed{1}$ $\boxed{1\ 0\ 0\ 1\ 0\ 0\ 0}$

+56, sign and absolute value $\boxed{0}$ $\boxed{0\ 1\ 1\ 1\ 0\ 0\ 0}$

$$32 + 16 + 8 = 56$$

BINARY MULTIPLICATION

The multiplication of binary numbers expressed as sign and absolute value is quite simple. Because the multiplier digits can only be 1 or 0, we either add or don't add the shifted multiplicand into the partial product, depending upon the value of each multiplier digit examined. If we work from least to most significant bit, the multiplicand is added and then shifted left to prepare for the next cycle. (We may also work from most to least significant, in which case the multiplicand is shifted right each time a multiplier digit is examined.) For instance,

$$
\begin{array}{r}
1010 = \quad 10_{10} \\
\underline{1100} \quad\quad 12_{10} \\
101000 \\
\underline{1010000} \\
1111000 = \quad 120_{10}
\end{array}
$$

In this example, both multiplier and multiplicand were considered to be positive. Where it is possible for the multiplier to be expressed in 2's complement form (negative), things become more complex. It is no longer enough to simply examine the multiplier bits, one by one, to control the addition, nor is it possible to simply invert the meaning of these multiplier digits when operating on numbers expressed in 2's complement form. Fortunately, several methods have been devised to handle this problem efficiently. The techniques described here can be used as the basis for multiplication subroutines as well as for hardware multiplication.

Example 1

First, let us consider the case where the multiplier is greater than zero and the multiplicand is less than zero.

$$
\begin{array}{r}
\text{multiplicand} -35 \quad \boxed{1}\ \boxed{1\ 0\ 1\ 1\ 1\ 0\ 1} \\
\text{multiplier} \times 75 \quad \boxed{0}\ \boxed{1\ 0\ 0\ 1\ 0\ 1\ 1} \\
175 \\
\underline{245} \\
-2625
\end{array}
$$

Since the arguments are each 8 bits long we must have available a double-length or 16-bit register to hold the partial product. In this example we will use the least significant digit of the multiplier to control the additions and shifts. This least significant digit is a one, so the multiplicand will be added into the product register, which was initially set to all zeros.

Step 1:

Product register

1	1	0	1	1	1	0	1	0	0	0	0	0	0	0	0

Shift right one place

1	1	1	0	1	1	1	0	1	0	0	0	0	0	0	0

(Insert a one in the highest order digit position when each right shift operation is performed.)

In order to isolate the least significant multiplier bit for control, the multiplier register may also be shifted right. Once the multiplier bit is used for control, it is of no further use and can be thrown away. If register space is at a premium, the partial product can be developed by using a single 8-bit register and shifting the lower-order bits into the vacated bit positions of the multiplier register. At any rate, we have now shifted the multiplier right, yielding

X	0	1	0	0	1	0	1

where X indicates "don't care."

Step 2: The least significant multiplier bit is a one, so we once again add the multiplicand into the partial product.

New partial product

1	1	0	0	1	0	1	1	1	0	0	0	0	0	0	0

Shift right one place

1	1	1	0	0	1	0	1	1	1	0	0	0	0	0	0

Shift multiplier right one place

X	X	0	1	0	0	1	0

Step 3: The least significant multiplier bit is a zero, so we shift the multiplier and product registers each right one place.

Product register

1	1	1	1	0	0	1	0	1	1	1	0	0	0	0	0

Multiplier

X	X	X	0	1	0	0	1

Step 4: Add multiplicand and shift right.

New partial product

1	1	0	0	1	1	1	1	1	1	1	0	0	0	0	0

33

Shift right
one place

| 1 | 1 | 1 | 0 | 0 | 1 | 1 | 1 | 1 | 1 | 1 | 1 | 0 | 0 | 0 | 0 |

Multiplier

| X | X | X | X | 0 | 1 | 0 | 0 |

Steps 5 and 6: The multiplier control digit is zero for both steps, so the partial product is shifted right twice:

New partial
product

| 1 | 1 | 1 | 1 | 1 | 0 | 0 | 1 | 1 | 1 | 1 | 1 | 1 | 1 | 0 | 0 |

Multiplier

| X | X | X | X | X | X | 0 | 1 |

Step 7: The multiplier control digit is a one.

New partial
product

| 1 | 1 | 1 | 0 | 1 | 0 | 1 | 1 | 0 | 1 | 1 | 1 | 1 | 1 | 1 | 0 |

Multiplier

| X | X | X | X | X | X | X | 0 |

The last control digit is a zero, but this is the sign of the multiplier. Since it is a zero in this case, the only result would be to shift the product right one place. So the final result is

| 1 | 1 | 1 | 1 | 0 | 1 | 0 | 1 | 1 | 0 | 1 | 1 | 1 | 1 | 1 | 1 |

Depending upon how we choose to scale the problem, this final shift may or may not be proper. If we follow the scaling rules of Chapter 4, we do not want to execute another shift and will terminate the multiplication here. The resulting binary point is then 14 digits to the right of the sign position (having multiplied two 7-digit numbers together). The product expressed in absolute value form is

| − | 0 | 0 | 1 | 0 | 1 | 0 | 0 | 1 | 0 | 0 | 0 | 0 | 0 | 1 | 0 |

$$- (2048 + 512 + 64 + 1) = -2625$$

We can now consider the general case, where either or both the multiplier and multiplicand can be negative.

Defining Conditions

The multiplier (x) and multiplicand (y) are contained in an 8-bit word with the sign as the most significant bit.

If the multiplier and multiplicand are both greater than or equal to zero, there is no problem. If the multiplier is greater than or equal to zero and the multiplicand is less than zero, negative partial sums are developed in complementary form and this is still not a problem (Example 1).

If the multiplier is less than zero, the register value is expressed as $2^8 - x$, so that a product (xy) is expressed as

$(2^8 - x) y$, or $2^8 y - xy$. The product can then be corrected by subtracting $2^8 y$ at the completion of the multiplication. This can be done by realizing that the sign digit is "1" if the multiplier is less than zero, so that we can subtract the product of the sign digit and y from the partial product, instead of multiplying by the sign digit of the multiplier.

All of this leads to a fairly simple rule:

> *To generate the product of two binary numbers where either, or both, may be negative and expressed as 2's complements, form the product as in Example 1, correcting the result by taking the product of the most significant digit of the multiplier and the complement of the multiplicand, adding this to a properly shifted partial product. The resulting final product will always be proper.*

Example 2

Using the preceding rule, we will generate the product:

$$\begin{array}{r} -35 \\ \times\ -75 \\ \hline 2625 \end{array}$$

1969085

Initial values are

Multiplicand

1	1	0	1	1	1	0	1

Multiplier

1	0	1	1	0	1	0	1

(Product register is set to all zeros.)

Step 1: Add multiplicand to product register and shift right one place.

Product register

1	1	1	0	1	1	1	0	1	0	0	0	0	0	0	0

Step 2: Shift product register right one place.

1	1	1	1	0	1	1	1	0	1	0	0	0	0	0	0

Step 3: Add multiplicand and shift.

1	1	1	0	1	0	1	0	0	0	1	0	0	0	0	0

Step 4: Shift right one place.

1	1	1	1	0	1	0	1	0	0	0	1	0	0	0	0

Step 5: Add multiplicand and shift.

1	1	1	0	1	0	0	1	0	0	0	0	1	0	0	0

Step 6: Add multiplicand and shift.

| 1 | 1 | 1 | 0 | 0 | 0 | 1 | 1 | 0 | 0 | 0 | 0 | 0 | 1 | 0 | 0 |

Step 7: Shift right one place.

| 1 | 1 | 1 | 1 | 0 | 0 | 0 | 1 | 1 | 0 | 0 | 0 | 0 | 0 | 1 | 0 |

Step 8: Subtract by adding the complement of the multiplicand to the partial product.

| 0 | 0 | 0 | 1 | 0 | 1 | 0 | 0 | 1 | 0 | 0 | 0 | 0 | 0 | 1 | 0 |

for the final correct product of +2625.

PRECISION

Binary requires more digits to express comparable precision than the digits of a decimal number. In fact, it requires approximately 10 bits to express the same information as contained in 3 decimal digits, since $2^{10} = 1024$, while $10^3 = 1000$. The actual number of bits required to satisfy the required precision can be determined by the general relationship, $2^x = 10^A$, solving for x when you know the required value of A. Taking the logarithm to the base 10 of both sides of the equation, we have

$$x \log_{10} (2) = A$$

or

$$x = A/0.30103$$

So a 5-digit decimal number would require approximately $5/0.301 = 16.6$ bits, which we would round up or down to 16 or 17 bits, as circumstances demanded, to express the equivalent precision of the decimal number.

If the decimal number does not range up to a full decade, you adjust for this by using a fractional value for A. For example, if the required precision is to express numbers up to decimal 500, then $500 = 10^A$, or $A = \log_{10} (500) = 2.7$. From this value we find that $x = 2.7/0.301$, or about 9 bits.

OCTAL AND HEXADECIMAL SYSTEMS

Because binary representations require long strings of digits to express numbers of useful precision, it has been found desirable to use other number systems having more admissible marks, and for which the conversions to and from binary are simple.

Table 2-4. Decimal, Octal, and Binary Equivalence

DECIMAL	OCTAL	BINARY
0	0	0
1	1	1
2	2	10
3	3	11
4	4	100
5	5	101
6	6	110
7	7	111
8	10	1000
9	11	1001
10	12	1010

Octal System

Since 8 is equal to 2^3, we can form the octal equivalent of a binary number by simply grouping the bits in sets of three and assigning symbols to each element of the set. Table 2-4 lists the equivalencies for small integral values.

The conversion from binary to octal is trivial. The binary number is marked off in groups of 3 and the conversion performed by reference to decimal digits 0—7 of Table 2-4. The equivalent octal and binary representations are

Binary	111	101	100	010
Octal	7	5	4	2

The octal number is then written as 7542_8.

The conversion from octal to binary is simply the reverse.

Octal	4	0	3	5	6
Binary	100	000	011	101	110

To add octal numbers we must use the rules for octal arithmetic. By reference to the octal addition table, Table 2-5, we can form sums. As two examples, we have:

$$
\begin{array}{r}
4{,}745_8 \\
+\,3{,}643_8 \\
\hline
10{,}610_8
\end{array}
\qquad
\begin{array}{r}
3{,}754_8 \\
+\,7{,}621_8 \\
\hline
13{,}675_8
\end{array}
$$

Complementation of octal numbers is performed in the same manner as complementation of decimal or binary. In the case of octal, the 7's complement may be taken by subtracting the number in question from all 7's, using octal arithmetic which, in this special case, is the same as decimal arithmetic.

Table 2-5. Octal Addition Table

+	0	1	2	3	4	5	6	7
0	0	1	2	3	4	5	6	7
1		2	3	4	5	6	7	10
2			4	5	6	7	10	11
3				6	7	10	11	12
4					10	11	12	13
5						12	13	14
6							14	15
7								16

The 8's complement is then formed by adding 1, also using octal arithmetic. For example, the 7's complement of 6720_8 is

$$
\begin{array}{r}
7777 \\
-6720 \\
\hline
1057_8
\end{array}
$$

The 8's complement is then

$$
\begin{array}{r}
1057 \\
+\ \ \ \ 1 \\
\hline
1060_8
\end{array}
$$

Octal complementation can also be performed by complementing the binary equivalent and converting to octal. Since the processor representation is binary, the latter is often more convenient. To form the 8's complement of 6720_8 we first form the 2's complement of $110\ 111\ 010\ 000_2$, which is $001\ 000\ 110\ 000_2$. Converting this result to octal we have 1060_8.

Octal multiplication is performed exactly as multiplication in the decimal system but using octal arithmetic. Referring to Table 2-6, we have

$$
\begin{array}{rcr}
1735_8 & = & 989_{10} \\
\times\ \ \ 46_8 & = & 38_{10} \\
\hline
13456 & & 7912 \\
7564 & & 2967 \\
\hline
111316_8 & = & 37582_{10}
\end{array}
$$

Table 2-6. Octal Multiplication Table

X	1	2	3	4	5	6	7
1	1	2	3	4	5	6	7
2		4	6	10	12	14	16
3			11	14	17	22	25
4				20	24	30	34
5					31	36	43
6						44	52
7							61

Hexadecimal

We chose 3-bit groups to form octal digits because we wanted a compact notation without introducing unusual symbols. While octal is commonly used as an intermediate notation for large computer systems having word lengths of 30 to 36 bits, microprocessors with 4-, 8-, and 16-bit organization for data words will more naturally use 4-bit groups. Since $2^4 = 16$, we can express numbers from 0 through 15_{10} in a *hexadecimal* group. To do so we must introduce new symbols for decimal numbers 10 through 15. Because IBM selected A, B, C, D, E, and F, most manufacturers have followed suit (Bendix chose U, V, W, X, Y, and Z for their G15 and G20 computer systems in the late 1950's, but it didn't stick). Hexadecimal ("hex" for short) digits and their binary and decimal equivalents are shown in Table 2-7. We must however, define rules for hexadecimal arithmetic as we did for the binary and octal operation. Table 2-8 and Appendix A are the hexadecimal addition and multiplication tables, respectively, and provide sufficient definition to begin to work within the hexadecimal system. The following are three examples of hexadecimal arithmetic.

Addition of two hexadecimal numbers:

$$
\begin{array}{rcr}
6E8_{16} & = & 1768_{10} \\
+3CD_{16} & = & +\ 973_{10} \\
\hline
AB5_{16} & = & 2741_{10}
\end{array}
$$

where the value of
$AB5_{16} = (10 \times 16^2) + (11 \times 16) + 5 = 2560 + 176 + 5 = 2741_{10}$

Table 2-7. Decimal, Hexadecimal (Hex), and Binary Equivalence

DECIMAL	HEXADECIMAL	BINARY
0	0	0
1	1	1
2	2	10
3	3	11
4	4	100
5	5	101
6	6	110
7	7	111
8	8	1000
9	9	1001
10	A	1010
11	B	1011
12	C	1100
13	D	1101
14	E	1110
15	F	1111

Multiplication of two hexadecimal numbers:

$$
\begin{array}{r}
1B3_{16} = \quad 435_{10} \\
\times\ 57_{16} = \times\ \ 87_{10} \\
\hline
BE5 \\
87F \\
\hline
93D5_{16} = 37{,}845_{10}
\end{array}
$$

To form the 16's complement of a hexadecimal number, we simply subtract that number from all F's and add 1. The 16's complement of D439 is

$$
\begin{array}{r}
FFFF \\
-D439 \\
\hline
2BC6 \\
+\ \ \ 1 \\
\hline
2BC7
\end{array}
$$

NUMBER CONVERSIONS

The preceding operational rules for addition, multiplication, and subtraction apply to binary and binary-compatible systems. Division can be performed by reference to addition and multiplication tables, but should be used sparingly.

So far, the discussion has been limited to operations with whole numbers. Once in a number system, using the arithmetic of that system, fractions and integers are handled identically. However, when converting from one system to another, where the conversions cannot be made directly, the rules for operating on fractions are different than those for integers. For purposes of establishing rules for converting from one system to another, we propose the following definitions:

radical point—the symbol separating the integer digits from the fraction digits. *Decimal point* and *binary point* are terms used for specific cases.

familiar number system—the system whose arithmetic rules we are following. If we are using hexadecimal arithmetic, then hexadecimal is the "familiar" system, at least for the moment,

foreign number system—any other system than what we happen to be using at the moment. If we are using binary arithmetic, then decimal would be a "foreign" system.

Using these definitions, we can reduce the number of different rules we must follow to obtain number equivalents in various systems.

Table 2-8. Hexadecimal Addition Table

+	0	1	2	3	4	5	6	7	8	9	A	B	C	D	E	F
0	0	1	2	3	4	5	6	7	8	9	A	B	C	D	E	F
1		2	3	4	5	6	7	8	9	A	B	C	D	E	F	10
2			4	5	6	7	8	9	A	B	C	D	E	F	10	11
3				6	7	8	9	A	B	C	D	E	F	10	11	12
4					8	9	A	B	C	D	E	F	10	11	12	13
5						A	B	C	D	E	F	10	11	12	13	14
6							C	D	E	F	10	11	12	13	14	15
7								E	F	10	11	12	13	14	15	16
8									10	11	12	13	14	15	16	17
9										12	13	14	15	16	17	18
A											14	15	16	17	18	19
B												16	17	18	19	1A
C													18	19	1A	1B
D														1A	1B	1C
E															1C	1D
F																1E

Converting Integers

To convert an integer expressed in a familiar base to an equivalent one in a foreign base, apply the following rule:

> *Successively divide by the foreign base expressed as a familiar number, using familiar arithmetic, pick, off the remainders and form the resulting foreign number from these remainders. The remainder, as a result of the first division, is the least significant digit and the remainder, resulting from the division yielding a zero quotient is the most significant digit of the new number.*

For example, convert 296_{10} to octal:

$$
\begin{array}{r}
37 \\
8\ \overline{)\ 296} \\
24 \\
\hline
56 \\
56 \\
\hline
0
\end{array}
$$

(1st remainder is 0_8)

$$
\begin{array}{r}
4 \\
8\ \overline{)\ 37} \\
32 \\
\hline
5
\end{array}
$$

(2nd remainder is 5_8)

$$
\begin{array}{r}
0 \\
8\ \overline{)\ 4} \\
0 \\
\hline
4
\end{array}
$$

(3rd remainder is 4_8)

The resulting equivalent octal number is 450.

Convert 450_8 to decimal:

$$
\begin{array}{r}
35 \\
12\ \overline{)\ 450} \\
36 \\
\hline
70 \\
62 \\
\hline
6
\end{array}
$$

(1st remainder is 6_{10})

$$12 \overline{\smash{\big)}\,35}$$
$$\frac{24}{11} \qquad \text{(2nd remainder is } 9_{10})$$

$$12 \overline{\smash{\big)}\,2}$$
$$\frac{0}{2} \qquad \text{(3rd remainder is } 2_{10})$$

The resulting equivalent decimal number is 296.

Hartmann Conversion

The following algorithm is quite useful for number conversion. It is called the Hartmann method and was originally published in *Computer Design*, April 1967, by Sigmund Hartmann. The advantage of this method is that it permits the use of *decimal* arithmetic when converting from a nondecimal to a decimal base. The rule can be stated as follows:

> *To convert an octal number to an equivalent number, using decimal arithmetic, first double the most significant digit of the octal number as though it were a decimal digit, then shift it one place right and subtract it from the original octal number using decimal arithmetic, successively choosing the resulting two most-significant digits, and then the three most-significant, etc. Continue this operation until subtraction is performed at the least significant digit position. The resulting number is the equivalent decimal integer.*

Examples:

$$
\begin{array}{r}
450 \;(\text{octal}) \\
-\; 80 \\
\hline
370 \\
-\; 74 \\
\hline
296 \;(\text{decimal equivalent})
\end{array}
\qquad
\begin{array}{r}
1762 \quad (\text{octal}) \\
-200 \\
\hline
1562 \\
-300 \\
\hline
1262 \\
-252 \\
\hline
1010 \quad (\text{decimal equivalent})
\end{array}
$$

The general rules are stated in Table 2-9 for converting to a decimal base, together with a binary example. (Conversion

Table 2-9. Rules for the Hartmann Conversion Technique

RULES	EXAMPLE
(Decimal arithmetic is used exclusively)	Convert 1011_2 to decimal
1. Subtract 10 from the old base. Call this difference M. 2. Multiply the Most Significant Digit of the number to be converted by M. 3. Shift the product from (2) one place to the right and add to the 2 most significant digits of the original number.	$M = 2 - 10 = -8$ $(1)(-8) = -8$ $\begin{array}{r} 10\lfloor 11 \rfloor \\ -\ 8 \hphantom{0} \\ \hline 2\lfloor 11 \rfloor \end{array}$
4. Multiply the result from (3) by M. 5. Shift the product from (4) one place to the right and add to it the product from (3) and the next most significant digit.	$(2)(-8) = -16$ $\begin{array}{r} 21\lfloor 1 \rfloor \\ -\ 16 \hphantom{0} \\ \hline 5\lfloor 1 \rfloor \end{array}$
6. Repeat the procedure of (4) and (5) until the least significant digit is reached. The result is the decimal equivalent.	$(5)(-8) = -40$ $\begin{array}{r} 51 \\ -\ 40 \\ \hline 11_{10} = 1011_2 \end{array}$

from decimal, of course, is quite conveniently done using conventional techniques.) For the mathematically inclined, a proof of this method can be found in Appendix B. The method can be used for conversion of hexadecimal numbers, but must be applied digit by digit because the symbols A through F are unique to hexadecimal making the method somewhat awkward. If desired, conversions can always be made by simply expressing the number in the new base as we have done earlier.

To convert $A16C_{16}$ to decimal, form the following sum of products:

$$A16C_{16} = A(16^3) + 1(16^2) + 6(16) + C$$

Since $A = 10_{10}$ and $C = 12_{10}$,

$$A16C_{16} = (40,960 + 256 + 96 + 12)_{10} = 41,324_{10}$$

Fractions

So far we have considered only integers, whereas numbers expressed in most systems consist of both integers and fractions. Further, we must expect to truncate or round infinite fractions if we are to be able to stay within the limited number of digits in our processor. The problem is that a finite fraction in one system may very well be an infinite fraction in another. For example, decimal 0.6 becomes octal 0.46314631... and hexadecimal 0.1 becomes decimal 0.166666... . The following rule applies:

To obtain an equivalent foreign representation of a fraction expressed in a familiar system, multiply the fraction in the familiar system by the foreign base expressed as a familiar number, using familiar arithmetic. Use the digit appearing to the left of the radical point as the most significant digit of the fraction, and express this in the foreign base. Again multiply the resulting fraction only, and repeat until either an adequate number of digits is obtained or the precision of the resulting foreign number is equivalent to that of the original familiar one.

Example: convert 0.7489_{10} to octal. We multiply by the octal base (8) expressed as a decimal number.

$$
\begin{array}{r}
0.7489 \\
8 \\
\hline
5\,|\,0.9912 \\
8 \\
\hline
7\,|\,0.9296 \\
8 \\
\hline
7\,|\,0.4368 \\
8 \\
\hline
3\,|\,0.4944 \\
8 \\
\hline
2\,|\,0.9552
\end{array}
$$

The resulting octal fraction is then 0.57732_8 .

Example: convert $0.A72_{16}$ to decimal. Since the decimal base is A expressed as a hexadecimal number, conversion is performed multiplying successively by A using hexadecimal arithmetic.

$$
\begin{array}{r}
0.A72 \\
A \\
\hline
6\,|\,874 \\
A \\
\hline
5\,|\,488 \\
A \\
\hline
2\,|\,D50 \\
A \\
\hline
8\,|\,520 \\
A \\
\hline
3\,|\,340
\end{array}
$$

The decimal equivalent is then 0.65283_{10} .

The Hartmann method may also be used to convert fractions by considering them to be composed of a numerator and denominator, converting the numerator as an integer, and dividing through by the denominator expressed as a decimal integer, using decimal arithmetic.

An alternate scheme for the conversion of an *octal fraction* to an equivalent decimal fraction is stated without proof:

> *Initially multiply the least significant "good" digit of the octal fraction by 0.025 and add the product to the octal fraction using decimal arithmetic. Then move to the next least significant "good" digit and all following digits—use this digit group as the multiplicand. Now continue the process until the most significant digit has been included as the multiplicand. The result is the equivalent decimal fraction.*

Example: convert 0.5773_8 to decimal.

$$
\begin{array}{ll}
\begin{array}{r}
0.577300 \\
+\ 000075 \\
\hline
0.57737500
\end{array} & = \quad (0.0003) \times (0.025) \\[1em]
\begin{array}{r}
+\ 00184375 \\
\hline
0.57921875
\end{array} & = \quad (0.007375 \times (0.025) \\[1em]
\begin{array}{r}
+\ 01980468 \\
\hline
0.59902343
\end{array} & = \quad (0.07921875) \times (0.025) \\[1em]
\begin{array}{r}
+\ 0.14975585 \\
\hline
0.74877928_{10}
\end{array} & = \quad (0.59902343) \times (0.025)
\end{array}
$$

This should be rounded to 0.7488_{10} (4 digits) to maintain nearly equivalent precision. (Some useless precision is implied, since 3 decimal digits aren't enough and 4 is too many.)

In addition to the converson methods discussed, a table of hexadecimal integer equivalents can be found in Appendix C together with a brief discussion of their use.

BINARY-CODED DECIMAL NUMBERS

Thus far we have been primarily concerned with binary and binary-derived systems used for the convenience of the processor. Because most of us prefer decimal, the binary-coded decimal (BCD) character set has been defined to permit communication with the processor in a decimal form. In fact, it is possible to perform an artificial arithmetic in this pseudo-decimal system. Most hand-held calculators work entirely in BCD even though the internal arithmetic is more cumbersome and requires additional memory when compared with straight binary arithmetic. The advantage is that the input/output conversions normally needed to obtain the binary equivalent on input, and the decimal equivalent on output, are trivial when BCD is used. BCD representation is nothing more than the familiar 4-bit equivalents used for hexadecimal, but restricted to the decimal digits 0-9, as shown in Table 2-10.

The AMP typewriter is driven using BCD from the CPU, one digit at a time. Other operations and symbols (e.g., carriage return, line feed space, decimal point, and minus sign) are controlled by remaining unused 4-bit characters. Similarly, the keyboard inputs are coded in BCD when they arrive at the CPU.

BCD Addition

In the case of a 4-bit processor, BCD addition of positive numbers is performed easily as long as the sum is less than 10.

$$
\begin{array}{rcr}
0101 & = & 5 \\
+0010 & = & +2 \\
\hline
0111 & = & 7_{10}
\end{array}
$$

But when the sum is 10 or greater, difficulties arise, as in

$$
\begin{array}{rcr}
0110 & = & 6 \\
+0111 & = & 7 \\
\hline
1101 & = & 13_{10}
\end{array}
$$

Here the sum is 13_{10}, which the CPU adder expresses as D_{16}. But two BCD characters are required to represent 13_{10}, and

Table 2-10. BCD and Decimal Equivalence

BCD	DECIMAL
0000	0
0001	1
0010	2
0011	3
0100	4
0101	5
0110	6
0111	7
1000	8
1001	9

these are formed by adding 6_{10} to an *illegal* BCD character (1010, 1011, 1100, 1101, 1111) and then adding the resulting carry to the next digit position. This in effect, "skips over" the illegal characters, forming the proper BCD representation.

$$1101 = 13$$
$$0110 = \ 6 \ (\text{binary to BCD correction})$$
$$10011 = 19_{10} = 13 \ \text{BCD}$$
$$\uparrow$$
carry

To obtain the proper answer of 0001 0011, zeros must be originally placed in the 4 bits of the most significant character set. When the C (carry flip-flop) is sampled, the resulting 1 is added in.

In the case of the AMP 8-bit adder, two instructions are provided to permit processing of BCD characters, two at a time. The first of these instructions is DC, and it causes a BCD 66 to be added to the accumulator prior to binary addition. The second instruction, DCC, is used after the addition has taken place, to correct the addition by adding a correction factor.

To provide sufficient information to determine whether or not a correction is needed, the AMP CPU uses two flag bits, called C and Q. The Q bit is set to one if a carry is generated in adding the four bits corresponding to the least significant BCD digit. The C bit is set to one if a carry is generated by the second BCD digit held in the CPU's 8-bit register. The Q is termed an *intermediate* carry, and this carry bit is set to zero after executing a DCC instruction. When the DCC instruction is issued, the states of the C and Q bits are examined, and the AMP hardware causes the appropriate correction factor (Table 2-11) to be added to the accumulator.

The following comments may help in understanding the rationale behind the correcton factors given in Table 2-11:

- If C = 0 and Q = 0 after the addition is complete, this indicates that no carries have been generated and that

Table 2-11. BCD Corrections

C	Q	BINARY	HEXADECIMAL
0	0	10011010	9A
1	0	10100000	A0
0	1	11111010	FA
1	1	00000000	00

the 66 added initially to the accumulator must be removed. The reason for adding the 66 in the first place was to automatically correct any sum exceeding decimal 99. But if no carries were generated, then the sum is obviously less than decimal 99, so each BCD digit is in error. This situation is corrected by subtracting 66 from the accumulator, which is accomplished by adding the 2's complement of 66_{16}, or $9A_{16}$. Carries generated by this operation are cleared by the CPU adder when the DCC instruction is completed.

- If $C = 1$ and $Q = 0$, the least significant digit (LSD) is correct, but the most significant digit (MSD) is in error. This is accomplished by subtracting 60_{16}, which is the same as adding the 2's complement, which is $A0_{16}$. The Q is reset to zero, while the C remains one to indicate that the accumulator has added two digits that total more than decimal 99.

- If $C = 0$ and $Q = 1$, the MSD is correct and the LSD is in error. Therefore 6 must be subtracted from the LSD by adding the 2's complement of 06_{16}, which is FA_{16}. The corrected sum is less than decimal 99, so both C and Q are reset to zero.

- If $C = 1$ and $Q = 1$, nothing more need be done since the sum is correct.

An example of BCD arithmetic is the addition of decimal 64 and 27, which would produce a carry in Q but not in C. The operations are as follows:

Load decimal 64	0110 0100 ($C = 0$, $Q = 0$)
Add 66 correction (DC)	0110 0110
Sum	1100 1010 ($C = 0$, $Q = 0$)
Add decimal 27	0010 0111
Sum	1111 0001 ($C = 0$, $Q = 1$)
Add correction (DCC)	1010 0000
Final sum is decimal 91	1001 0001 ($C = 0$, $Q = 0$)

BCD Subtraction

Subtraction is performed in the same manner as addition except that the subtrahend must be complemented. The sign is contained in C and the result is expressed in BCD 10's complement if the number is negative. The one-digit (4-bit) case follows directly from 4-bit BCD addition. The 8-bit case is a bit more complex.

Example: $(-4) + (-7) = -11$.

Load -4 (2's complement)	1100
Add -7 (2's complement)	1001
Sum	1 0101 (note carry bit at left)
Add --6 correction	1010
Sum (complementary form)	1 1111

Example: $25 - 76$.

Load 25 (absolute value)	0010 0101 ($C = 0, Q = 0$)
Add -76 (10's complement)	1000 1010
Sum (both digits)	1010 1111 ($C = 0, Q = 0$)
Add correction (Table 2-11)	1001 1010
Final sum is -51 (complemented)	0100 1001 ($C = 0, Q = 0$)

Notice that a preliminary correction (adding 66) is not necessary for subtraction. The compensation defined by Table 2-11 is sufficient.

Conversions

Binary-to-BCD conversions may be performed by the methods discussed earlier in the chapter. For example, let's convert 0.11011101 to BCD.

Since the conversion is to a form of decimal number, the binary fraction should be multiplied by 1010 (10_{10}) using binary arithmetic, and the most significant BCD digits are picked off 4 bits at a time after each multiplication. Using the simpler form of binary multiplication by 1010,

We shift right once	0110 11101
Then right twice more	0001 1011101
	1000 1010001

We have multiplied by 10_{10}, so the radical point is now shifted four places right. (Chapter 4 addresses the rules). The first BCD digit is 1000, or 8_{10}. The remaining number, 0.1010001 is now multiplied by 1010

Shift right	0101 0001
Shift right twice more	0001 010001
Sum	0110 010101

The next BCD digit is 0110, or 6. Since 8 binary digits have the same precision as 2.4 decimal digits, it is only necessary to find 3 BCD digits, so the final step is

Shift right	0010 101
Shift right twice more	0000 10101
Sum	0011 01001

The final BCD digit is 0011 or 3_{10} for a BCD equivalent of 0.863. This can be checked by observing that

$$0.11011101_2 = 0.5 + 0.25 + 0.0625 + 0.0312 + 0.0156 + 0.0039$$
$$= 0.08632_{10}$$

Integers can be converted as well, with the methods of this chapter, using division and picking off remainders. Remainders are not always easy to come by in a microprocessor, so a preferred method is to convert a fracton by assuming the binary point to be at the *left end* of the register, then moving the decimal point to the correct position after the conversion is complete. The danger here is the conversion may be in error by round-off or truncation, affecting the value of the least significant integral digit.

Further operations using binary, hexadecimal, and BCD in various programs will be discussed in later chapters dealing with the AMP instruction set and programming techniques.

Chapter 3
Basic
Microprocessor Logic

Logical operations can be reduced to a structured form, which is the basis for the mechanization of processor functions and for the organization of the program. These operations are performed on "sets" of things , where a *set* is defined as a collection of objects, all of which possess (or don't possess) an attribute or property. For example, all integers form a set, and all 8-bit microprocessors form another set. Sets may be combined by algebraic methods to form other sets. To discuss these operations, we will need a few definitions:

> U is the *universal set*; it has everything in it.
>
> N is the *null set*; it has nothing in it.
>
> A *subset* is a set wholly contained within another set. For example, the set of prime numbers is a subset of the set of integers. Similarly, the null set is a subset of all sets, while all other sets are subsets of the universal set, and every set is a subset of itself.
>
> The symbol $\subset$ is used to denote a subset. For example, $N \subset U$ means that N is a subset of U. If A is a set, then $A \subset A$. If B is a set and if $A \subset B$ and $B \subset A$, then $A = B$, meaning that the two sets are equivalent.
>
> The *union* of sets A and B is often termed the *logical sum* of sets A and B. This operation is denoted by writing $A + B$, and the result is another set which consists of all the things in A or B or both.

The *intersection* of A and B is often termed the *logical product* of sets A and B. This operation is denoted by writing A•B, A × B, (A)(B), or simply AB, and it defines a set which consists only of those things in both A and B.

We can now list some additional important properties of sets, using the preceding defined operations:

$$A + B = B + A$$
$$AB = BA$$
$$AA = A$$
$$A + A = A$$
$$AU = A$$
$$AN = N$$
$$A + N = A$$

If $C \subset D$, then $C + D = D$, $CD = C$

Some of these properties are identical with those of ordinary algebra; others such as $AA = A$ and $A + A = A$ are not.

Another operation, termed complementation, is needed. The *complement* of A consists of all things which are not in A, and the complement of A is normally denoted as $\bar{A}$ or A'. Thus,

$$A + \bar{A} = U$$
$$A\bar{A} = N$$

If $C \subset D$, then $\bar{D} \subset \bar{C}$

One last operation definition is quite useful. It is normally termed the *exclusive OR,* often written as $\oplus$. $A \oplus B$ consists of those things which belong to A or to B, but not to both. If A and B are binary numbers, the exclusive OR can be thought of as an *add without carry.* This function is useful in mechanizing binary adders, as we shall see a bit later.

A truth table for the $\oplus$ function is:

A	B	$A \oplus B = C$
0	0	0
0	1	1
1	0	1
1	1	0

An interesting property of $\oplus$ is if $C = A \oplus B$, then $B = A \oplus C$ and $A = B \oplus C$.

A	C	$A + C = B$	$B + C = A$
0	0	0	0
0	1	1	0
1	1	0	1
1	0	1	1

This property has been used to encrypt and decrypt messages using the same secure bit pattern at both sender and receiver.

INTRODUCTION TO BOOLEAN ALGEBRA

The techniques described here were first organized by George Boole in 1847 and published in *Laws of Thought* in 1854. Boolean algebra considers variables that exist in one of two states (0 and 1), and this is directly applicable to the binary integers. This Algebra may be defined in terms of two *binary* operations (an operator mapping two Boolean variables into one Boolean variable) and a *unary* operation (an operator mapping one Boolean variable into one Boolean variable). The binary operators are + (OR) and • (AND).

$$0 + 0 = 0 \qquad 0 \bullet 0 = 0$$
$$0 + 1 = 1 \qquad 0 \bullet 0 = 0$$
$$1 + 0 = 1 \qquad 1 \bullet 0 = 0$$
$$1 + 1 = 1 \qquad 1 \bullet 1 = 1$$

The unary operator is variously called the *prime*, *bar*, *complement*, or *NOT* operator, which are defined as

$$0' = \overline{0} = 1$$
$$1' = \overline{1} = 0$$

The OR operator is analogous to switches in parallel, while the AND operator is analogous to switches in series, if we define a "1" as representing a closed switch and a "0" as representing an open one. Logically, both OR and AND have intuitively satisfying meanings, that is, if a "1" is defined as representing a true statement and a "0" one which is false, then the Boolean AND operator becomes equivalent to the logical "and," and the Boolean OR to the logical "or."

The laws or operations of Boolean algebra follow immediately from the following operator definitions.

1. Complementation:
$$A + \bar{A} = 1 \quad A \cdot \bar{A} = 0$$
2. Involution:
$$\bar{\bar{A}} = A$$
3. Intersection:
$$1 \cdot A = A \quad 0 \cdot A = 0$$
4. Union:
$$1 + A = 1 \quad 0 + A = A$$
5. Idempotent:
$$A + A = A \quad A \cdot A = A$$

Boolean variables also possess certain of the common algebraic properties.

6. Boolean operations are *commutative*:
$$A \cdot B = B \cdot A \quad A + B = B + A$$
7. Boolean operations are *associative*:
$$A + (B + C) = (A + B) + C = (A + C) + B$$
$$A(BC) = (AB)C = (AC)B$$

(We drop the dot symbol at this point and replace it by parentheses or the juxtaposition of AB).

8. Boolean operations are *distributive*:
$$A(B + C) = AB + AC$$

The verification of the commutative associative, and distributive operations can also be done by truth tables. Armed with this knowledge, we can prove identities by algebraic manipulation.

Example 1:
$$\begin{aligned} A(A + B) &= AA + AB \text{ distributive law} \\ &= A + AB \text{ idempotent law} \\ &= A(1 + B) \text{ distributive law} \\ &= A \text{ union and intersection laws} \end{aligned}$$

Example 2:
$$\begin{aligned} A + \bar{A}B &= A(1 + B) + \bar{A}B \\ &= A + AB + \bar{A}B \\ &= A + B(A + \bar{A}) \\ &= A + B \end{aligned}$$

The identity of Example 2 is an important one to recognize and is commonly used to simplify Boolean expressions.

Example 3: Does $\bar{A} + \bar{B}$ equal $\overline{AB}$?
Here we will prove that $\bar{A} + \bar{B} + AB = 1$, and $(\bar{A} + \bar{B})(AB) = 0$, and deduce that since both examples are true, then

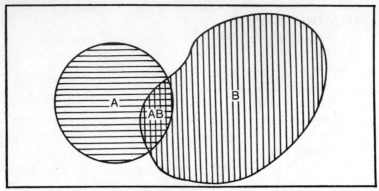

Fig. 3-1. Venn diagram.

AB is the complement of $\bar{A} + \bar{B}$ and therefore $\overline{AB} = \bar{A} + \bar{B}$ (involution law).

$$\bar{A} + \bar{B} + AB = (\bar{A} + AB) + \bar{B}$$
$$= (\bar{A} + B) + \bar{B} \text{ since } \bar{A} + AB = \bar{A} + B \text{ (see example 2)}$$
$$= \bar{A} + (B + \bar{B})$$
$$= \bar{A} + 1$$
$$= 1$$

$$(\bar{A} + \bar{B})(AB) = \bar{A}AB + AB\bar{B}$$
$$= (\bar{A}A)B + A(B\bar{B})$$
$$= (0)B + A(0) \text{ since } X\bar{X} = 0$$
$$\text{(complementation)}$$
$$= 0 + 0$$
$$= 0$$

This and its dual, $(\overline{A + B}) = \bar{A}\bar{B}$, are examples of De Morgan's theorem and are especially useful. It may be illustrative at this point to introduce and use Venn diagrams to provide a visual realization of De Morgan's theorems.

In Fig. 3-1 consider all A as contained within the area having horizontal shading and B within the area having vertical shading. The unshaded area represents those elements which belong neither to A nor to B. Then A + B is denoted by the entire shaded area (whether horizontal or vertical). The representation of $(\overline{A + B})$ is exactly the unshaded area, which of course is *not A and not B* ($\overline{AB}$).

VEITCH DIAGRAMS

This form of graphical presentation, also referred to as a Karnaugh map, is very useful in the reduction of Boolean expressions. Consider the Boolean expression $\overline{A}\overline{B}C + AB\overline{C} + A\overline{B}$. A reduction is not immediately obvious from inspection and will only result from more or less inspired algebraic manipulation. Suppose we represent each two-level state of A, B, and C by an area on a diagram organized as Fig. 3-2, where the two left-hand columns represent A true, the top row B true, and the two middle columns C true. There are 2^3 or 8 different states available as we would expect. Each segment of the diagram is marked with the associated state. Note that the diagram can also be thought of as being composed of larger segments; for example, the left column is exactly $A\overline{C}$. This can also be seen by observing the following identity:

$$AB\overline{C} + A\overline{B}\overline{C} = A\overline{C}(B + \overline{B}) = A\overline{C}$$

A term of the form ABC is called a *minterm* since it covers the minimum area of the diagram. Conversely, A, B, and C are called *maxterms* since they cover the maximum area that can be occupied by a single term.

Returning to the original expression $\overline{A}\overline{B}C + AB\overline{C} + A\overline{B}$, shown in Fig. 3-3, by recognizing the areas covered, we can regroup as $A\overline{C} + \overline{B}C$, which is certainly simpler by most criteria than the original expression. A reduction by algebraic manipulation would require several steps:

$$\overline{A}\overline{B}C + A\overline{B} + AB\overline{C} = \overline{A}\overline{B}C + A(\overline{B} + B\overline{C})$$
$$= A(\overline{B} + \overline{C}) + \overline{A}\overline{B}C$$
$$= \overline{B}(A + \overline{A}C) + A\overline{C}$$
$$= \overline{B}(A + C) + A\overline{C}$$
$$= A\overline{B} + \overline{B}C + A\overline{C}$$

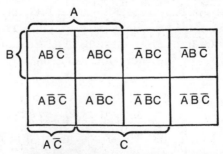

Fig. 3-2. Three-term Veitch diagram.

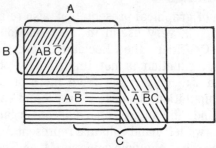

Fig. 3-3. ABC + AB + ABC plotted using a three-term Veitch diagram.

Here, if we had not seen the Veitch diagram, we might have been tempted to stop. However, it is clear from the diagram that $A\bar{B}$ is wholly contained within $A\bar{C} + \bar{B}C$. This can be shown by multiplying $A\bar{B}$ by a "well chosen" unity, $C + \bar{C}$, so that:

$$
\begin{aligned}
A\bar{B} + \bar{B}C + A\bar{C} &= A\bar{B}\,(C + \bar{C}) + \bar{B}C + A\bar{C} \\
&= A\bar{B}C + A\bar{B}\bar{C} + \bar{B}C + A\bar{C} \\
&= A\bar{C}\,(1 + \bar{B}) + \bar{B}C\,(1 + A) \\
&= A\bar{C} + \bar{B}C
\end{aligned}
$$

Veitch diagrams can be used for the graphical reduction of Boolean expressions of any number of variables. However, as the number of variables increases, the use of the Veitch becomes more cumbersome and the recognition of equivalences more difficult. But minterms can always be combined if they are adjacent in the same row or column, or at opposite ends of the same row or column.

BINARY ADDERS

An elemental function of the AMP processor is one of adding two 8-bit numbers. To perform the addition as fast as possible, the AMP processes all eight bits during one major clock period. This is called *parallel addition*. However, to better understand the summing operation and the logic required, we will first describe a one-bit-at-a-time or *serial adder*.

The Serial Adder

The serial adder consists of a shift register in which inputs are partial 1-bit sums. These are inserted at one end, then shifted one digit position each clock pulse. A means of generating each partial sum and associated carry is provided

58

by logic external to the shift register. We have chosen for discussion an 8-bit, right circular shift register (Fig. 3-4), identifying the bit positions as A_0 through A_7, and the controlling clock as ϕ.

Data modification can take place only when the clock pulse is true assuring synchronous operation. The logic for the shift register is then

$$A_7 = A_0\,\phi \qquad A_3 = A_4\,\phi$$
$$A_6 = A_7\,\phi \qquad A_2 = A_3\,\phi$$
$$A_5 = A_6\,\phi \qquad A_1 = A_2\,\phi$$
$$A_4 = A_5\,\phi \qquad A_0 = A_1\,\phi$$

where each memory position in Fig. 3-4, except A_7, merely copies the one to its left.

Since we want the clock to be enabled only during the time we wish to perform the addition, the storage elements must be able to hold data for long periods of time. Such storage elements are termed *static* elements, as opposed to *dynamic* elements that must be actively refreshed periodically. The adder mechanizes the binary sums appearing in Table 2-3, where the inputs to the adder are the addend (A), the augend contents of memory (M), the carry bit (C), the initialization timing pulse (T_0), and the sum digit (S). Then from Table 2-3 the 1-set and 0-set terms for the sums are

$$1^S = (A_0\,MC + A_0\,\overline{M}\overline{C} + \overline{A}_0\,MC + \overline{A}_0\,\overline{M}C)\phi$$
$$0^S = (\overline{A}_0\,\overline{M}\overline{C} + A_0\,M\overline{C} + A_0\,\overline{M}C + \overline{A}_0\,MC)\phi + T$$

The 1-set and 0-set terms for the carry (C) are

$$1^C = (A_0\,MC + A_0\,M\overline{C} + A_0\,\overline{M}C + \overline{A}_0\,MC)\phi$$
$$0^C = (\overline{A}_0\,\overline{M}C + \overline{A}_0\,M\overline{C} + A_0\,\overline{M}\overline{C} + \overline{A}_0\,\overline{M}\overline{C})\phi + T_0\,\phi$$

Figures 3-5 and 3-6 are the Veitch diagrams for the 1-set sum and carry logic. The clock is not shown since it is common to all terms. Also T_0 (which resets the sum and carry to start off the addition with a clean slate) is not shown either. The pattern in Fig. 3-5 suggests no simplification since no adjacent squares are covered. Many alternate forms, including the use of the exclusive OR, have been used. Their attractiveness is

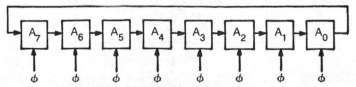

Fig. 3-4. Clocked right-circular shift register.

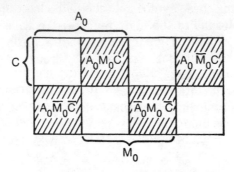

Fig. 3-5. Veitch diagram: One-set sum logic terms.

dependent upon the hardware used to mechanize the adder, but for our purposes this is an adequate form.

The pattern in Fig. 3-6 suggests the following simplification:

$$1^C = (A_0 C + MC + A_0 M)\phi$$

The 0-set sum logic covers the Veitch squares not covered by the 1-set terms, so no further simplification is evident by this analysis. The 0-set carry, however, can be simplified to:

$$0^C = (\overline{M}\overline{C} + \overline{M}\overline{A}_0 + \overline{A}_0 \overline{C})\phi + T_0 \phi$$

The functional or schematic mechanization of microprocessor systems is often depicted using symbolic logic elements to represent the required Boolean expressions. In addition to the functions discussed, the use of NAND and NOR logic is quite common. (NAND is a contraction for NOT AND, and NOR for NOT OR.) Logic symbol conventions have been locally adopted (but are by no means standard) to represent the various logic functions: one commonly used set is shown in

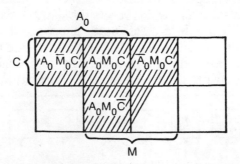

Fig. 3-6. Veitch diagram: One-set carry logic terms.

Fig. 3-7. Using these symbols a schematic diagram of a serial adder is shown in Fig. 3-8.

The Parallel Adder

With today's integrated circuit technology, there is no longer a need to accept the time delay associated with one-bit-at-a-time operation in order to save hardware. All microprocessors use parallel arithmetic. The AMP (Rockwell PPS-8) adder is 8 bits in length, accepts 2 parallel inputs

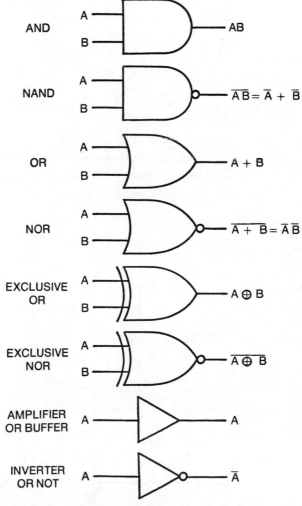

Fig. 3-7. Logic element symbols.

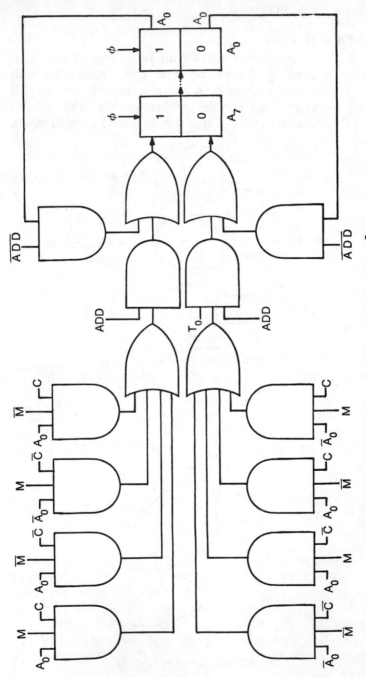

Fig. 3-8. Schematic diagram of an 8-bit serial adder, 1^C and 0^C not shown.

Table 3-1.

a_i	b_i	c_i	$s_i = a_i + b_i$	$s_i = s_i + c_i$
0	0	0	0	0
0	0	1	0	1
0	1	0	1	1
0	1	1	1	0
1	0	0	1	1
1	0	1	1	0
1	1	0	0	0
1	1	1	0	1

(A and B) and an initial carry (C_0). From this data, the adder generates a sum (S). The process is as follows:

A and B are both binary fractions such that

$$A = a_7/2 + a_6/4 + a_5/8 + \bullet \ \bullet \ \bullet + a_0/2^8$$
$$B = b_7/2 + b_6/4 + b_5/8 + \bullet \bullet \bullet + b_0/2^8$$

The sum is:

$$S = A + B = S_7/2 + 2_6/4 + \bullet\bullet\bullet + S_0/2^8$$

The 1^c term from the serial adder is

$$c_{i+1} = a_i b_i + a_i c_i + b_i c_i$$

As an alternate mechanization to the more straight-forward AND and OR Logic, the AMP uses exclusive-OR elements to simplify the mechanization somewhat, with the result that

$$S_i = a_i \oplus b_i \oplus c_i$$
$$c_i = (a_{i-1} \oplus b_{i-1})c_{i-1} + a_{i-1} b_{i-1}$$

The generation of a sum digit using exclusive-OR logic is done according to the truth table in Table 3-1. A mechanization of the sum generation is illustrated in Fig. 3-9, where the *carry into* (CIN) terms represent the inputs generated by the c_i equations.

For the parallel adder, the logic equations for c_i are generated as CIN_i terms, the first four of which are as follows:

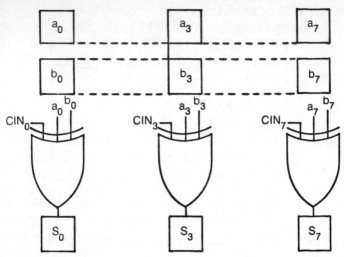

Fig. 3-9. Partial schematic diagram showing generation of sum terms with exclusive-OR gates.

$$CIN_0 = (C) (ADD)$$
$$CIN_1 = (C) (ADD) (a_0 \oplus b_0) + (a_0 b_0) (ADD)$$
$$CIN_2 = [(C) (ADD) (a_0 \oplus b_0) + (a_0 b_0) (ADD)]$$
$$(a_1 \oplus b_1) + (a_1 b_1) (ADD)$$
$$CIN_3 = \{[(C)(ADD) (a_0 \oplus b_0) + (a_0 b_0)$$
$$(ADD)](a_1 \oplus b_1) + (a_1 b_1) (ADD)\}$$
$$(a_2 \oplus b_2) + (a_2 b_2) (ADD)$$

Figure 3-10 illustrates the logic generation of the first three CIN terms. By now you can see that a pattern is evident in both the logic and equations. Instead of setting the carry flip-flop, as was done in the serial adder, the set logic is duplicated in each stage and combined with the A_i and M_i terms. As a result, the carry into bit position 8 looks like quite a mess, but Fig. 3-10 illustrates that the various CIN terms are generated successively and used as the input to the next group of logic gates. Thus, while the logic equations may look formidable, the actual logic circuits consist merely of repetitive stages, each of which generates another CIN term.

The ADD input in Fig. 3-10 is the add mode control, which is made true when an addition is commanded. Note that the stage of the carry flip-flop itself need not change during the 8-bit addition, but it will normally be set or reset depending upon the presence or absence of a carry out from the eighth bit position at the completion of the addition. The AMP uses this carry flip-flop in the instruction ADI (add immediate and skip or carry out), which is explained in Chapter 5. With this instruction, the previous state of the carry flip-flop is preserved, even though an addition has taken place.

Four-Phase MOS Logic

It is now necessary to say a few words about the use of four-phase MOS logic. The basic processor clock is composed of two separate, but synchronized clocks, A and $\bar{B}$. From these two timing sources, four clock signals are determined, and these are denoted ϕ_1, ϕ_2, ϕ_3, ϕ_4. The time during which each is true in relationship to A and $\bar{B}$ is shown in Fig. 5-14.

The use of separate, phased clocks permits multiple functions to be performed serially in one major clock period. The parallel adder takes advantage of this fact to propagate

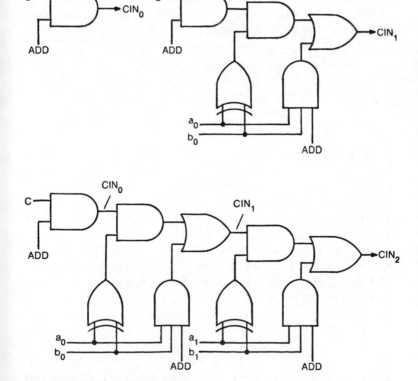

Fig. 3-10. Generation of carry-in terms for bits 0, 1, and 2.

the carry from the least to the most significant digit position in one major clock time. Carry determination is the hang-up of parallel adders, since the carry into bit position i is not known until position $i-1$ has been processed. If this delay is accepted, an 8-bit adder cannot generate a sum in four minor clock periods. But because MOS logic is used, it is not necessary to propagate both 1-set and 0-set terms. Instead, only the 1-set need be considered. (It so happens that the complement is propagated in the PPS-8, but this is simply a matter of needing the complement itself for other logic.)

MOS dynamic logic operates by gating signals. Either a particular gate conducts or it does not. For four-phase MOS logic, the clock times are used to control three sequential modes of operation: precharge, sample (or evaluate) and hold. During precharge, selected gate capacitors are charged negatively. During sample, a controlled set of capacitors are discharged, allowing their previous stage to determine the voltage on other capacitors, thus transferring the information. During hold, the capacitors simply hold their charge.

Chapter 4
Fixed-Point Arithmetic

An observant programmer once remarked that "life is too short to write more than one fixed-point program." The trouble lies in the fact that the microprocessor does not keep track of the position of the radical point (or binary point). It neither knows nor cares where the programmer places it. This means that the programmer must provide a method of keeping such records externally or write a separate program designed to keep the records for him. Obviously, the nuisance involved might not appeal to some programmers, but there are many simple applications where fixed-point arithmetic is quite satisfactory.

CONVENTIONS

The usual convention is to consider all numbers in the processor memory as being less than or equal to one in absolute value. This definition permits the establishment of a reference position by placing the binary point between the most significant digit and the sign bit of the data word. Thus the sign bit is zero if the number is positive, and one if the number is negative. For example, the numbers +0.5 and −0.25 would be represented like this:

$$\boxed{0\ \vert\ 1\ \ 0\ \ 0\ \ 0\ \ 0\ \ 0\ \ 0} = +0.5$$

$$\boxed{1\ \vert\ 1\ \ 1\ \ 0\ \ 0\ \ 0\ \ 0\ \ 0} = -0.25$$

where the arrowheads mark the location of the binary point.

It is this "fixing" of the reference that gives rise to the term *fixed point*. Other more convenient techniques are available in which the service program keeps track of the binary point for you. These techniques are known as *floating point*, and they are discussed in Chapter 7.

A 2's complement processor cannot contain a +1 under these rules, but it can hold a −1, as 10000000. Note that this is truly a −1, for if it is added to +0.5, which is 01000000, the result is −0.5, or 11000000.

The preceding numbers are considered as being in *machine units*, or in a *binary scale* of zero. We shall define this binary scale, using the letter B, as the number of digit positions to the right of the zero position that the binary point must be shifted to obtain the proper value of the number. Thus for each piece of fixed-point data, there must be an associated binary scale.

The reason for requiring a binary scale is illustrated by the following number held in memory, for which different binary scales may be assigned.

$$\boxed{0}\;\boxed{1\quad 1\quad 0\quad 1\quad 0\quad 0\quad 0}$$
$$-B \longleftarrow \blacktriangle \longrightarrow +B$$

For B = 0, the value of this number is +0.1101.
For B = 1, the value is +1.101
For B = 7, the value is +1,101,000.
For B = 10, the value is +1,101,000,000.
For B = −3, the value is +0.0001101.

Note that the binary point of the number need not fall within the register. Leading or trailing zeros may be attached to the number in memory as required to form the proper magnitude. Normally numbers should be held at a scale such that there are no leading zeros in memory (or leading ones if the number is negative and in complementary form), which is to insure maximum utilization of the available bit positions. This situation is termed the *minimum* binary scale, for which values can be found in Appendix D.

A number cannot be held at a scale less than the minimum scale. Any attempt to do so will result in an incorrect representation by the processor. When this occurs during an arithmetic operation, the unfortunate result is known as *overflow*. For example, the number 30_{10} can be held at B = 5, for which the binary representation is

| 0 | 1 | 1 | 1 | 1 | 0 | 0 | 0 |

But the number cannot be properly held at B = 4, or the result would look like this

| 1 | 1 | 1 | 1 | 0 | 0 | 0 | 0 |

which the processor might interpret as a negative number because of the one shifted into the sign bit position.

Fixed-point arithmetic involves a deliberate effort on the part of the programmer to maintain a running account of the magnitudes of the variables encountered throughout the program. Fortunately, this effort can be organized according to well-defined rules.

SCALING RULES FOR FIXED-POINT ARITHMETIC OPERATIONS

Whenever fixed-point arithmetic is used, the binary scale of the quantity at every step in the calculation must be considered. To assist in keeping accurate account of the magnitudes, it has been found useful to include the binary scale of the result of each arithmetic operation in the program comments. (In the following examples, the binary scale associated with each number is shown in parentheses.)

Addition

The binary scale of the addend must be equal to that of the augend. This also happens to be the binary scale of the sum, though an adjustment in scale may be required in the sum to prevent an overflow condition. For example, $8_{(+4)} + 2_{(+4)} = 10_{(+4)}$) appears in the processor as

| +8 | | 0 | 1 | 0 | 0 | 0 | 0 | 0 | 0 | | (B = +4) |

| +2 | | 0 | 0 | 0 | 1 | 0 | 0 | 0 | 0 | | (B = +4) |

| +10 | | 0 | 1 | 0 | 1 | 0 | 0 | 0 | 0 | | (B = +4) |

|← +4 →|

Example: Add $7_{(+3)}$ and $9_{(+4)}$. Since the addend is stored at a different binary scale than the augend, it will first be necessary to shift at least one position in order to have equal binary scales. But shifting the 7 to the right one place to give both numbers a binary scale of +4 is not adequate since the sum of the two numbers is 16, or 2^4, and so requires a minimum binary scale of +5 to prevent overflow. Only by shifting both numbers to obtain a binary scale of +5 will the accumulator be able to accommodate the sum without overflow. Thus the addition must take place as $7_{(+5)} + 9_{(+5)} = 16_{(+5)}$.

Subtraction

The binary scale of the subtrahend must be equal to that of the minuend. This is also the binary scale of the difference. The binary scale for each subtraction should be chosen to accommodate the subtrahend, minuend, and difference.

Example: $36 - (-40) = +76$.   The   minuend   and subtrahend both have a minimum binary scale of +6 since they are numerically less than $2^6 = 64$. However, the difference is equal to +76, which has a minimum binary scale of +7. Thus, the minuend and subtrahend must be shifted so that $B = +7$ for each, and then the difference will be accommodated in the accumulator without overflow.

Multiplication

The binary scale of the product is equal to the sum of the binary scale of the multiplicand and the binary scale of the multiplier.

A few current processors have multiplication capability built into their hardware, but most require programmed subroutines. In either case the rule for the binary scale must be adhered to if overflow is to be prevented. This rule will also yield the largest possible number of significant digits for the product, though the potential presence of leading zeros in the product may mean that the product will not always be at its minimum binary scale. The number of digits that are significant, of course, depends upon the number of significant digits in the original data.

Example: $(-526) \times (3867) = -2,034,042$. Here the binary scales of the multiplicand and multiplier are +10 and +12, so the product must have $B = +22$. In this case the product is more than 2^{20} but less than 2^{21}, indicating that the adjusted scale of the product is $B = +21$ since there is one leading zero when $B = +22$.

Division

The binary scale of the quotient is equal to the binary scale of the dividend minus the binary scale of the devisor. The divisor must be greater in magnitude than the dividend as they are positioned in the registers.

Few commercially available processors at this writing have hardware division capability. There are algorithms available from which to program a division subroutine (see Chapter 6), but all will require adherence to the division rule.

Example: $124 \div 63 = 1.97$. Here the dividend has $B = +7$ and the division has $B = +6$. The quotient then has $B = 7 - 6 = +1$. Since a subtraction is involved in figuring the binary scale of the quotient, it is possible for the quotient to have a binary that is larger than that of the dividend.

When performing division, the binary representation is often written in groups of four, to correspond to hexadecimal notation, but this grouping is only for our convenience and does not exist in the processor. The numbers in the preceding example would then be written as

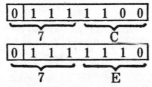

Note that even though the divisor is larger than the dividend, both are positioned in their respective registers as required by their minimum binary scale. This is a necessary and sufficient condition to insure proper division. Of course, after completion of the division, it may be necessary to shift the position of the quotient to obtain a proper minimum binary scale.

Exponentiation

The binary scale of a number raised to a positive integral power is equal to the product of the original binary scale and the power to which the number is raised.

Most operations of evaluating powers of numbers involve raising a number to a positive integral power, such as a^2 and n^8. But this process really amounts to successive multiplications in which the number is multiplied by itself the required number of times. Thus n^3 would be evaluated as $n \times n \times n$, where the scaling rule is applied to each successive product. For example, if n is at a binary scale of 4, the binary scale of n^2 would be $4 + 4 = 8$, by the scaling rule for multiplication, or $4 \times 2 = 8$, by the scaling rule for exponentiation. To form n^3 with one more multiplication, the base of n^2 , which is 8, would be added to the base of n, which is 4, to obtain a new base of 12. However, using the exponentiation rule, the same result would be arrived at since $4 \times 3 = 12$. And since the entire operation is the result of successive multiplications, overflow cannot occur in this simple form of exponentiation.

Root Extraction

Root extraction is, of course, a form of exponentiation using *fractional* exponents, such as $a^{1/2} = \sqrt{a}$. The same scaling rule applies to root extraction as to the case of simple exponentiation, but with one catch—the resulting binary scale must be modified if the product of the number base and the exponent results in an answer that is not an integer. This modification can take one of two forms:

1. The mantissa can be shifted, with corresponding additions or subtractions to the binary scale.
2. The fractional portion of the binary scale can be converted into an equivalent multiplying factor that is used to correct the mantissa value.

Example: Find the square root of 5. The number 5 would be held in the register at $B = 3$, so the mantissa, or fraction, would appear as

0	1	0	1	0	0	0	0

But $3 \times 0.5 = 1.5$, and this is not an acceptable base. This problem can be fixed in this case by shifting the mantissa one place, thereby changing the base to 4, and $4 \times 0.5 = 2$, which is an integer. The mantissa would then appear as

0	0	1	0	1	0	0	0

The calculated square root (2.236...) is then held at $B = 2$ as

0	1	0	0	0	1	1	1

There is also an alternate method for computing the square root of 5, and this method entails taking the square root of the mantissa as if it were a number held at $B = 0$. In the preceding example, the binary number would be interpreted as 0.101_2 or 0.625_{10} . The square root is computed directly and is approximately 0.791_{10} and this would appear in the register as

$$\boxed{0} \;\; \boxed{1 \quad 1 \quad 0 \quad 0 \quad 1 \quad 0 \quad 1}$$

Now by applying our rule, the binary scale of the answer should have been $3 \times 0.5 = 1.5$. The fractional part (0.5) can be removed by simply multiplying the mantissa of our answer by a predetermined constant of $2^{0.5} = \sqrt{2}$ at a binary scale of 1, following the usual rules of multiplication. Thus, $0.791 \times 1.414 = 1.118_{10}$. Increasing the base by the remainder (that is, $1.5 - 0.5 = 1$) doubles the result, yielding 2.236_{10} which is held at $B = 2$ as before.

Similarly, all real exponents can be expressed as the sum of an integer and a fraction (negative exponents included), so the real cases are covered here. It may happen that the multiplicative constant needed is a bit difficult to compute, such as $2^{0.31415}$, but it will nevertheless be a constant and can always be calculated beforehand.

The advantage of using a multiplicative constant to take care of the fractional part of the exponent lies in the fact that it does not require excessive shifting of the mantissa, as the first example required. Any shifting will usually be to the right, and if the root is a nasty one, say $n^{1/11}$, several right shifts (11, 22, 33, etc.) may have to be made to find an integer number for the binary scale. In fact there is real danger that the mantissa may disappear altogether as it is shifted entirely out of the register. So, even though method 1 may be simpler, method 2 affords more precision.

Precision

So far, we have been primarily concerned with avoiding an overflow condition. Also damaging, in the sense that the result will be in error, is loss of precision. In the extreme case, you may find an erroneously computed result of zero because sequential calculations have been performed at binary scales greater than the minimum, and the register length was insufficient to hold enough significant digits with numbers so scaled. This sad condition is termed *underflow* though purists restrict the use of this term to floating-point arithmetic (see Chapter 7). In either event, the result is an unexpected zero.

Most processors have an overflow flag that can be tested to determine whether or not an overflow has occurred since that last time the flag was tested or reset. AMP uses the carry flip-flop for this purpose. No microprocessor today provides a similar protection for underflow.

To maximize precision and avoid underflows, use binary scales as near the minimum as possible. Where the result of a previous computation is not at the minimum scale, it is better to shift the result left and then perform the required arithmetic, rather than doing further operations prior to rescaling.

It may be that the word length that was originally chosen was simply insufficient to hold enough bits to maintain the required precision, even though minimum or near-minimum scales were used throughout. If this occurs, there is no option other than to increase the operating word length by adding bytes. This is generally awkward to do once the program is written. Memory fields must be expanded, counter limits changed, and addresses modified to accommodate these new bytes. Careful analyses will help, but there are no sure-fire systems that easily yield the minimum required word length. Two configurations to be wary of are:

1. The subtraction of two nearly equal numbers. Look for a possible problem, reordering or reformulating the program to avoid this precision loss or by deferring it as late as possible in the computational cycle.

2. Division. This is very often troublesome since the problem must be scaled to provide for the combination of the smallest denominator and the largest numerator. Other number pairs will yield smaller quotients and hence significance is likely to be lost at these points in the problem. While similar precision loss can occur all operations, the range of quotient values is often larger than the range of sum and difference values for many real problems. The best answer is to use the divide operation sparingly. Where necessary, a test may be added in the program to examine the values of the numerator and denominator and, where necessary, to rescale either or both to provide for a smaller scale to properly contain the quotient.

For most real problems the scale factor will have included a physical quantity (minutes, feet, radians, etc.). These units of course are handled externally in identical fashion to the familiar dimensional analysis. For example,

$$\frac{[A_{(+2)} \text{ feet}] [B_{(+3)} \text{ pounds}]}{[M_{(+1)} \text{ seconds}] [N_{(0)} \text{ seconds}]} = P_{(+4)} \text{ ft-lb/sec}^2$$

The first topic of Chapter 12 will be concerned with more complex (less natural) numeric scale factors when there is an advantage to be gained from their use in instruction count or computational speed.

Chapter 5
Basic Microprocessor
Programming

Program development can be thought of as occuring in four steps—specifying requirements, flow charting, coding, and testing. These steps are explained as follows:

Specifying Requirements. The programmer should have available, at the start, a complete set of demands on the program. Input data magnitudes and format; maximum allowable solution times; equations to be solved; output requirements and formats. The problem should usually be well understood before the programmer proceeds any further.

Flow Charting. The flow chart is a picture of the program paths. It is a very necessary tool. Flow charts are often prepared in conjunction with the generation of specifications and modified as the requirements change to fit within the hardware constraints. Because you are using a microprocessor, you will find that you will be concerned about available time and memory to a greater degree than when programming a larger computer system. This is part of the fun—to successfully solve a constrained problem using ingenuity. A complete but not necessarily detailed flow chart should be available before the coding is begun.

Coding. Using the manuals prepared by the manufacturer, examine the programming aids and input forms, then decide which form you wish to use. Virtually no one generates code in pure machine binary or hexadecimal since assembly programs are available for all microprocessor systems on the market. Assembly programs usually generate one machine instruction for each input statement, also providing some rudimentary error checks, a more-or-less readable listing (see Fig. 5-1), and the ability to conveniently replace or relocate blocks of code. Assembly programs often can be run on the microprocessor for which they assemble code, provided sufficient memory and the right peripheral equipment are available. More often, they are run on other, larger machines, generating outputs that can be read into the PROM or used to generate ROM masks. Such assemblers are known as *cross assemblers*.

Testing. The testing or checkout phase normally begins with a code check at the desk to remove obvious errors. The program is then entered into a PROM and executed to assure that it functions logically and runs to completion. When the program passes these preliminary tests, numerical results from the program are compared with predetermined answers from a set of test problems. The complexity of this checkout is normally determined by the programmer himself—he should be reasonably assured that there are no errors or "bugs" remaining. Trace routines, simulators, emulators, etc., are often made available by the manufacturer to somewhat simplify the task of detecting and removing program errors (see Chapter 8). A common misconception among programmers concerns the time required to adequately check out a program. Almost all seriously underestimate this effort for significant programs—the checkout phase will normally take about half of the total calendar time needed to develop the program.

Let's assume that the program requirements have been properly stated, since we can't do much about that step here, and proceed to a discussion of program organization and flow charting.

FLOW CHARTS

The flow chart in Fig. 5-2 doesn't represent a mathematical problem, but does demonstrate the pictorial value of such a chart. Sequences of activities can be easily seen, as can points at which decisions are made, yielding one of two or more possible courses of action. Loops are defined where one of the two possible paths is to go back and perform and same (or almost the same) activity again. Functional as

```
ROM     ..CODE..        ARG     STMT    SOURCE STATEMENTS
ADOR    I1 I2 I3                NUMBER

                                593              ORG

                                595     ******** HL    NMLZX* ***************************************
                                596     *PERFORMS LEFT SHIFTS AND EXPONENT, ADJUSTMENTS OF X* REGISTER *
                                597     *UNTIL MSD IS NONZERO
0300    E8(8B AB)   0314        598     NMLZX*   BL    R=0?        |X*| = 0 ?
0301    9F                      599              DW    X*M
0302    8H          0308        600              B     LFTJST
0303    A0(20 40)   005E        601              LXI   X*S
0304    A6(26 72)   0000        602              LAI   0
0305    74                      603              SD
0306    75                      604              S
0307    5E                      605              RT
0308    85(05)9F    0060        606     LFTJST   LXI   X*M        X*M = 0 ?
030A    A6(26 72)   0000        607              LAI   0
030B    45                      608              MDL
030C    62                      609              SKZ
030D    5E                      610              RT
030E    E6(86 A6)   00E1        611              BL    LSFT       SHIFT LEFT X* REG.
030F    90          0063        612              DW    X*0
0310    A0(20 40)   005E        613              LXI   X*S
0311    E7(R7 A7)   031F        614              BL    EM1        EXP <- EXP - 1
0312    21                      615              NOP
0313    8H          0308        616              B     LFTJST
```

Fig. 5-1. Assembler listing for Rockwell PPS-8 system.

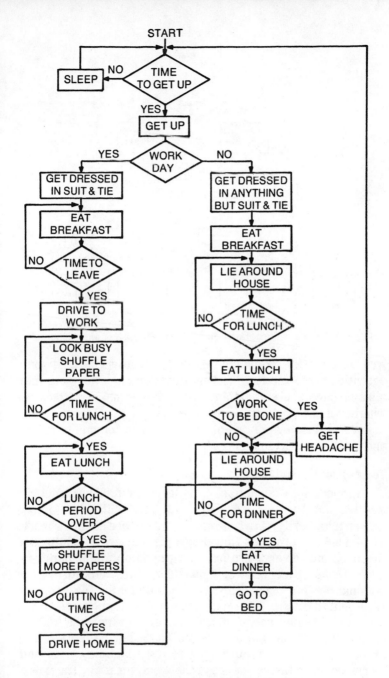

Fig. 5-2. Flow chart of an ordinary day.

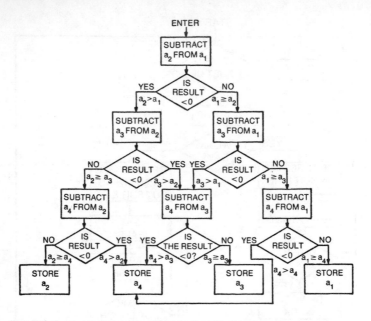

Fig. 5-3. An explicit program flow to find the largest of four numbers.

well as pictorial efficiency results from observing that some activities performed at different times are *common*—our man always does the same thing from dinner on, regardless of whether it is a work day or the weekend.

We will now apply some of these observations to logical and mathematical sequences.

To Loop or Not to Loop

Suppose we wished to find the largest number of a set of 4 positive numbers (A_1, A_2, A_3, A_4). (We will settle for one chosen arbitrarily, if two or more numbers are equal.) Figures 5-3 and 5-4 are program flow diagrams that define solutions to this problem. Even when operating upon only four numbers, these flows have become unwieldly, and both forms are unthinkable for use with, say, 100 numbers. The program represented by Fig. 5-3 is quite wasteful of memory, requiring an inordinate number of instructions, which increase linearly as the size of the number set to be tested increases. This program, however, requires the fewest machine cycles and, therefore, runs faster than any other configuration. The flow of Fig. 5-4 is better than that of 5-3 in terms of instruction count because common storage is used to hold the largest number

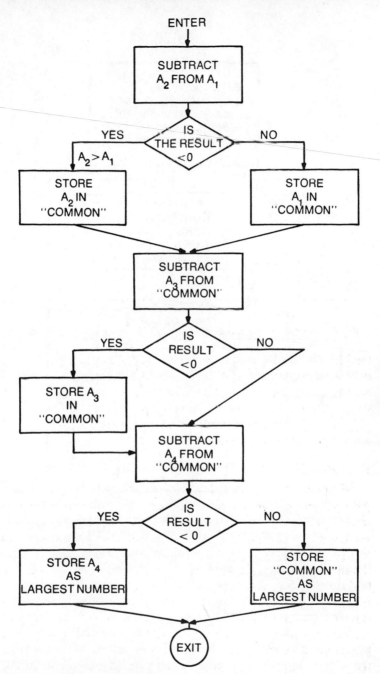

Fig. 5-4. A second explicit program flow to find the largest of four numbers.

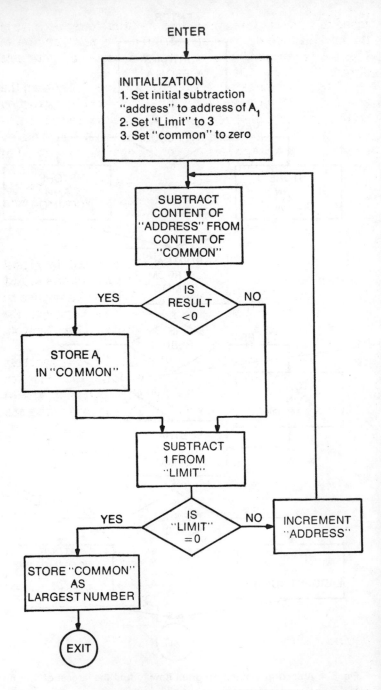

Fig. 5-5. A program loop to find the largest of a set of numbers.

found to date, but the program runs a little slower because of the intermediate data storage required. The program flow in Fig. 5-4 is not particularly useful for substantial data sets either.

Figure 5-5 represents a loop that will run slower than the preceding configurations, but it is more efficient in instruction count and can handle large strings of data by merely changing the limit variable during initialization. The use of a loop places a constraint upon data storage, in that data must be stored in orderly fashion in the data memory. Use of adjacent cells as depicted here is common but not mandatory. Any orderly process that can be used to predict the address of the next data element can be used.

Iteration

Iterative techniques are particularly suited to digital processors. They are commonly used for optimization, and where explicit solutions are either difficult or impossible in terms of known functions. As an example of this technique, the determination of a quadratic root (R_1) by the Newton-Raphson method is described.

The plan of attack is pictured in Fig. 5-6. The parabola chosen for the example is described by the equation $x^2 = (y + 1)/2$. We choose a first guess, $M_1 = (x_1, y_1)$, then determine the tangent to the curve at M_1 and move down the

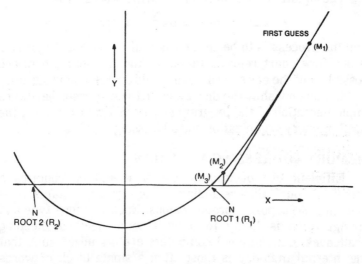

Fig. 5-6. Iterative Newton-Raphson technique for finding quadratic roots.

tangent to $y = 0$, finding the corresponding x. We now move back to the curve, holding x constant, and get a new value, $M_2 = (x_2, y_2)$. The process is repeated as many times as necessary until the magnitude of resulting y_N is less than a predetermined error limit, ϵ. When this occurs, the corresponding x_N is the root we were after.

We must be careful, however, to pick M_1 large enough such that we don't find the wrong root (we could be iterating toward R_2). In the case used here, any positive x would work, but to be safe, we chose the largest positive number the processor can hold as the first guess (x_1).

The general form of Newton-Raphson quadratic approximation is:

$$x_{N1} = x_N - (y_N / y_N')$$

where n and $n + 1$ denote the successive guesses, and y_N' is the slope of the curve at point n:

$$y_N = 2x_N{}^2 - 1$$

$$y_n' = 4x_N$$

We have also decided that we will be satisfied that x_N is our root when the corresponding value of y_N is less than $2^{-8} = 1/256$, a fairly crude approximation, so ϵ is set equal to $1/256$.

The equation to be mechanized in the processor is

$$x_{N+1} = x_N - (2x_N{}^2 - 1)/4x_N$$

And the process is to be continued until $y_N \leqslant 1/256$. Figure 5-7 is one flow chart representation for the solution; others are possible, but the one shown should yield an efficient program.

Let us now shift the discussion to the processor hardware implementation of the program sequence, first examining the AMP memory organization and addressing.

MEMORY ADDRESSING AND PAGING

Efficient use of microprocessor memories requires a rather thorough understanding of the memory organizations and special-purpose storage regions. Each memory type and configuration is likely to present some new bookkeeping challenges. Conventional computers are organized such that the internal memory is most often a single block of words beginning at address 0, and numbered sequentially through to the last word. Both instructions and data are generally contained in the same high-speed memory. The only distinction occurs at access time, depending upon whether the computer is in an *instruction read* or an *operand read* state at the time the information is extracted from memory.

The microprocessor will normally use some type of ROM for storing most instructions and fixed data, and a RAM for holding variable data. The content of the data address (or B) register is used to address RAM, while the contents of the program address (or P) register is used to address ROM. These two memories are addressed independently by the basic AMP CPU. In fact, when using the AMP the independence is so strong that arithmetic instruction modification is not possible. This precludes treating an instruction as data, modifying it, and then executing the modified instruction. While this is a limitation that might prevent the programmer from creating some clever code, it also prevents some rather subtle errors that might arise from this kind of operation. However, this is a

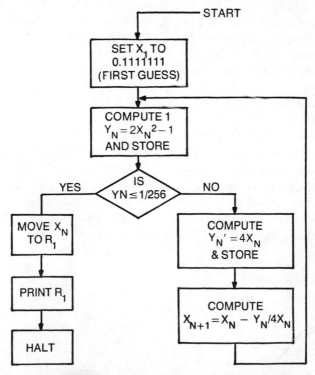

Fig. 5-7. Newton-Raphson iteration flow diagram.

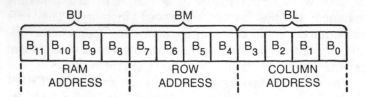

Fig. 5-8. Organization of data address (B) register.

limitation not found in processors that permit a freer interchange of data.

RAM Addressing

The AMP data address word is contained in the 12-bit B register, which is logically separated into three 4-bit partial registers, BU, BM, and BL—B upper, middle, and lower—as depicted in Fig. 5-8. The BU Field specifies one particular 256×8-bit RAM from a maximum of 16 possible addressed memory chips. (0000 in BU selects RAM-0; 1111 selects RAM-15.) BM and BL provide the coordinates for one of 256 available 8-bit words in accordance with Fig. 5-9.

Since our AMP has only one RAM chip, it will be identified as RAM-0. The address of word 6A in RAM-0 would then appear in B as $06A_{16}$. Word 6A is logically located as shown in Fig. 5-9. The B register can be modified in several ways. It is initially set to all zeros when power-on becomes true. It can be set to known addresses by use of a pair of *load B* instructions (see Appendix E), which put predetermined fixed information from the ROM into B. It can also be modified under control of a set of register exchange instructions, which cause data exchange between B and A, or B and X, permitting variable information from data memory to be transferred into B. BL can also be incremented or decremented under program control.

ROM Addressing

The P register is a 12-bit register that contains sufficient information to address the ROM program memory. Unlike the B register, the P register contains counter logic that increments the P counter each time an instruction is executed. The P register is set to zero after power reset, and it can also be set under program control to an arbitrary value by the execution of one of several *control transfer* instructions or incremented by an additional count as a result of the execution of *conditional transfer* instructions when the specified condition is met.

The P counter is composed of only the least significant 6 bits of the P register, so that upon power reset, the P register can count only from 0 to 63_{10}. It then cycles back through 0. Only the execution of a transfer instruction can alter the most significant 6 bits of P. The reason for this kind of operation is to save instruction word length, and hence program memory. A more complete addressing capability would imply that each control transfer instruction contains enough bits to fully address any word within a ROM (or a block of ROMs).

The *address compaction* method used here is known as *paging*. The ROM can be thought of as a book divided into pages that are directly addressable without requiring the execution of a transfer instruction. The P register organization is shown in Fig. 5-10, and the hexadecimal address to page and ROM numbers in Table 5-1. The *word address* corresponds to the counter portion. A page then consists of 64 words. All words on a page can be addressed using the 6-bit counter.

Upon power reset, the P register, like the B register, is set to zero. This means that the first instruction to be executed will be taken from ROM-0, page-0, word-0. The ROM-0 data is further subdivided into special-purpose pages (see Fig. 5-11),

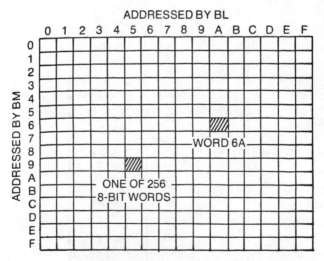

Fig. 5-9. RAM address organization.

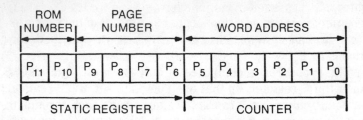

Fig. 5-10. Program (P) register organization.

but this is not true of any other ROM. While pages 0, 1, and 2 of
ROM-0 can contain general instructions, page 3 (beginning at
address $0C0_{16}$ and ending at address $0FF_{16}$ contains *address
pointers*—8-bit groups that indicate (point to) a subroutine

Table 5-1. ROM Address Equivalences

ROM	PAGE	HEX RANGE
0	0	000-03F
0	1	040-07F
0	2	080-0BF
0	3	0C0-0FF
0	4	100-13F
0	5	140-17F
0	6	180-1BF
0	7	1C0-1FF
0	8	200-23F
0	9	240-27F
0	10	280-2BF
0	11	2C0-2FF
0	12	300-33F
0	13	340-37F
0	14	380-3BF
0	15	3C0-3FF
1	16	400-43F
1	17	440-47F
1	18	480-4BF
1	19	4C0-4FF
1	20	500-53F
1	21	540-57F
1	22	580-5BF
1	23	5C0-5FF
1	24	600-63F
1	25	640-67F
1	26	680-6BF
1	27	6C0-6FF
1	28	700-73F
1	29	740-77F
1	30	780-7BF
1	31	7C0-7FF

entry address, used in conjunction with the *transfer and mark* (TM) instruction.

Data stored in locations $OC0_{16}$ through OCF_{16} (the first 16 words in ROM-0, page-3) may be addressed by the LB instruction, which occupies only one ROM word. This provides a very efficient access to these locations. To save additional program memory, TM instruction entry addresses are provided in pages 4 through 7 of ROM-0 (addresses 100_{16} through $1FF_{16}$).

The use of special-purpose instructions having limited scope is typical of microprocessor organization and adds to the challenge of programming.

INSTRUCTION SET

The AMP processor recognizes 44 distinct instructions or commands. The majority are 1-byte (8-bit) instructions. These 8 bits are used as *operation code* (op-code) designators,

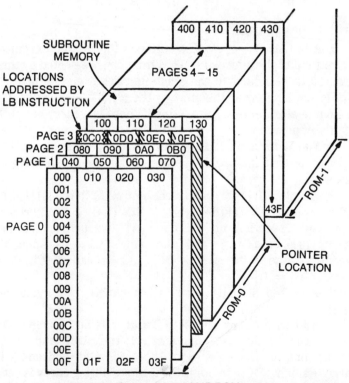

Fig. 5-11. Schematic of AMP ROM system.

although some of the 256 possible combinations are used in conjunction with a few instructions to specify addresses, or for bit patterns used to partially load registers. Five of the AMP instructions require 2 bytes (16 bits), where the added information is used to specify addresses or to load the accumulator with data from a ROM. All microprocessors have a somewhat similar instruction structure, although the 8-bit instruction formats may be restricted to a 4-bit operation code, permitting as few as 16 primary operations, with the other 4 bits used as partial addresses and modifiers to designate instruction subclasses.

The AMP instructions are logically separated into the groups introduced earlier (with some overlap) and summarized in Appendix E. We begin the discussion of the instruction set with the 14 instructions that comprise the arithmetic and logic group, identifying each instruction, giving a brief description of the function, the mnemonic code, and the number of machine cycles used in execution.

Arithmetic and Logic Group

1. Add (A). One cycle. Execution of this instruction causes the content of the addressed RAM memory M selected by the B register to be added to the accumulator. The state of the C flip-flop is ignored at the start of the addition; however, C is set to one at execution completion if there is a carry out of the eighth bit position.

2. Add With Carry (ADC). One cycle. Operates similarly to *add* except that the previous state of C is used in forming the new sum.

Example: If [M], (read "content of M") is 11011110 (or BE_{16}) and [A] = 11101001 ($E9_{16}$), then [C] = 1. Therefore, upon the execution of the add (A) instruction, the new [A] = 11000111 ($C7_{16}$) and the new [C] = 1. Upon the execution of add with carry (ADC), [A] = 11001000 ($C8_{16}$) and the new [C] = 1.

3. Add and Skip if Carry is Set (ASK). One cycle. See ADSK.

4. Add with Carry and Skip if Carry is Set (ADSK). One cycle. The arithmetic functions of the ASK and ADSK instructions are identical with those for add, and add with carry, (A and ADC). In addition, if the resulting carry is set to one, the next ROM word is ignored, providing a program branch on the state of C.

5. Decimal Correct 1 (DC). One cycle. See DCC.

6. Decimal Correct 2 (DCC). One cycle. The DC and DCC instruction pair is used to generate BCD sums. Their operation is described in Chapter 2 and is not repeated here.

7. Add Immediate and Skip on Carry Out (ADI). Two cycles. This instruction provides a means for using data obtained from the ROM. It is not particularly efficient since only 8 bits can be obtained at a time, at the expense of 16 bits of memory and two machine cycles; however, the skip or branching operation compensates somewhat. The 8-bit content of ROM immediately following the byte containing the op-code is added to the content of A (C is ignored). If the *carry out* is a one, the next instruction in sequence is ignored. (*Carry out* is used here to describe the logic information that would normally be used to set C, although C is not used or changed.)

Example: Initially $[A] = 76_{16}$ and $[C] = 0$. After the execution of ADI, the new $[A] = 22_{16}$, which is 76 + AC. The carry out is one, so the next ROM location is skipped, but the [C] is still zero.

8. Logical AND (AND). One cycle. See EOR.

9. Logical OR (OR). One cycle. See EOR.

10. Logical Exclusive OR (EOR). One cycle. Instructions 8, 9, and 10 cause the stated logical operation to be performed on the [A] and [M] with the result becoming the new [A]. [M] is unchanged.

Example: [A] = D9 and [M] = 72. The execution of AND will cause the new [A] = 50. The execution of OR will cause the new [A] = FB. The execution of EOR will cause the new [A] = AB.

11. Complement (COMP). One cycle. The execution of COMP causes the [A] to be replaced with the *1's complement* of [A]. For example, if [A] = D9, the execution of COMP will cause the new [A] = 26. This instruction is used to perform subtraction and is normally used in conjunction with the SC instruction to obtain the 2's complement. But if you prefer, you can program the AMP to perform 1's complement subtraction.

12. Set Carry Flip-flop (SC). One cycle. See RC.

13. Reset Carry Flip-flop (RC). One cycle. The SC and RC instruction pair cause C to be set to a known state. The execution of SC causes C to be set to one. The execution of RC causes C to be set to zero.

14. Accumulator Right Shift (ARS). One cycle. This instruction shifts the [A] one place to the right. The bit shifted out of A replaces the original [C]. The value initially placed in C is shifted into the most significant bit position of A. The bit retention in C enables multibyte shifts. The ability to place either a one or zero in C prior to the execution of ARS permits the proper arithmetic shifting of both positive and negative numbers.

Example 1: The word being operated on in AMP consists of 4 bytes (32 bits):

| S | byte 3 | byte 2 | byte 1 | byte 0 |

(Byte 3 contains the sign bit in the most significant position.)

To shift the entire word right one place and preserve the proper arithmetic configuration, first determine the sign of the word to be shifted. If it is negative, a one is initially placed into the C flip-flop, which will cause a one to be shifted into the sign position. If the number is positive, a zero should be initially put into C to propagate into the sign. If byte 3 of a negative number contains

| 1 | 1 | 0 | 1 | 1 | 0 | 0 | 0 |

Prior to execution of ARS, $1 \rightarrow C$, meaning a one is loaded into C. After execution of ARS,

$$[A] = \boxed{1 \quad 1 \quad 1 \quad 0 \quad 1 \quad 1 \quad 0 \quad 0}$$

and the new $C = 0$.

If byte 2 contains

| 1 | 0 | 1 | 1 | 0 | 1 | 0 | 1 |

C is left unchanged from one. After execution of the second ARS,

$$[A] = \boxed{0 \quad 1 \quad 0 \quad 1 \quad 1 \quad 0 \quad 1 \quad 0}$$

and the new $C = 1$.

Data Transfer Group

There are nine instructions in this group. The basic or "primitive" forms are *load* and *exchange*.

The load instructions describe an instruction set which causes the selected 8-bit content of RAM or of a CPU register to replace the content of the accumulator or another CPU register. Time for execution of this instruction set is one major cycle or about 5 microseconds (μsec).

The exchange instructions will cause the selected 8-bit (12-bit in the case of SA and SB) content of RAM or of a CPU register to be exchanged with the content of the accumulator of another CPU register. Where the exchange is between CPU registers, these instructions are executed in one cycle. Where the exchange occurs between RAM and the accumulator, two major cycles are required since 8 bits of data must be transferred in each direction over an 8-line instruction/data bus. (The PPS-4 System, which is the basis for AMP architecture, operates using a 4-bit data word; 4-bit transfers can be made over the 8-bit bus each way in only one machine cycle by PPS-4.)

A *cycle* instruction is in the AMP repertoire. This is CYS, which causes an 8-bit right shift of the content of the SA Register, with the least significant 8 bits originally in SA replacing the content of A. Meanwhile the original content of A is shifted into the most significant 8 bits of SA. This is typical of the cycle or "long shift" instruction found on many microprocessors. Several of this class of instructions are often included in the instruction set to facilitate addressing and information transfer.

In addition to the basic function of these instructions, a secondary or tertiary operation may also be performed. These permit the programmer to save both time and memory where the auxiliary functions are useful to him. It also may create a problem for him when he finds that the instruction he selected destroyed information that he was counting on using later. Three instructions in the data transfer group are of this genre.

With this introduction let us now examine the set. The instructions are:

1. **Load Accumulator (LD).** One cycle. See EX.

2. **Exchange the Contents of A and RAM (EX).** Two cycles. Upon execution of LD the content of the 8-bit memory word addressed by the B register replaces the content of the accumulator. The original content of A is destroyed. Upon executing both EX and LD, the content of addressed RAM replaces the content of A. In the case of EX, the content of A also replaces the original content of the addressed memory word.

In addition to the primary functions, an accompanying secondary operation is performed by LD and EX, which is that of modifying the BM register. The new content of BM after executing either instruction is determined by the previous content of BM combined by an exclusive OR with the least significant 3 bits of the instruction word.

Example: At the time of reading an LD instruction, the AMP registers and RAM contained the following hexadecimal information:

P	B	A	RAM Byte 056	ROM Btye 02C
02C	056	62	7F	36

After executing the LD instruction, the register contents are modified as follows:

02D	036	7F	(RAM and ROM are unchanged)	

The result is:

1. The P register is incremented by one in preparation for reading the next instruction in sequence.
2. BM (the middle byte of B) is 5, or 0101_2, and the lower 3 bits is exclusive-OR-ed with the least significant 3 bits of the instruction word read from ROM, which is 6, or 110_2. Performing an exclusive OR between 101 and 110 yields the result 011, and this replaces the original lower 3 bits of BM, making B equal 036 instead of 056.
3. The content of location 056 in ROM is then loaded into register A.

While the reason for the exclusive-OR modification of the B register is not immediately clear, it is sufficient at this time to merely observe that B must be modified in some manner unless we wish to access the same information again. This modification of B is one method, and as you will see it turns out to be quite convenient.

3. Exchange and Decrement B (EXD). Two cycles. This is one of the complex multifunction instructions and it operates as an extension of the EX instruction. In addition to all of the **EX** functions, **EXD** causes a further modification to the B register by subtracting one from BL, and if BL = 111111_2 the next instruction is skipped, thus generating a branch command. EXD requires 2 machine cycles because of the 8-bit memory interchange. In this one instruction, data is modified, the middle portion of the data address register is modified, the lower portion is decremented, and a program branch point is established.

4. Load Accumulator Immediate (LDI). Two cycles. LDI is a 2-byte instruction. The first byte is read in one cycle. Once the instruction is decoded, P is incremented and the second byte is read during the next cycle, replacing the accumulator content. Only the first in a string of LDI's is executed (see discussion of LB and LBL). The use of LDI is the primary means of obtaining constant data stored in program memory.

5. Load A From X (LAX). One cycle. The content of the accumulator is replaced by the 8-bit content of the X register. The original content of the accumulator is destroyed.

6. Load X From A (LXA). One cycle. The content of the X register is replaced by the content of the accumulator. The original content of the X register is destroyed.

7. Exchange X and A (XAX). One cycle. The contents of X and A are exchanged.

8. Exchange SA and SB (XS). One cycle. The 12-bit contents of SA and SB are exchanged.

9. Cycle SA and A (CYS). One cycle. SA is a 12-bit program register. As we will see later, its primary function is to hold the address of the instruction to which control will be returned after executing a subroutine. It is necessary to provide a means of communication between this register and the accumulator to allow address modification, and to "save" the save register for multi-level subroutine work. This instruction causes the least significant 8 bits of SA to be shifted into A; meanwhile the content of A is shifted into the most significant 8 bits of SA (the original most significant 4 bits are shifted down into the least significant 4-bits of SA).

Data Address Modification Group

There are nine instructions in this Group. Eight of them permanently modify all or part of the B register. The ninth, SAG, causes a temporary (one-shot) modification of the B register output, without affecting the content of the register itself.

1. Load B Indirect (LB). Two cycles. Execution of this instruction causes BM and BL to be loaded with a selected byte from page 3 of ROM-0. The byte address is contained in the lower 4 bits of the 8-bit instruction field (0_{16} addresses byte 0, F addresses byte 15). BU is set to 0. SB, the second of the program-address save registers, is destroyed as a result of shifting program through it.

This destruction of SB by the execution of LB is an example of an instruction that does some bad things along with the good. Microprocessors have many instructions of this ilk that sometimes have undesirable side effects. There is no reason apparent on the surface why SB should be destroyed—it is simply a function of the CPU logic. Most of the time we will not be relying on the content of SB to be retained over an LB instruction, so the damage is minimized. But unless the programmer is alert to this subtlety, when the content of SB is important, the program will be in error after the execution of an LB.

2. Load B Long (LBL). Two cycles. Because of the need to use 8 bits of data to load BL and BM this instruction uses 2 bytes of ROM. The second ROM byte is loaded into BL and BM. BU is set to 0.

A special condition is associated with the LDI, LB, and LBL instructions. When a string of these instructions occurs, only the *first* instruction encountered is executed—all others are considered as "no operations" (no-op's). This permits the programmer to address a specific data word by entering a string at the desired point. Consider the following simple program.

INSTRUCTION LOCATION	OPERATION	OPERAND
A	LBL	01
A + 1	LBL	05
A + 2	LBL	09
A + 3	LBL	0D
A + 4	LBL	11
A + 5	LD	

Entering this string at the top, the processor would encounter the first LBL instruction, loading the B register's lower 2 bytes with 01 and causing the processor to fetch the next data from RAM address 001. Had the string been entered at point A + 3, the LBL instruction would have loaded 0D into the B register, and the next address would have been 00D.

3. Increment BL and Skip (INCB). One cycle. The content of BL will be incremented by one, providing the capability of stepping through 16 pieces of data. If the new content of BL is

0000, the next ROM word will be ignored, providing a branch point in the program.

4. Decrement BL and Skip (DCB). One cycle. This instruction operates much as INCB and causes a one to be *subtracted* from BL. If the new content of BL is 1111, the next ROM word will be ignored.

5. Load BM and LB with A (LBA). One cycle. See LBX.

6. Load BM and BL with X (LBX). One cycle. The LBA and LBX pair of instructions causes the least significant 8 bits of the B register to be loaded with the contents of A and X respectively. The execution of LBA also causes the content of the currently addressed RAM location to be copied into A.

7. Exchange BL, BM, and A (XBA). One cycle. See XBX.

8. Exchange BL, BM, and X (XBX). One cycle. The XBA and XBX pair of instructions causes the least significant 8 bits of the B register to be exchanged with the contents of A and X respectively.

9. Special Address (SAG). One cycle. The lines containing address data from BU and BM are set to zero, regardless of the content of B. This forces data to be read from row 0 of RAM-0 for the next cycle only. The purpose of this instruction is to provide a convenient means of addressing these locations. The contents of B are unaffected.

The Control Transfer Group

There are eight instructions in this group. No instruction has a function other than to change the content of the P, SA, or SB registers. Some of the previously discussed instructions also affect these registers, but they did more than just modify the registers. The instructions are:

1. Transfer Control (T). One cycle. Execution of this instruction causes the next instruction to be read from the designated ROM word on the current page. This is accomplished by replacing the content of the least significant 6 bits of P by the least significant 6 bits of the instruction word (the "immediate field" of the instruction). The transfer control instruction uses 64 of the 256 bit patterns available for instruction designation.

2. Transfer and Mark (TM). Two cycles. See RTN.

3. Return (RTN). One cycle. The TM and RTN instruction pair is used to transfer control to a subroutine, while at the same time providing for a return to the proper spot in the main

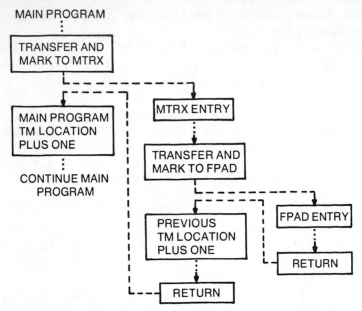

MAIN PROGRAM

TRANSFER AND
MARK TO MTRX

MAIN PROGRAM
TM LOCATION
PLUS ONE

CONTINUE MAIN
PROGRAM

MTRX ENTRY

TRANSFER AND
MARK TO FPAD

PREVIOUS
TM LOCATION
PLUS ONE

FPAD ENTRY

RETURN

RETURN

Fig. 5-12. Control sequence of transfer and return operations.

program. The address of the return location is one greater
than the address of the TM instruction. Upon executing TM,
the return location is placed in the SA register for safekeeping
during the subroutine execution. The existing content of SA is
transferred to SB to accommodate linking when two
subroutine levels are used. Transfer of control to the
subroutine is accomplished by first loading the content of one
of the 48 consecutive addresses in page 3 of ROM-0
(hexadecimal locations 0D0 through 0FF) in the least
significant 8 bits of the P register, and setting the 4 most
significant bits to 0001. This causes the subroutine entry to be
in ROM-0, pages 4 through 7. Further, 256 words are identified
for subroutine memory by expending only 48 instruction codes.

The return (RTN) instruction transfers the content of SA
to P, and the content of SB to SA, in effect reversing the link
storages set up by TM. The next instruction executed after
obeying an RTN will be taken from the location of the
last-executed TM instruction plus one.

Example: It is required to transfer from the main
program to a subroutine entitled *MTRX*, which in turn uses a
subroutine entitled *FPAD*. Control will be transferred back to
the main program upon the completion of the MTRX function.

The flow of the transfer and return operations is shown in Fig. 5-12. The absolute code represented by the flow chart would look like this:

ROM Location	Instruction	Comments
300	TM (DO)	Transfer to start of MTRX, location 100 [16th word of page 3, ROM-0]*P, 301→SA
301	LXA	Return from MTRX
•	•	•
•	•	•
•	•	•
0D0	00	MTRX entry address, location 100
100	LB	MTRX entry (SA has return address to main program)
•	•	
•	•	
•	•	
130	TM (F1)	Transfer to start of FPAD, location 140 (50th word of page 3, ROM-0)→P, 131→SA, 301→SB
131	COMP	Return from FPAD
•	•	
•	•	
•	•	
13F	RTN	Return to main program. 301→P
0F1	40	FPAD entry address, location 140
140	LXA	FPAD entry (SA has return address to MTRX, SB has return address to main program)
•	•	
•	•	
•	•	
16D	RTN	Return to MTRX. 131→P, 301→SA

4. Transfer Long (TL). Two cycles. This instruction will cause control to be transferred to any ROM word in AMP. Unfortunately, TL must use two ROM words to have sufficient addressing capability and thus uses two machine cycles. The first byte contains the operation code and address data to modify bits 9 through 12 of P. The second byte replaces bits 1 through 8 of P.

5. Return and Skip (RTSK). One cycle. RTSK operates similarly to RTN. The only difference is that the return is to the second ROM word following the location of the TM instruction, which permits a controlled return based upon the

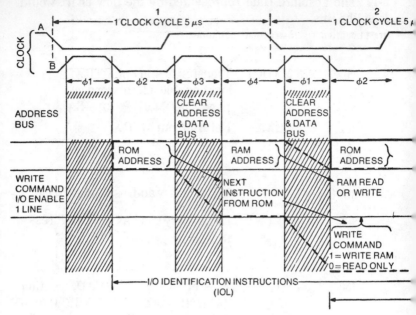

ADDRESS BUS

WRITE COMMAND I/O ENABLE 1 LINE

CLEAR ADDRESS & DATA BUS

ROM ADDRESS

NEXT INSTRUCTION FROM ROM

RAM ADDRESS

CLEAR ADDRESS & DATA BUS

ROM ADDRESS

RAM READ OR WRITE

WRITE COMMAND
1 = WRITE RAM
0 = READ ONLY

←——————I/O IDENTIFICATION INSTRUCTIONS——————→
(IOL)

outcome of an event in the subroutine. This is quite handy for error returns; for example, if the main program asks a SQRT subroutine to find the square root of a negative number, SQRT may RTSK back to the main program rather than RTN to express its contempt. (Be sure when RTSK is used that the instruction in TM location plus one is a 1-byte command, otherwise RTSK will transfer control to the second half of a 2-byte instruction, with attendant surprises.)

6. Skip on Carry Flip-Flop (SKC). One cycle. Execution of this instruction causes the next ROM word to be skipped if $C = 1$.

7. Skip on A Equal to Zero (SKZ). One cycle. Execution of SKZ causes the next ROM word to be skipped if $A = 0$.

8. Skip on BL (SKBI). One cycle. Execution of SKBI causes the next ROM word to be skipped if the content of BL is equal to the SKBI immediate field. This instruction is designed to provide a convenient means for branching out of a loop where BL is being incremented or decremented. Of course, no more than 16 passes through the loop are allowed if an SKBI is to be used without an additional test to define the branch.

(The caution stated for RTSK applies also to SKC, SKZ, and SKBI. No instruction requiring more than one byte should follow any skip instruction.)

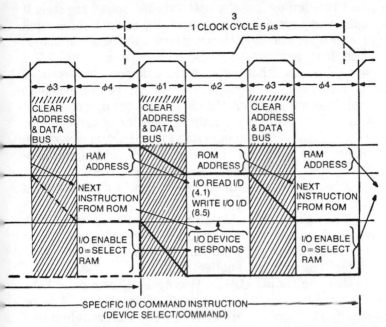

3
1 CLOCK CYCLE 5 μs

φ3 | φ4 | φ1 | φ2 | φ3 | φ4

CLEAR ADDRESS & DATA BUS

CLEAR ADDRESS & DATA BUS

CLEAR ADDRESS & DATA BUS

RAM ADDRESS

ROM ADDRESS

RAM ADDRESS

NEXT INSTRUCTION FROM ROM

I/O READ I/D (4.1) WRITE I/O I/D (8.5)

NEXT INSTRUCTION FROM ROM

I/O ENABLE 0=SELECT RAM

I/O DEVICE RESPONDS

I/O ENABLE 0=SELECT RAM

SPECIFIC I/O COMMAND INSTRUCTION
(DEVICE SELECT/COMMAND)

Fig. 5-13. Timing diagram for AMP input/output and long instructions.

Input/Output Group

The remaining AMP instruction group to be discussed is the input/output group. There are four instructions in this group. They are:

1. **Output Long (OL).** Two cycles. See IL.
2. **Input Long (IL).** Two cycles. Both OL and IL are two-word instructions. They control data transfer between the accumulator and the instruction/data (I/D) bus, and at the same time enable and direct the IOC device. The content of the first word identifies the instruction as an IL or OL and causes the second word to be ignored by the normal processing logic. First-word data also preconditions the RAM and IOC to expect input/output activity. The second word is directed onto the I/D bus. Bits 1−4 are used to define the input/output operation. Bits 5−8 are reserved for addressing more than one IOC. (Since our AMP uses only one IOC device, these bits are effectively ignored.)

During the data transfer time following an OL instruction (see Fig. 5-13) the content of the accumulator is copied onto the ID bus. If the operation code sent to the IOC designates an output (teleprinter operation), the content of the accumulator is gated through to the teleprinter via the output register. If the operation code asks for an input, the content of the input register is placed on the ID bus and copied by the accumulator.

The IOC configuration described here is a simplified version of a real input/output control device. Because it is highly desirable for a microprocessor to be connected to several different peripheral units at once, the operation code structure of an IOC will normally include the selection of one of several such units, and may also include a data conversion capability to condition information exchanged, accommodating special timing constraints that are functions of the external hardware (print motor select signals, display strobes etc.)

3. Discrete Input (DIA). One cycle. Execution of DIA causes the content of the 4-bit discrete input register to be copied into the least significant 4 bits of A. The most significant 4 bits of A are unaffected.

4. Discrete Output (DOA). One cycle. Execution of DOA causes the least significant 4 bits of the contents of A to be transmitted to the discrete output register. The discrete output register can be altered only by a DOA instruction, or by the removal of power. The input register follows the information presented on the four lines tied to the external world.

INTRODUCTION TO ASSEMBLERS

An assembly program represents an attempt on the part of the manufacturer (or the user) to remove some of the drudgery associated with programming, by supplying a program to handle input data in a fashion more amenable to the programmer than hexadecimal or binary. A simple or basic assembler will permit entering instructions and data in a usable symbolic form; it will provide for symbolic and relative addressing; and it will provide some form of error checking. These provisions are each discussed in the following topics.

Entering Instructions and Data

It is easy to enter instructions and data using an assembler that provides for symbolic codes. The use of mnemonics is a prime example. The assembler will accept *RTN* as designating the return instruction rather than making the programmer enter the code 05. Numerical data may also be entered symbolically—a *ZRO* or similar designator will likely be used to enter a zero into some addressed location, and other designators may be used for π, ϵ, etc.

Decimal data can also be entered directly using an identifier such as *DEC*. The assembler would then convert the number to binary or hexadecimal and store it for use as an integer. But the assembler could also accept symbolic codes to convert decimal numbers to their minimum binary scale (see Chapter 4), printing out the scale factor used. On the other hand, the assembler may require that the number be entered at a binary scale of zero, and this requires that the decimal number be divided by an integral power of two, such that the magnitude of the resulting fraction is less than one.

Example: We wish to store the decimal number 75.291. The assembler wants a number at a binary scale of zero. This is accomplished, in this case, by dividing the decimal number by $2^7 = 128$, so that

$$75.291/128 = 0.58821$$

and the resulting number is less than one, as required. We will then either note that the number is stored at a binary scale of 7 or rescale the problem to insure that all input data is less than one in magnitude. If we choose to rescale, we could of course have picked a decimal scale factor, rather than binary, and merely divided the input data by a power of 10. But unless we are working in BCD, we will probably be using binary and scaling the numbers internally, so there is little sense in working with two scaling systems, one for converting input/output data and another for machine arithmetic.

Normally, instructions having complex forms are made easier to specify when using the assembler. If the programmer desires the transfer to be to a particular word in ROM, the *T* (transfer) instruction might be written as *T 081* or *T02, 1* in absolute assembler code for a transfer to ROM-0, page 2, word 1. (AMP pure machine code would require specifying the last 6 bits of the hexadecimal operation code for a transfer.) Further, the assembler will check to see if the specified location can be reached by a *T* command, and if not, will generate a diagnostic.

Symbolic and Relative Addressing

The assembler will provide some facility for symbolic and relative addressing. It is often inconvenient to be required to specify the exact memory location or locations used, and when coding in pure machine language, that of course is precisely what must be done. The assembler provides for labeling of addresses to simplify communication within and among programs, and to facilitate moving blocks of code in memory. The flow chart of Fig. 5-14 represents the logic of the following assembly code, whose purpose is to relocate a group of bytes in the AMP RAM.

LABEL	OP CODE	OPERAND	COMMENTS
REL	LBL	BREL	Specifies address of register to be moved
	LDI	F	Causes 15 (address of receiving register) to be loaded into A
	XBA		$0 \rightarrow BM$, $F_{16} \rightarrow BL$, [BM, BL]$\rightarrow A$
	LXA		[A]$\rightarrow X$
	XBX		[X]$\leftrightarrow$[BM, BL]
	LD		[M]$\rightarrow A$
	DECB	0	[BL] $-$ 1$\rightarrow$BL, skip if [BL] = 1111
	T	* + 1	
	XBX		[X]$\leftrightarrow$[BM, BL]
	EXD		[M]$\leftrightarrow$[A] [BL] $-$ 1$\rightarrow$BL, Skip if [BL] = 1111
	T	* $-$ 6	Continue the move
	RTN		Return to calling program
BREL	DEC	(16)	Identifies decimal number entry

At the time the assembler source program is generated, a set of labels are decided upon by the programmer to define the starting points of various blocks of code. These labels may be numeric, alphabetic, or a combination of alphabetic, numeric, and symbolic (+ , −, <, %) characters. Each label can mean only one thing for each assembled program. In the example, *REL* and *BREL* are such labels. This subroutine is entered at *REL*, while *BREL* locates a particular piece of data, which in this case is a decimal 16 (or hexadecimal 10.) (The *DEC* pseudo op code tells the assembler to treat the operand as decimal data.)

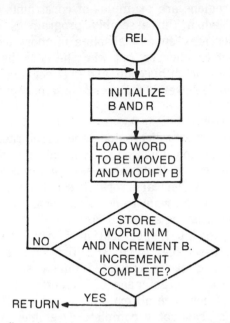

Fig. 5-14. The flow chart relocating a group of bytes in the AMP RAM.

The *T* instructions use *relative addresses* such as * + 1 and * − 6. This addressing form tells the assembler that control is to be transferred to the statement occurring ahead or behind the present statement by a predetermined amount. For example, * + 1 means the very next statement in sequence, while *−6 means to go back 6 statements. But note that the statement count is not necessarily the same as the actual number of memory locations, since more than one byte location may be needed to implement one assembly statement.

It is not necessary, or even desirable, to identify each statement with a label. It is only necessary if that statement is to be referred to by other parts of the program. To aid in bookkeeping, most assemblers will also print out cross-reference tables identifying the routines that refer to or use each labeled statement.

As long as all addresses are either symbolic or relative to a symbolic lable, the assembler has some freedom in locating or relocating the program. The idiosyncracies of the microprocessor hardware will often constrain the available locations. Initial power-on rules, paging, and special-use ROM and RAM regions are examples of constraints that must be considered when the assembly program is written. The programmer may specify absolute memory location to the assembler if he chooses, but when he does, he has fixed in memory that part of his code, and in effect removed from use one of the more powerful features of assembly programs.

Error Checking

The assembler will provide some error checking facility but don't count too much on the assembler finding program errors. The sort of things that assemblers are designed to catch are mostly clerical errors. After all, the assembler does not know what you want to do, so it normally flags out only obvious inconsistencies, such as two different statements giving the same label; specification of an op code that does not exist in the assembler table; specification of a number that cannot be held at an indicated binary scale; addressing locations in a different page of memory with a short-form instruction. These are all examples of errors that should be caught by a reasonably complete assembler. Where errors exist, the assembler should (although not always) assemble what it can, supplying dummy labels where necessary, increasing the binary scale to the minimum, and using a long-form instruction to attempt to correct, or at least work around, some of the preceding error examples.

There will be a bit more said about assemblers in Chapter 8. This introductory discussion was intended to give a cursory understanding of the general functions of assembly programs.

Chapter 6
Programs
and Subroutines

Now that we have examined in some detail the basic microprocessor (microcomputer) functions, number systems, the AMP instruction list, and introduced the use of assemblers, we are now ready to tackle some simple illustrative programs. The format chosen is a combination of assembler input code and machine absolute hexadecimal. Depending upon the system and the assembler used, hexadecimal may be printed out by the assembler as an aid to debugging. (Everyone will find it necessary at one time or another to examine binary information directly from the microprocessor memory, if only to make certain that the assembler really knew what it was doing.) Flow charts are provided for most programs. Comments are included to explain the code in a step-by-step, although abbreviated, fashion with a discussion of the salient points of each programming example following the sample code.

INITIALIZATION ROUTINE (ST)

The following is typical of the initialization program entered immediately after power is turned on. The states of the various registers and outputs cannot be guaranteed and so must be set to known conditions under program control. The transfer in location 000 is a logically unnecessary instruction, but is used here to provide a 5 μsec delay, allowing power transients to settle before data generation and transfer are started.

LABEL	ROM LOCATION	OP CODE	OPERAND	HEX	COMMENTS
ST	000	T⎯⎯	*+1	81 ⎫	Transfer to 001
	001	LBL◄	0	00 ⎬	B register set
	002			00 ⎭	to 0 (0→B)
	003	LDI	0	70 ⎫	Accumulator set
	004			00 ⎭	to 0 (0→A)
	005	DOA	0	1D	Discrete outputs set to 0
	006	RC		24	Carry set to 0 (0→C)
	007	OL	0	21	Set outputs to 0
	008			01	
	⋮	⋮	⋮	⋮	

ZERO RAM SUBROUTINE (ZORM)

This subroutine, which we will call ZORM, puts zeros in a group of sequential bytes in RAM. The flow chart for this simple routine is shown in Fig. 6-1.

LABEL	ROM LOCATION	OP CODE	OPERAND	HEX	COMMENTS
ZORM	100	┌►LDI	0	70	0→A
	101	│		00	
	102	│ EXD─┐	0	28	0→M, [M]→A
	103	└──T	ZORM (*−2)	80	Transfer back
	104	RTN◄		05	Return to main program

This subroutine must be entered using the TM (transfer and mark) instruction. Upon completion, execution of the return command will cause the return address previously stored in SA by the main program to replace the content of P. The B register must also have been loaded to the location of the first word to be set to zero.

EXD causes the content of A to be exchanged with the addressed memory word, placing a zero in memory. Simultaneously, the content of M replaces the content of A, but since A is set to zero before the next word is stored, this is of no

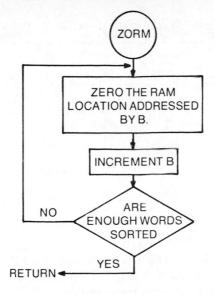

Fig. 6-1. ZORM flow diagram.

consequence. EXD further causes the content of BL to be decremented by one during each execution. The content of BM is unchanged since a zero is coded as the EXD operand.

When the content of BL is 1111, the T instruction is skipped, causing the RTN to be executed. Note that the final RAM location to be set to zero must have a hexadecimal zero in the least significant digit of its address, since the ZORM subroutine will continue until the content of BL is 1111, and the zeros are stored *before* the content of BL is decremented and tested.

The operand of the transfer (T) instruction indicated in the ZORM program is *−3, which is a form of relative addressing. But this particular feature of the program depends upon the assembler configuration, so either relative or absolute addressing may be required to transfer control back to the ZORM label address.

WORD SHIFT SUBROUTINE (WRS)

This WRS program shifts a group of 7 bytes in RAM, moving them down by one word space. Prior to entry into the routine, B must be loaded with the address the first byte to be moved. In addition, BL must be set to zero. The flow chart for this program is shown in Fig. 6-2.

LABEL	ROM LOCATION	OP CODE	OPERAND	HEX	COMMENTS
WRS	120	→EX	0	38	[A]→M, [M]→A
	121	INCB		17	[BL] + 1→BL, skip if [BL] = 0
	122	SKBI┐	8	48	Skip if [BL] = 8
	123	└─T	WRS	A0	Transfer back
	124	LBL◄─	0	00	Load B to 0
	125			00	
	126	RTN		05	

Upon entry, the content of M, designated by B, is copied into A by the exchange instruction. The content of A, which could be anything, is copied into M, but since the useful information from M is now in A, no harm is done. BL is now incremented (INCB). The new value can never be zero, so the skip will not occur. We will skip out, however, when [BL] = 8, having shifted information from addresses XX0 through XX6 to addresses XX1 through XX7, where XX0 represents the address of the first byte. At completion, we set B to zero, as a courtesy to the next routine, and then exit.

BIT DESIGNATION SUBROUTINE (BDS)

The BDS subroutine causes one of the four least significant bits specified by the entry address to be artibrarily set to one. Such a routine may be used to prepare for a discrete output (DOA). The content of B must be set by the calling program to

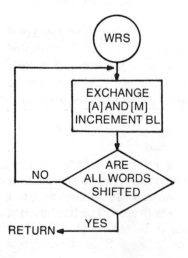

Fig. 6-2. WRS flow diagram.

specify the byte location. The BDS logic is sufficiently simple that no flow chart is shown.

LABEL	ROM LOCATION	OP CODE	OPERAND	HEX	COMMENTS
BDS1	130	LDI	1	70	1→bit 1
	131			01	
BDS2	132	LDI	2	70	1→bit 2
	133			02	
BDS3	134	LDI	4	70	1→bit 3
	135			04	
BDS4	136	LDI	8	70	1→bit 4
	137			08	[M] OR-ed with [A]
	138	OR		0F	
COM1	139	EX	0	38	[A]→[M]
	13A	LDI	0	70	0→[A]
	13B			00	
	13C	RTN		05	

Labels are used here to designate a set of entries into the BDS subroutine. The label COM1 is further used to facilitate entry by other programs into the last part of the BDS subroutine, to execute a commonly used string of code at the end of BDS. The entry locations of BDS1 through BDS4 are specified by pointers located in ROM-0, page 3, which can also be addressed symbolically using the assembler.

SKIP ON CARRY ZERO SUBROUTINE (SKCZ)

This simple subroutine demonstrates the use of the return and skip (RTSK) instruction. The function of the SKCZ routine is to provide a means to skip the next instruction in the main program if the carry is zero.

LABEL	ROM LOCATION	OP CODE	OPERAND	HEX	COMMENTS
SKCZ	140	SKC		15	Skip if C = 1
	141	RTNSK		07	
	142	RTN		05	

If C = 0, return to the main program is via the RTNSK instruction, which will cause the normal return location to be skipped and the next instruction in sequence to be the first one executed. If C = 1, the exit is via the familiar RTN. The existence of an instruction of the form of RTNSK permits a decision to be made in a subroutine, with the result of that decision modifying a sequence in the main program.

Increment/Decrement Byte Subroutine (IDBS)

This subroutine will increment or decrement any designated byte in RAM-0. The subroutine can be entered at several points, two of which (IDBS3 and IDBS4) require the B register to be loaded by the calling program.

LABEL	ROM LOCATION	OP CODE	OPERAND	HEX	COMMENTS
IDBS1	144	LBL	2F	00	Load
	145			2F	Byte address for decrement (or *+3)
	146	T	IDBS4	8B	
IDBS2	147	LBL		00	Load
	148			C3	Byte address for increment
IDBS3	149	LDI	1	70	Incrementation constant
	14A			01	
IDBS4	14B	LDI	FF	70	Decrementation constant is 255_{10}
	14C			FF	
	14D	A		0B	Add without carry
	14E	EX	0	38	Adjusted byte→M
	14F	T	COM1	B9	Exit to COM1

The IDBS1 entry loads the B register with the address of the byte to be decremented. IDBS2 does the same for the byte to be incremented. The IDBS3 and IDBS4 entries perform the incrementation or decrementation and store the result back in RAM-0. Note that IDBS uses a common exit (COM1) with BDS saving a few instructions.

BINARY LEFT SHIFT (BLS) SUBROUTINE

AMP has no left shift instructions, so this shifting function must be mechanized by a subroutine. The technique used here is based on the fact that a binary left shift is equivalent to multiplication by two, which is the same as adding the number to itself. The BLS subroutine requires the B register to contain the RAM address of the byte to be shifted, and the content of C to be set to zero upon *initial* entry.

LABEL	ROM LOCATION	OP CODE	OPERAND	HEX	COMMENTS
BLS	105	LD	0	30	[M] addressed B→A
	106	ADC		0A	Add with carry
	107	EX	0	38	[A]→[M]
	108	RTN		05	Exit

BLS can also be used to perform a right shift by successive reentries without resetting the carry.

Examples: Shift 11101110 left one place on initial entry of BLS and C = 0 During execution of BLS, 11101110 is added to itself:

[C]	[A]	
0	11101110	Initial value in A
	11101110	Add A to itself
1	11011100	Final value in A

The original number is shifted left, with the "1" that started in the most significant bit position, ending up in the carry. In the event that the byte just shifted is part of a longer word, the reentry of BLS addressing the next byte should not reset the carry. The carry one will then propagate into the least significant bit position of the next byte.

The shift method is also legitimate arithmetically if we are processing a single byte. Since the number is negative and expressed in 2's complement form, the leading 1's (except for the sign bit) are not significant. By complementing the initial and final values, we see the final value is twice the initial.

Sign and complement	1 1 1 0 1 1 1 0	Initial
Sign and absolute value	1 0 0 1 0 0 1 0	Values
Sign and complement	1 1 0 1 1 1 0 0	Final
Sign and absolute value	1 0 1 0 0 1 0 0	Values

Binary Right Shift

Although AMP has a right shift instruction (ARS) mechanized in the hardware, it is possible to use the BLS routine unchanged to shift a byte one bit to the right at the expense of execution time. Inasmuch as some 4-bit processors do not have a right shift in their instruction repertoire, an example is in order.

Example: Let us assume, for the sake of the example, that the processor in question has a 4-bit arithmetic register, but is otherwise configured as the AMP. BLS is initially entered as before, and on subsequent entries, the carry is left alone:

[C]   [M]

| 0 | 0111 | Initial value
| | 0111 | Add

| 0 | 1110 | Value after 1st execution
| | 1110 | Add

| 1 | 1100 | Value after 2nd execution
| | 1100 | Add

| 1 | 1001 | Value after 3rd execution
| | 1001 | Add

| 1 | 0011 | Value after 4th execution

The original number is shifted one bit to the right, with the digit shifted from the right hand of the register, ending in the carry flip flop. This bit is available to propagate into the most significant position of the next lower order byte. Notice that if the number is negative, that the carry flip flop must be one-set on initial entry to propagate a one into the sign bit position.

General Register Exchange (GX)

The GX subroutine exchanges the contents of designated RAM-0 multibyte registers. The register sets are further addressed by the two LBL instructions, with the entry point determining which are to be exchanged. If the entry is at GX3, the LBLs in the calling program are used to designate the register set.

LABEL	ROM LOCATION	OP CODE	OPERAND	HEX	COMMENTS
GX1	120	LBL	R1	00	Address of R1
	121			( )	
GX2	122	LBL	R2	00	Address of R2
	123			( )	
GX3	124	LDI	( )	70	
	125			( )	D_i address→A
	126	XBA		19	Address of first byte→B
	127	LXA		1B	R_i address→X, address of first exchange→A

114

LABEL	ROM LOCATION	OP CODE	OPERAND	HEX	COMMENTS
	128	→LD	0	30	Byte→A
	129	XBX		18	Exchange addresses
	12A	EX	0	38	D→R
	12B	DECB		1F	[BL] − 1→BL
	12C	T	* + 1	AD	Transfer to avoid skip
	12D	XBX		18	Exchange address again
	12E	EXD	0	28	Complete byte exchange, decrement B
	12F	T	*−7	A8	
	130	RTN		05	
R1		DEC	( )		
R2		DEC	( )		

This GX subroutine shares a common memory with the earlier WRS subroutine, so if both GX and WRS are to be used in the same program, one or the other routine will have to be relocated.

The last two addresses given for R_1 and R_2 are indicated (with parentheses) as being decimal, but most assemblers permit symbolic operands to be used.

The contents of the registers are specified within the subroutine by the GX1 and GX2 entries, or the contents of one internally specified and one externally specified register are exchanged. The latter exchange requires that the B register be loaded with the address, and then the subroutine is entered at GX3. Note that the second LBL will not be executed on a GX1 entry, so that in effect GX1 addresses R_1 as one of the registers to be exchanged, while GX2 addresses R_2. Note also that this routine may be used to address registers that "wrap around" a page of memory, for if the last page address is exceeded, the subsequent addresses are taken from the beginning of the page.

It is often helpful to examine the contents of the CPU registers at critical steps in the computation cycle to determine if the program will function as anticipated. As an example of this kind of analysis, consider the first pass of the

Table 6-1. Step-by-Step Analysis of GX Subroutine

| | REGISTER CONTENTS | | | | |
INSTRUCTION	P	B	X	A	COMMENTS
LBL	120	R	–	–	R₁ address→B
LBL	122	R	–	–	Second LBL ignored
LDI	124	R	–	D	Dᵢ address→A
XBA	126	D	–	R	
LXA	127	D	R	R	
LD	128	D	R	[D]	First byte of Dᵢ →A
XBX	129	R	D	[D]	Exchange B and X
EX	12A	R	D	[R]	[D]→R
DECB	12B	R –¹1	D	[R]	Decrement B
T	12C	R – 1	D	[R]	Transfer control
XBX	12D	D	R –1	[R]	Exchange B and X
EXD	12E	D – 1	R – 1	[D]	[R]→D
T	12F	D – 1	R – 1	[D]	Transfer control
LD	128	D –1	R – 1	[D –1]	Second byte of Dᵢ →A

GX subroutine, beginning with a P register value of 120 after execution of the instruction at that location. This analysis results in Table 6-1.

FIXED-POINT BCD ADDITION SUBROUTINE (FXA)

The FXA flow chart is shown in Fig. 6-3 and the RAM map in Fig. 6-4. This subroutine is an example of a $2n$ digit, BCD arithmetic routine. In this case, $n = 7$ for a 14-decimal-digit number. Note that the digits are stored in reverse order (N_{11} and N_{21} are the least significant digits of words N_1 and N_2), to take advantage of the EXD instruction that causes BL to be decremented.

LABEL	ROM LOCATION	OP CODE	OPERAND	HEX	COMMENTS
FXA	110	RC		24	0→C
	111	LB	N1	C4	N_1 address→B
N	112	→LD	1	31	N_1 →A, N_2 address→B
	113	DC		6D	66_{16} + [A]→A
	114	ADC		0A	Add N_2
	115	DCC		6E	Correct to valid BCD
	116	EXD—	1	29	Store BCD sum digit, decrement, and modify B
	117	└ T	N	92	Continue addition
	118	RTN←		05	Return to main program
N1	0C4	EQU	6	06	Hex integer pointer

116

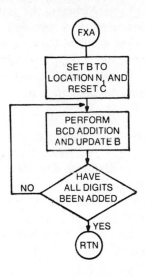

Fig. 6-3. FXA flow diagram.

The LD instruction causes BM to be modified by the exclusive-OR of the contents of BM and the last 3 bits of the LD op code field. In this case, a one was chosen in the LD field, setting BM to one after the first execution of LD ($1 \oplus 0 = 1$). After the EXD execution, BM is reset to zero ($1 \oplus 1 = 0$, permitting addressing of the second digit of the first number since BL has been decremented. The sum digits are stored over the N_2 digits since the B register was not modified

Fig. 6-4. FXA RAM map.

	BM CONTENTS			
	0	1	2	3 → ⋯
0	N_{17}	N_{27}		
1	N_{16}	N_{26}		
2	N_{15}	N_{25}		
3	N_{14}	N_{24}		
4	N_{13}	N_{23}		
5	N_{12}	N_{22}		
6	N_{11}	N_{21}		
7				
8				
9				
A				
B				
C				
D				
E				
F				

BL CONTENTS

between the pickup of N_2 digits and the storage of the sum. In the event both N_1 and N_2 are greater than zero, and the addition results in an overflow, C is set to one at the completion of the routine. Both N_1 and N_2 must be at the same decimal scale (the decimal points must be aligned), and the scale must be adequate to accommodate the magnitude of the sum.

SORTING PROGRAM (SORT)

To further demonstrate data addressing, and as an excercise in the use of X, A, and B registers, assume that it is required to sort through a 64-word block of 8-bit data. All numbers greater than 73_{16} in magnitude must be moved to a storage region for further processing. The sorting operation is to be made several times on the data as it is continuously loaded by the processing program, so the use of a subroutine is indicated. The flow chart is shown in Fig. 6-5, and the AMP code is as follows.

LABEL	ROM LOCATION	OP CODE	OPERAND	HEX	COMMENTS
	310	TM		DO	Transfer to SORT
	ODO		OC	OC	SORT entry (1OC)
	311	LB			Return from SORT
	•	•		•	
	•	•		•、	
	•	•		•	
SORT	10C	LB		CO	Load B
	10D	LD1	( )	70	Destination address →A
	10E			( )	Destination address, D
	10F	EX	0	38	D→050, gibberish →A
	110	LDI	( )	70	Source address→A
	111			( )	Source address, S
	112	INCB		17	[051]→B
	113	EX	0	38	S→051, gibberish→A
SORT 1	114	LD	0	30	S→A
	115	ADI	1	6C	Increment S and test
	116			01	
	117	T	*+2	99	Continue
	118	RTN		05	Return when complete
	119	LXA		1B	Incremented S→X

LABEL	ROM LOCATION	OP CODE	OPERAND	HEX	COMMENTS
	11A	EX	0	38	Incremented S→051 051, →A
	11B	XBX		18	S→B, [051]→X
	11C	LD	0	30	S→A
	11D	ADI	8C	6C	Add complement of 73
	11E			8C	
	11F	T	*+15	AF	S ≤ 73 (Note decimal relative address)
	120	LD	0	30	S > 7 , S→A
	121	XBX		18	[051]→B
	122	DECB		1F	[050]→B
	123	LXA		1B	S→X
	124	LD	0	30	D→A
	125	ADI	1	6C	D + 1 (new D)→A
	126			01	
	127	XBA		19	new D→D, [050]→A
	128	XAX		1A	050→X, S→A
	129	EX	0	38	S→new D location
	12A	XBX		18	[050]→B, D→X
	12B	LAX		12	D→A
	12C	EX	0	38	D→050
	12D	INCB		17	[051]→B
	12E	T	SORT1	94	Transfer back
	12F	XBX		18	[051]→B
	130	T	SORT1	94	Transfer back
	OCO			50	

In this SORT program, destination address D is assigned to memory location 050, while source address S is held in memory location 051. While this code is not intended to be an example of an efficient technique, it does show a straight-forward arithmetic method to pick up and store addresses from the 64-byte block, taking into account the unpredictability of the store addresses. Because the AMP has no store instruction (only an exchange of the accumulator and memory contents), it is necessary to save the accumulator content in the X register if it is needed after the EX instruction is executed—an example of a multipurpose instruction that does too much for the case at hand.

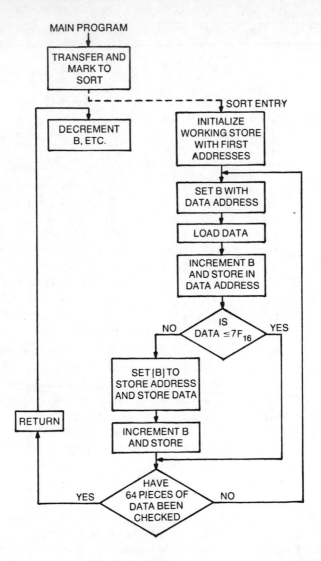

Fig. 6-5. SORT flow diagram.

FIXED-POINT BCD SUBTRACTION SUBROUTINE (FXS)

The FXS subroutine is very similar to the FXA. The flow chart logic and the data storage map are the same as those shown for the FXA. Because the COMP instruction causes the 1's complement of A to be formed, C must be one-set (SC) and added in initially to form the 2's (or 10's) complement.

LABEL	OP CODE	OPERAND	COMMENTS
FXS	SC		$1 \rightarrow C$
	LB	N1	N_1 address $\rightarrow B$
FXS1	LD←	1	$N_1 \rightarrow A$, N_2 address $\rightarrow B$
	COMP		1's complement of N_1
	ADC		$N_2 - N_1$
	DCC		Correct to valid BCD
	┌ EXD	1	Decrement BL, modify BM, and store partial sum
	T ──	FXS1	Continue
	└→ RTN		Return
N1	EQU	C6	Hex integer data, location of LB pointer address

For this and the following routines, the absolute octal addresses and codes are not shown. The coding here is thus representative of the input data fed to an assembler, which then assigns such addresses as it compiles the actual machine-language programs.

RETURN ADDRESS SAVE SUBROUTINE (PSHP)

This sequence establishes a third-level subroutine hierarchy.

LABEL	OP CODE	OPERAND	COMMENTS
PSHP	XS		$[SA] \leftrightarrow [SB]$
	LBL	SC	SC address $\rightarrow B$
	CYS←		8 least significant bits of SA $\rightarrow A$
	┌ EXD	0	$[A] \rightarrow RAM$
	T ──	*−2	Not finished
	└→ XS		Restore $[SA]$
	RTN		Third-level save
SC	EQU	( )	register address

The execution of the XS instruction causes the content of SA to be exchanged with SB. This places the second-level subroutine return address in SA and the first-level address in SB. The LBL causes B to be loaded with the address of a RAM location that will be used as the third-level subroutine save register (SC). Eight bits of the original content of SB (now in SA) are cycled into the accumulator and then into RAM by the first execution of the CYS and EXD instructions. The

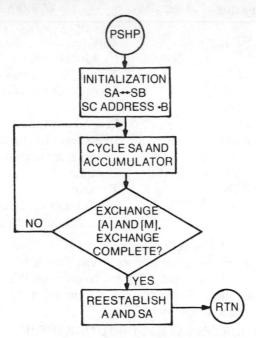

Fig. 6-6. PSHP flow diagram.

remaining 4 bits are placed into RAM during the second pass. The final XS execution reestablishes the original content of the SA register (see Fig. 6-6). The resulting content of the SB register is of no value.

FIXED-POINT BINARY ADDITION SUBROUTINE (FBA)

This subroutine is quite similar to the BCD addition routine (FXA), using essentially the same program logic, but since the addition is in natural binary, the coding is more straightforward.

LABEL	OP CODE	OPERAND	COMMENTS
FBA	RC		$0 \rightarrow C$
	LB	N1	N_1 address $\rightarrow B$
	LD	1	$N_1 \rightarrow A$, N_2 address $\rightarrow B$
	ADC		$N_1 + N_2 + C \rightarrow A$
	EXD	1	Sum $\rightarrow N_2$, N_1 address $\rightarrow B$
	T	*-3	Not Complete
	RTN		Exit
N1	EQU	C3	Address of pointer to N_1

122

With the value of 3 chosen for the initial address of N_1, four bytes are added before the content of BL is 1111 and the routine is exited. The RAM map is similar to Fig. 6-4, with N_{14} and N_{24} the least significant digit locations used by FBA.

FIXED-POINT BINARY SUBTRACTION SUBROUTINE (FBS)

FBS differs from FBA only in the setting of the carry and the formation of the 1's complement of N_1. FBS causes the 4-byte N_1 to be subtracted from N_2. Addressing is identical to that of FBA, as shown in Fig. 6-7.

LABEL	OP CODE	OPERAND	COMMENTS
FBS	SC		$1 \rightarrow C$
	LB	N1	N_1 address $\rightarrow B$
	LD	1	$N_1 \rightarrow A$, N_2 address $\rightarrow B$
	COM		1's complement of N_1
	ADC		$N_2 - N_1 \rightarrow A$
	EXD	1	Sum $\rightarrow N_2$
	T	*–3	
	RTN		

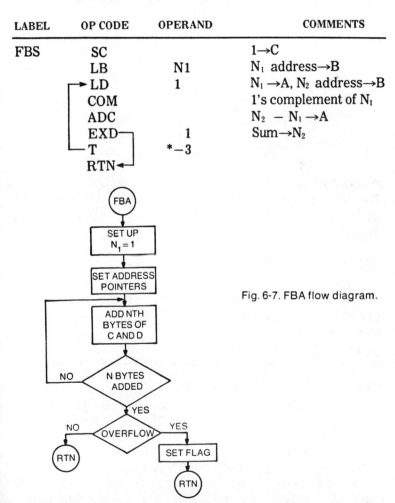

Fig. 6-7. FBA flow diagram.

123

This is the last of the specific AMP program examples, though reference will be made throughout the book to AMP functions as examples of microprocessor operation and architecture. The discussion of larger and more sophisticated programs is beyond the intent of this book, although the complex codes are nearly always generated by dividing the problem into manageable subsets (subroutines) similar to the ones of our examples, and then building a calling program to utilize the subroutines in proper sequence. Because of a desire to illustrate as much of the AMP instruction repertoire as possible, minimal coding was not always achieved.

Chapter 7

Floating-Point
Arithmetic

While it is always possible to solve problems using fixed-point arithmetic, the difficulties involved provided incentives to both hardware designers and programmers to mechanize methods by which the arithmetic unit or a service program could keep track of the radical point during computation. The technique is known as *floating-point* and is simply an extension of scientific notation, where a number is expressed as the product of a number lying between 1 and 10 (or alternately 0.1 and 1) and an integral power of 10. For example,

$$375.92 = 3.7592 \times 10^2 = 0.37592 \times 10^3$$
$$0.0001764 = 1.764 \times 10^{-4} = 0.1764 \times 10^{-3}$$

Binary numbers can be expressed in a like manner:

$$1011101.11_2 = 1.01110111 \times 10_2{}^6 = 0.101110111 \times 10_2{}^7$$
$$0.00000110101 = 1.110101 \times 10_2{}^{-6} = 0.1110101 \times 10_2{}^{-5}$$

Where $10_2{}^6 = 2^6$ and $10_2{}^{-6} = 2^{-6}$. This notation can be further shortened by not writing down the 10 since regardless of the number system used, the most natural multiplier is an integral power of 10 in any base. Thus we can write:

$$0.1110101 \times 10^{-5} = 0.1110101 \mid -5$$

This suggests a format where the *mantissa* (the number lying between 0.1 and 1 in this case) and the *characteristic* (the

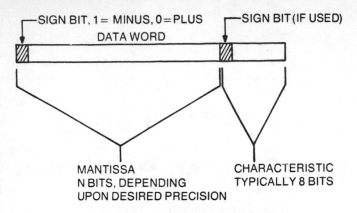

SIGN BIT, 1 = MINUS, 0 = PLUS
DATA WORD
SIGN BIT (IF USED)

MANTISSA
N BITS, DEPENDING
UPON DESIRED PRECISION

CHARACTERISTIC
TYPICALLY 8 BITS

Fig. 7-1. AMP floating-point word format.

power of 10 of the multiplier) are contained in adjacent sets of bytes and operated upon according to the scaling rules of Chapter 5.

CONVENTIONS

Like most things in the digital computing world, there are no firm standards. But common usage (and common sense) have given rise to formats similar to that in Fig. 7-1. The characteristic, or *floating-point scale*, is quite often held as an 8-bit number whose value is equal to 128-B, where B is the binary scale discussed in Chapter 4, and 128 is a constant that permits B to range from -127 to $+128$. An equivalent and more straightforward approach is to divide the 8 bits into a sign bit with 7 magnitide bits, as in complement notation.

The mantissa is constrained to be less than one in absolute value. If it is negative, it is held in 2's complement form. The mantissa is nearly always held at the minimum binary scale (normalized). If we assume that a precision of one part in 2^{24} is adequate, we will then require a 24-bit mantissa (including sign). Expressed in decimal form, this corresponds to about one part in 16,000,000. Most problems to be addressed by a microprocessor can be adequately handled by a mantissa that is 24 bits or less.

This system will then accommodate fairly large numbers ranging from 2^{-128} to 2^{+128}, corresponding to a decimal range of approximately 10^{-38} to 10^{+38}. The symmetry of this range results from our definitions. The smallest magnitude that can be held under these rules is $0.1_2 \times 2^{-127}$ or 2^{-128}, and the largest magnitude is $0.1111...\times2^{128}$ or almost 2^{128}. It is possible to hold numbers smaller in magnitude than 2^{-128} if normalization is not required, for then insignificant leading zeros would be permitted.

For discussion, assume that one floating-point word occupies four 8-bit bytes—three bytes for the mantissa and one byte for the characteristic. In keeping with common terminology, we will talk about this word as residing in a register, although in fact the "register" is merely a group of bytes held in RAM, having a size determined by our program. For example, the number 255_{10} would appear in memory as four 8-bit bytes:

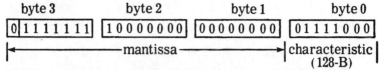

byte 3   byte 2   byte 1   byte 0

Byte 3 contains the sign bit, which is zero since 255 is positive. Bytes 3, 2, and 1 hold the mantissa at minimum binary scale, so 255_{10} appears as 0.11111111_2. From observation or from Appendix D, the minimum binary scale is found to be 8; therefore in our example the characteristic is $128 - 8 = 120_{10}$ or 1111000_2. In hexadecimal this floating-point number can be expressed as four two-digit bytes: 7F 80 00 78.

ARITHMETIC

In performing arithmetic on floating-point numbers, the rules for binary scaling are mechanized together with operations necessary to prevent overflow. Thus the mantissa and characteristic arithmetic are both done in fixed point. The result is a combination nearly always yielding maximum precision. While all large computers and most small ones have floating-point capability in their hardware, today's microprocessors are, without exception, fixed-point systems. Floating-point arithmetic must be accomplished by subroutines.

In the case of addition and subtraction, the subroutine must examine each of the two numbers to be added and determine the appropriate scale such that the sum can be contained without overflow. The subroutine should also recognize when overflow or underflow are inevitable, and act accordingly. It must normalize or left-adjust the result such that there are no leading zeros, and also adjust the scale.

A second class of so-called floating-point routines may be encountered where BCD arithmetic is used. Preparatory to BCD addition or subtraction, these routines simply line up the radical points, which may be identified using an illegal BCD character or by a counter whose contents point to the position. Overflow will normally be checked. The BCD numbers are held in a manner that will allow maximum precision as long as the radical point is contained in the register, so data will not be normalized, but rather held with the radical point at the position required by the latest operation.

We will now discuss the operation of a typical true n-byte floating-point subroutine where the addend and augend are in binary 2's complement form, and held as normalized numbers.

FLOATING-POINT ADDITION AND SUBTRACTION

The flow chart of Fig. 7-2 is indicative of the logic required for a binary floating-point addition and subtraction subroutine. Execution of the routine is separable into three parts. Part 1 handles the setups and any shifts necessary to equate the characteristics by lining up the binary points of the two arguments, C and D. Part 2 performs the addition or subtraction. Part 3 adjusts the sum or difference so that it is contained in the assigned register with no insignificant leading digits, restores the necessary data, and exits to the main program.

The subroutine is entered at FPAD for addition or FPSB for subtraction, where a flag (F1) is set either to a one or to zero for the add/subtract control used in Part 2. The required common initialization is also performed. The two characteristics are then examined to determine if they are equal. If the format of the number is that of Fig. 7-1, the characteristics are each held in one 8-bit byte and a simple accumulator zero-test on the difference will suffice. If the characteristics are unequal, then the number associated with the smaller scale (larger characteristic) will be shifted right one bit at a time by the RS (right shift) second-level subroutine until the scales are equal. The RS test for the proper characteristic must pass here because we are only modifying one characteristic to be equal to a known valid one. With this mechanization, it is quite possible that the mantissa may be shifted out of the register, one bit at a time, until it is zero. Shifting will then continue until the scales are equal, using up unnecessary time. A test may be inserted at the return from RS in Part 1 to count the number of right shifts performed, with a test limit equal to the number of bits in the register. Or alternately, you could examine the mantissa for a zero. If either test were satisfied, the smaller characteristic could be used for both numbers, or the remaining non-zero number would be used for the sum or difference (complemented if necessary). When the two scales are found to be equal, Part 1 has done its job and control is transferred to Part 2.

In Part 2, any required setup is performed, and F1 is examined to determine if addition or subtracton should take place. If addition, the carry is zero-set and byte-by-byte addition is performed; if subtraction, the carry is one-set, the 1's complement of D is taken, and once again byte-by-byte addition is performed. (Depending upon the processor used, some efficiencies may be realized by making some of this coding common).

Part 3 tidies up the arithmetic by correcting any overflow and by normalizing the scale of the sum. After the arithmetic is performed, it is possible that a potential overflow has occurred, with the overflow bit residing in the most significant digit position (sign bit). This overflow can be corrected by recognizing the existence of the overflow condition, shifting the mantissa right one place, recovering the sign bit from the carry, and adjusting the characteristic. (There is only the possibility of a 1-bit overflow, so the shifting operation need be done only once.) Where the resulting signs are different (like signs of subtraction arguments), an overflow is not possible. The programming in the "is sign proper" box must look for the sign combinations of Table 7-1 that result in overflow. Fortunately, the only combinations needed result in a

Table 7-1. Addition and Subtraction Overflow Sign Combinations

	ADDITION				SUBTRACTION					
Sign of C**	+	+	+	−	+	+	−	+	−	−
Sign of D**	+	−	−	−	+	+	+	−	−	−
Sign of result	+	−	+	−	+	−	−	+	−	+
MSB for no overflow	0	1	0	1	0	1	1	0	1	0
MSB for overflow	1	*	*	0	*	*	0	1	*	*

*Overflow is not possible.
**C and D are interchangeable under addition, so the four redundant cases are not shown.

129

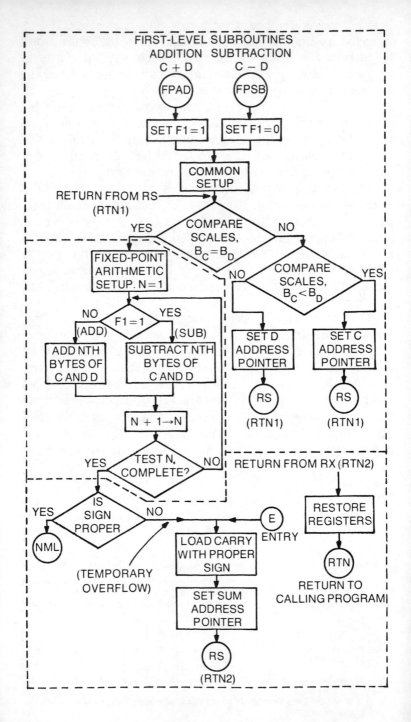

FIRST-LEVEL SUBROUTINES
ADDITION   SUBTRACTION
C + D   C − D

(FPAD)   (FPSB)

SET F1 = 1   SET F1 = 0

COMMON SETUP

RETURN FROM RS (RTN1)

COMPARE SCALES, $B_C = B_D$

YES — FIXED-POINT ARITHMETIC SETUP. N = 1

NO — COMPARE SCALES, $B_C < B_D$

NO — SET D ADDRESS POINTER → (RS) (RTN1)

YES — SET C ADDRESS POINTER → (RS) (RTN1)

F1 = 1
NO (ADD) — ADD NTH BYTES OF C AND D
YES (SUB) — SUBTRACT NTH BYTES OF C AND D

N + 1 → N

TEST N, COMPLETE?

YES — IS SIGN PROPER
NO

IS SIGN PROPER
YES — (NML)
NO — (TEMPORARY OVERFLOW)

RETURN FROM RX (RTN2)

(E) ENTRY

LOAD CARRY WITH PROPER SIGN

SET SUM ADDRESS POINTER

(RS) (RTN2)

RESTORE REGISTERS

(RTN)

RETURN TO CALLING PROGRAM

130

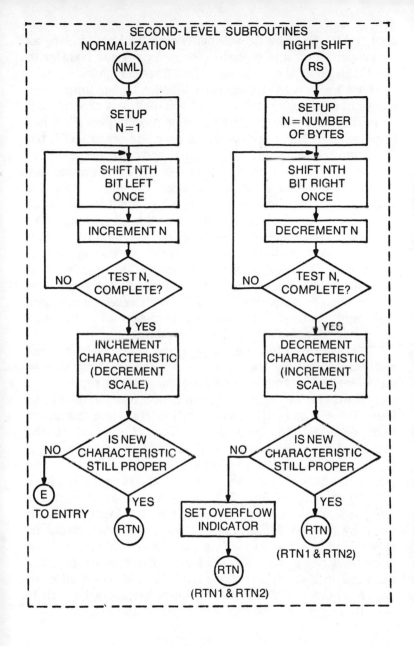

Fig. 7-2. Floating-point addition-subtraction subroutine flow chart.

131

predictable sign. The RS will put everything right, as long as the proper sign bit is placed in the carry prior to transfer to RS. At this point, the functions of Part 2 are complete.

Part 3 also provides for normalization by left-shifting the mantissa until no leading insignificant digits are present, and by modifying the characteristic. If no potential overflow has occurred, the NML subroutine is entered, which shifts the mantissa left one bit at a time and also adjusts the characteristic. After each reentry into the main routine, the sign bit is checked to determine when it changes state, for when this occurs, the mantissa has been shifted one place too many and must be shifted back one by the RS subroutine. At this point, the mantissa contains no leading insignificant digits, providing maximum precision of the arithmetic operations. Of course, the precision of the number just normalized was not enhanced, since insignificant zeros were shifted into the right-hand end of the register as the mantissa was being shifted left, but the precision of subsequent opeations using this data is probably improved.

It is possible that the range of the characteristic is not sufficient to handle the magnitude of the resulting sum or difference. While this occurrence is not likely, it represents a true *floating-point overflow* and must be recognized. In this case, the characteristic will overflow from the maximum positive scale indication of 00000000 (B = +128) to the maximum negative indication of 11111111 (B = −127). Or, if we try to establish a scale more negative than −127, an indicated scale of +128 will result. Both RS and NML have tests for these conditions. If found by RS, the overflow flag is set and the add/subtract routine is exited immediately. If found by NML, it simply means that the number cannot be normalized within the range we have chosen for the characteristic. It was decided for the example to leave the mantissa unnormalized in this case, but not to set an error flag. A bit more will be said about characteristic arithmetic in the following discussion on floating-point multiplication.

FLOATING-POINT MULTIPLICATION

The AMP has no multiplication capability. Whether we choose to program in fixed or floating point, a subroutine must be generated to enable multiplication. Floating-point multiplication was chosen to develop a typical program flow. The

132

technique used is based on the multiplication example in Chapter 2. Recall that fixed-point overflow cannot occur as a result of multiplication, so no overflow tests are necessary to insure a proper mantissa. However, floating-point overflow or underflow can occur, with the product characteristic exceeding the allowable range as a result of addition of the characteristics of the multiplier and multiplicand. Binary multiplication algorithms handling more than one bit at a time are available for those who wish to trade complexity for speed. BCD techniques are also available.

The FMP subroutine is a one-bit-per-basic cycle subroutine. It is entered with a transfer and mark (TM) with address pointers set for the IER (multiplier) and ICAND (multiplicand) registers. The word format is open, but the program flow was generated with the format described earlier in the chapter in mind.

Upon entry into FMP, the necessary initialization is performed, including setting the PROD (product) register to zero. Normally, PROD would be a double-length register to hold the product, but the high-order bit positions of the IER register are vacated (see Chapter 2, Multiplication) as the partial product is shifted right, so a single-length PROD register attached to IER in the following manner will suffice:

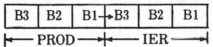

As in floating-point addition, the new characteristic is computed by using fixed-point addition on the characteristic byte. If the binary scale is contained in the characteristic in the form of 128-B, a bit of thought must be given to determining the rules for overflow or underflow. The characteristic will have the configurations for selected binary scales shown in Table 7-2. Note that overflow occurs when the characteristic is forced to pass through zero or to exceed 255, as when B is $+128$ or -127. Adjusting the characteristic of the product is more straightforwardly accomplished by adding the characteristics of the two numbers, and then adding 128_{10} or 80_{16} to correct the result. For example, if the scales of the two numbers are 30 and 50, their characteristics would be 98 and 78, respectively. The sum of the two characteristics is then 176, and when 128 is added, the result is 48 (actually 304, but the overflow in the 8-bit register is ignored). A characteristic of 48 corresponds to

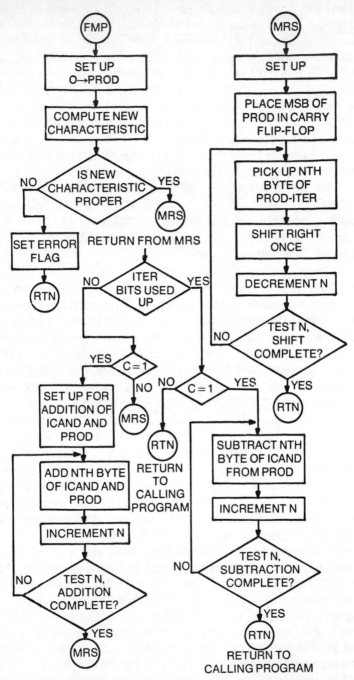

Fig. 7-3. Floating-point multiplication subroutine flow chart.

Table 7-2. Comparison of Selected Binary Scales and Their Characteristics

BINARY SCALE (B)		CHARACTERISTIC	
DECIMAL	HEXADECIMAL	DECIMAL	HEXADECIMAL
0	0	128	80
64	40	64	40
−64	40	192	C0
−64	−40	192	C0
128	80	0	00
−127	−7F	255	FF

a base of 80, which is the sum of the two original bases, as required. If the characteristic was equal to the base (not 128−B), then the characteristics of the numbers can be added directly without correction.

Once the characteristic of the product is judged proper, control is transferred to the MRS (multiply, right shift) subroutine. The MRS examines the most significant bit of the PROD register and places it into the carry flip-flop so that the bit will be re-entered into the most significant digit position when the contents of the PROD and ITER are shifted right. The shift begins with the most significant byte of PROD, and ends with the least significant digit of ITER; the next multiplier control bit ends up in the carry flip-flop.

If the new value of the carry is zero, then no addition is performed and MRS is re-entered, once again shifting the combination of PROD and ITER right and obtaining a new multiplier control digit. If the new value in the carry is a one (C = 1), the content of ICAND is added to PROD before MRS is re-entered. When the iterative portion of the multiplication is complete, MRS is entered for the last time, with control returning to the final correction routine.

To complete the operation, the carry bit is once again examined, and if found to be one, a subtraction is performed to correct for any error resulting from a multiplicand or multiplier, or both, appearing in 2's complement notation. The subtraction takes place by adding the complement of ICAND to the PROD. When the subtraction is completed, or if the carry was initially zero, the subroutine returns control to the calling program.

Chapter 8

Programming Aids

Programming a microprocessor is a more involved task than programming a "full service" digital computer. By comparison, the aids and services available to the programmer of a microprocessor are still incomplete. Microprocessors are new, therefore the associated hardware and software have not yet had time to mature. However, most manufacturers have recognized that one of the more powerful sales tools for the hardware is the availability of a full line of programming aids. Those companies that intend to stay in the business are now spending a significant portion of their research and development budget to add both software and hardware aids to their product line. So we can soon expect to see major improvements in ancillary microprocessor systems.

LOADERS

The loader is probably the simplest form of programming aid. The loader may be nothing more than a few hand-entered or permanently stored instructions, but it is usually a moderate-sized routine that permits direct entry of instructions or variable data by keyboard or tape, with absolute address information for the data to be stored. The problem, of course, is how to load the information. When approaching a microprocessor with a completely empty memory, you must find a way to begin to enter the information, for the microprocessor will not have a loading program to assist you. But once the program has been permanently stored in ROM, any required loading routine will be part of the normal instruction sequence, so the problem is solved.

The loader is a set of instructions that enables the input media to set up a starting address, read in one byte at a time, and store it in either RAM or PROM. The loading address is incremented either by the hardware or by the loader, depending upon the routine and the microprocessor used. The loader should also be able to recognize the end of a block of data and to prepare for addressing a new block. For processors using paged memory, data is normally entered one page at a time.

A relocatable loader is one that will reposition *blocks* of code in absolute memory, to make room for additions or to compact the code, thereby eliminating some transfer instructions. These loaders, however, require block start and stop information and so are not used much for microprocessor programming since the relocatable loader functions are normally satisfied by reassembling the source code.

THE MICROPROCESSOR AS AN ASSEMBLER HOST

The most common microprocessor programming aid is the assembler. (Typical assembler functions have been briefly discussed in Chapter 5.) There are several different vehicles used to provide convenient access to an assembler. There are also editors, simulators, emulators, etc., so that the assembled program may be executed on the spot, and any errors found easily corrected.

The microprocessor itself can be used to host the assembler accessing a larger machine in a time-share mode via a smaller, but still intelligent terminal. Such assemblers have been written to run on most of the commercially available microprocessors, but they have limited computational ability (primarily limited by throughput and memory capacity, and secondarily limited by available peripheral equipment). Consequently, an assembler written for a microprocessor host will be limited in relation to the functions of one written to take advantage of the features of more complex machines.

The Resident Assembler

A typical resident assembler is a two-pass program. The first pass converts the symbolic op codes and nonbinary data to binary, stores this information away in absolute machine addresses, and establishes a label table. Clerical errors are flagged out, such as misspelled or nonexistent op codes. The second pass equates addresses to the assigned labels, setting up equivalences and assigning absolute addresses to the binary code. Processor idiosyncrasies are accounted for, and additional error checks are performed. Examples of errors detected at the second pass are failure to define a label, and finding a label defined twice.

Most assemblers use as input data the 128-character ASCII set (Table 9-1). The input data is formed in *statements*. The statement in turn is subdivided into *fields*. A typical assembler format is used in Chapters 5 and 6, and the fields used there were *label, op code, operand,* and *comments.* The absolute ROM location and hexadecimal data equivalents were shown only to indicate the relationship of the mnemonic and absolute information; they are not normally included with the input data.

LABEL FIELD

The format of the label field is determined by the assembler. There is usually a limit of six alphanumeric characters, with a maximum of 256 or 512 labels, depending upon available memory.

The label field may also be used to designate a comment statement, where the entire statement is treated as a comment rather than data for information appearing in the fourth field. In this case, the assembler passes over the comment statement without allocating memory or assigning an address to it.

Because of the assembler structure, there can be illegal combinations of characters that, though not logically incorrect, will cause an error diagnostic. For example, some assemblers look for only alphabetic characters in the label field, so if others are used, an error will be flagged.

Op Code or Operator Field

The mnemonic codes for the processor op codes, together with *pseudo instructions* to the assembler, make up the data in this field. Pseudo instructions, often called *pseudo ops* or *assembler instructions*, do not result in assembly of microprocessor op codes, but rather tell the assembler to perform certain functions. Examples of pseudo instructions are:

EQU—Causes a designated label to be equated to the indicated hexadecimal number.
DEC—Causes a designated label to be equated to the indicated decimal number.
ORG—Defines the starting point of a block of code.
END—Designates the end of the source program.

Most rudimentary assemblers are critical of simple input errors. For instance, if the op code is an LBL and it is entered with a space as LB L, an error flag will most likely be set. Likewise, if the assembler wants a comma after the op code and no comma is there, an error will be indicated. Conversely, if the assembler does not want a comma and one is present, an error will also be set.

Operand Field

This field is used to indicate the addresses of operands, immediate data, and to further define execution of certain instructions not requiring address information. These instructions are typified by shift instructions, where the number in the operand field tells the processor the number of places to shift the operand right or left. Since hexadecimal numbers can be alphabetic, the assembler must be notified by an auxiliary agreed-upon symbol, whether by an alphabetic combination in the operand field as a label or by an absolute number (a *literal*). The symbols "1" or "*" in front of the operand entry is commonly used to designate hexadecimal data.

Comment Field

Comments are used only for readability in the program listing. They are usually held for printing by the assembler during its first pass and is ignored during the second pass. Comments can utilize any character set that the peripherals recognize.

Figure 8-1 is a representative listing prepared by a resident assembler for the Rockwell PPS-4 microprocessor.

```
*FIXED-POINT BINARY ADDITION SUBROUTINE  ⎫
FBA RC*        0 to C                     ⎪
LB N1          N1 ADDRESS TO B            ⎪
LD 1           N1 TO A,N2 ADDRESS TO B    ⎪
ADC            N1 + N2 + C TO A           ⎬ INPUT
EXD 1          SUM TO N2, N1 ADDRESS TO B ⎪
T *−3          NOT COMPLETE               ⎪
RTN                                       ⎪
N1 EQU C3                                 ⎪
END                                       ⎭

100W1

*FIXED-POINT BINARY ADDITION SUBROUTINE      ⎫
0100  24   FBA RC*   0 TO C                   ⎪
0101  C0   LB N1     N1 ADDRESS TO B          ⎪
0102  30   LD 1      N1 TO A,N2 ADDRESS TO B  ⎪
0103  0A   ADC       N1 + N2 + C TO A         ⎬ ASSEMBLER
0104  28   EXD 1     SUM TO N2, N1 ADDRESS TO B  OUTPUT
0105  80   T *−3     NOT COMPLETE             ⎪
0106  05   RTN                                ⎪
           N1 EQU C3                          ⎪
           END                                ⎭

100W2                      ⎫
0100L0                     ⎬ OBJECT CODE
24 C3 31 0A 29 82 05       ⎭
```

Fig. 8-1. Sample resident assembler printout.

The first data group is the input information as it is typed into the assembler. The second data group is the first pass response, and it includes the assigned addresses and basic hexadecimal equivalent op codes. The third data group is the assembled object code with the starting address of location 0100. This last group is preserved on paper tape punched by the assembler for loading the PROM (programmable read-only memory). The address of N1, content of location OC3, has been omitted.

DIAGNOSTICS

As we have observed, error detection and diagnosis by assemblers are usually less than the best; however, a few words are still in order regarding some specific errors that should be caught by the assembler and brought to the attention of the programmer.

Memory Contents Exceeded

The assembler will be keeping track of the memory usage, and therefore almost certainly will be able to provide diagnostics that say:

Page Is Full—You must use a long transfer to continue.

ROM or RAM Is Full—This one can be real trouble. If the program cannot be compressed or functions deleted, the only answer is more memory for the system.

Special Memories Are Full—Where literal or command pools, stack pointer memory, special input/output buffers, or other special-purpose memories are used, this message will alert the programmer to the fact that the world is finite.

Invalid Codes

These messages will usually indicate some kind of clerical error.

Invalid Op Code—Usually a typing or keypunch error.

Syntax Error—Too many or not enough commas, parentheses, asterisks, spaces, etc.

Undefined Symbol—Usually an input typing or keypunch error.

Symbol Defined More Than Once—Poor bookkeeping.

Improper Program Structure

Label Not Present Or Undefined—Labels are required on pseudo-ops such as EQU. If a label is not used, this diagnostic message is likely. If control is transferred to an undefined label, a similar message should be used.

Transfer Is Beyond Page Boundary—Here the programmer inadvertently addressed a location that could not be reached by the type of transfer instruction he was using.

There will be other message types referring to specific errors created by the limitations of the particular microprocessor and assembler combination used. None of these messages are welcome, but it is much easier to find and correct an error when it is pointed out.

Typical Operation

As an example of resident assembler operation using paper tape as the storage media, we will briefly discuss the operation of the PPS-8 assembler. This assembler uses paper tape as the primary input and storage media. Standard operating procedure dictates that the source program be prepared off-line using a teletypewriter.

Once the tape has been punched, it can be placed on the reader and read by Pass 1 of the assembler. The PPS-8MP assembler uses the 128-character ASCII set. (Any one of the first group of 16 codes is treated as a statement delimiter, and if two or more appear in succession in the source program, all but the first are ignored.) Pass 1 creates the symbol table but does not store source data. The tape must be once again positioned on the reader and Pass 2 addressed from the teletypewriter. Pass 2 generates the source-object listing. Both Pass 1 and 2 provide some error checks and printout diagnostics where errors are found. Pass 3 provides an object program in a format suitable for use with the loader provided for the PPS-8.

THE SIMULATOR OR EMULATOR

Simulators provide a program execution sequence which is identical to that of the microprocessor, but for which the programmer has considerably more visibility. If the program is initially run on the microprocessor, monitoring of program execution is most often done by observing a bank of lights or a simple digital display providing the hexadecimal location of the last instruction executed and values of selected register constants.

Unless Transfers, Halts, Printout Commands and Pauses are inserted into the assembled code, no intermediate results are directly observable. The act of modifying the code to add visibility for checkout is commonly done, even where simulators are used, but additional opportunities for error are created when the patches are removed and the final "checked out" code is compressed.

THE TEXT-EDITOR

For those systems using a bulk input media (paper tape, magnetic tape, punched cards) to the assembler, it is inconvenient to go back and recreate the entire source data set when corrections are to be made. The test-editor provides a system that modifies designated pieces of data and prepares a new corrected tape or deck, together with a printed record of the changes made and of the resulting complete data set.

The editor operates by reading the test to be altered into a buffer. The buffer is usually limited in memory such that the source data must be handled in pieces that will fit in the buffer, and the loading process is repeated until the entire text has been edited. A typical set of commands available to the user of an editor are as follows.

1. Set buffer pointer.
2. Add or append n lines of text.
3. Delete n lines of text.
4. Move buffer pointer n character positions forward.
5. Punch specific characters (end-of-file, no-ops, etc).
6. Punch buffer contents.
7. Search for specific string in buffer.
8. Insert text into specific location in buffer.
9. Delete mth through nth character.
10. Insert specific character into buffer.

TIME-SHARED SYSTEMS

Manufacturers and service bureaus have cooperated in providing rather complete assembly, compilation, and simulation programs that are resident on large computers and accessed by terminals in the customer's plant. The access is nearly always over telephone lines and is initiated by dialing the telephone number of the remote computer facility. This mode of operation requires a fairly intelligent local terminal.

The terminal equipment should include a paper tape or card reader, a teletypewriter, a cathode-ray tube (CRT) display, some auxiliary memory (disc or magnetic tape), and a reasonably competent minicomputer to control the peripherals and operate interactively with the big computer.

The user will pay for the terminal equipment, the telephone line rental, and the main-frame time actually used at the central computer. During normally busy periods, several programs are running nearly simultaneously on the big machines, but each user pays only for the portion of the central processor time directly involved with this program. Even though rental of machines in this class is quite expensive ($200–$1000 per hour, depending upon machine configuration), the total cost to assemble a 500-statement program is generally less than $10, excluding the cost of the terminal.

Fig. 8-2. Photograph of PPS-4MP assemulator system. (Courtesy Rockwell International)

Time-shared systems require the creation of an initial input data file for the assembler source code, which is maintained at the central facility and updated as the file is accessed. In addition to the source code, secondary files are generated and normally consist of one or two assembler output files and a simulator input file compatible with the machine configuration or configurations simulated at the central computer. This permits the source code to be assembled, and a simulation verification performed in a single sitting.

Use of a time-shared system is initiated by "logging on," which consists of calling the number of the central computer, identifying the terminal, and identifying the specific user. The exact procedure is dependent upon the company providing the service, the executive program used, and the terminal configuration.

THE ASSEMULATOR

Another class of programming aid utilizing a combination of hardware and software techniques is known as an *assemulator*. The title is a contraction of the terms *assembler* and *simulator* (or *emulator*), which describes the services rendered. A typical example is the PPS-4MP assemulator system shown in Fig. 8-2. The assemulator processing center is composed of the PPS-4 CPU, 256 4-bit words of scratch-pad RAM, two general-purpose I/O devices, and a clock generator.

144

The PPS-4MP block diagram is shown in Fig. 8-3. The CPU has access to all internal blocks shown in the diagram and takes its instructions from either the ROM or the RWM (read-write memory).

The selection of the program set used is switchable from the console. The ROM programs are those which make up the operating system. The program in the RWM are the *object codes* (the programs being developed or checked out). At the programmer's option the assemulator will assemble or edit the program, or permit it to be executed on the spot. The assembly and utility programs in ROM are referred to as the *chip-based operating system* (CBOS). The permanent storage media used with the basic assemulator is paper tape, and both source and object code are preserved as punched holes on paper tape.

Source Program

The source program is in assembler language and consists of mnemonic-coded data similar in form to the AMP routines discussed earlier. Specific formats are necessary to instruct the CBOS system as to which data are comments, operands, or labels.

Upon entering the source data into PPS-4MP memory via paper tape, a second paper tape is punched to preserve the assembled information. Program errors will likely be found during the debugging process, so the programmer will want to punch yet another tape containing the newly discovered corrections. To facilitate the process, the *edit* function is provided, permitting corrections to be made and a new tape to be punched by reading in the old tape and manually entering only changes, deletions, or additions.

Assembly

Assembly of the source program is performed by the utility assembler, which is a two-pass assembler. Passes 1 and 2 operate independently, and each requires separate initialization. Upon the completion of pass 2, an object tape will be punched that can be loaded into the RWM of the assemulator ready for execution and emulation by PPS-4MP.

Simulation

During initial program execution, a *single step* or *single cycle* mode of operation is very useful in permitting the

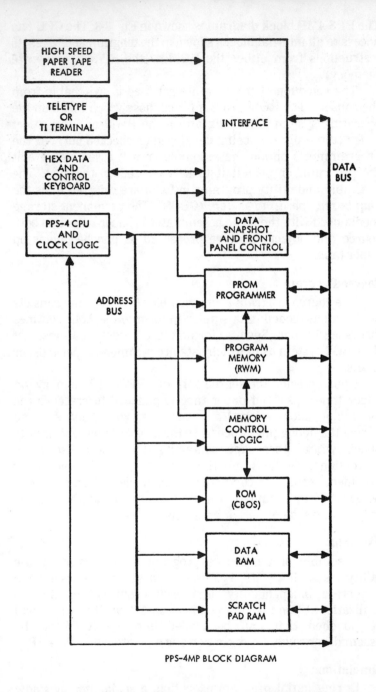

Fig. 8-3. PPS-4MP block diagram. (Courtesy Rockwell International)

programmer to observe the execution of his program, one command at a time. He can view the register contents at the completion of each instruction to determine the goodness of his code. In addition to the single-cycle mode, the programmer may dump all of the program memory on paper or magnetic tape (if available) or on printed hard copy.

Program data may be entered into the PROMs when the checkout has progressed to the point where the programmer is satisfied with the accuracy of his program. Capability exists within the PPS-4MP to verify the proper entry of this data by comparing the PROM contents bit-by-bit with the latest contents of the RWM.

Chapter 9

Data Exchange and Use of Peripherals

An important and growing use of the microprocessor is in data formatting and control. Information must be put into forms that the outside world can accept. Data must be received in similar forms and then translated into the 2's complement binary that is natural to the processor. Further, transmitted data is subject to contamination from several sources, and in general, the longer and more complex the transmission link, the higher the error rate. So the microprocessor may be assigned the task of determining whether or not a data group is likely to contain errors. For example, it may be asked to select the "best" available data from several redundant sets, or to "correct" an apparently faulty reception using partially redundant data.

DATA FORMAT STANDARDS

Some data format standards exist. Punched card and paper tape formats have been established for some time and have wide acceptance. Two of the most used standard code systems are ASCII (American Standard Code for Information Interchange) and EBCDIC (Extended Binary-Coded Decimal Interchange Code).

ASCII is a 7-bit code used to provide a numeric representation of alphanumeric and formatting data. ASCII is an *incomplete* set in that several of the possible codes are without meaning. Hexadecimal to ASCII equivalencies are listed in Table 9-1.

EBCDIC (pronounced either **ee**-be-dick or **ib**-si-dick) is an 8-bit code yielding 256 possible combinations, but as in ASCII, many of the combinations are not used. EBCDIC can be thought of as being divided into two 4-bit groups—the high-order group contains the *zone bits*; the low-order group, the *digit bits*. This grouping corresponds to the zone and digit

Table 9-1. ASCII Character Codes

HEX	ASCII CHARACTER	HEX	ASCII CHARACTER	HEX	ASCII CHARACTER
0 - 1F	No equivalence	3F	?	5F	
20	blank or space	40	@	60	
21	!	41	A	61	a
22	"	42	B	62	b
23	#	43	C	63	c
24	$	44	D	64	d
25	%	45	E	65	e
26	&	46	F	66	f
27	'	47	G	67	g
28	(	48	H	68	h
29	)	49	I	69	i
2A	*	4A	J	6A	j
2B	+	4B	K	6B	k
2C	'	4C	L	6C	l
2D	–	4D	M	6D	m
2E	.	4E	N	6E	n
2F	/	4F	O	6F	o
30	0	50	P	70	p
31	1	51	Q	71	q
32	2	52	R	72	r
33	3	53	S	73	s
34	4	54	T	74	t
35	5	55	U	75	u
36	6	56	V	76	v
37	7	57	W	77	w
38	8	58	X	78	x
39	9	59	Y	79	y
3A	:	5A	Z	7A	z
3B	;	5B	[		
3C	<	5C	\		
3D	=	5D	]		
3E	>	5E			

149

Table 9-2. EBCDIC Alphabetic and Numeric Character Codes

CHARACTER	EBCDIC ZONE BITS	DIGITS BITS	HEX
A	1100	0001	C1
B	1100	0010	C2
C	1100	0011	C3
D	1100	0100	C4
E	1100	0101	C5
F	1100	0110	C6
G	1100	0111	C7
H	1100	1000	C8
I	1100	1001	C9
J	1101	0001	D1
K	1101	0010	D2
L	1101	0011	D3
M	1101	0100	D4
N	1101	0101	D5
O	1101	0110	D6
P	1101	0111	D7
Q	1101	1000	D8
R	1101	1001	D9
S	1110	0010	E2
T	1110	0011	E3
U	1110	0100	E4
V	1110	0101	E5
W	1110	0110	E6
X	1110	0111	E7
Y	1110	1000	E8
Z	1110	1001	E9
0	1111	0000	F0
1	1111	0001	F1
2	1111	0010	F2
3	1111	0011	F3
4	1111	0100	F4
5	1111	0101	F5
6	1111	0110	F6
7	1111	0111	F7
8	1111	1000	F8
9	1111	1001	F9

punches of punched-card code. Hexadecimal to EBCDIC equivalencies for alphabetic and numeric characters can be found in Table 9-2. For format characters, other zone bit combinations are used.

Punched cards are probably the most common form of data input to digital equipment. Cards are not the overwhelming source media in the microprocessor community as they are for the larger systems, but are still in very general use. The most common code used for punched cards today is due to H. Hollerith who used cards for data handling in the 1890s. The cards are often called *Hollerith cards*, and the code the *Hollerith card code*. One column is used for each character, so that 80 characters are contained on an 80-column card. As seen in Fig. 9-1, the numbers are represented by a punch in rows 0-9. The letters are represented by double punches—A through I by a row-12 punch and a digit punch in rows 1–9, and J through R by an row-11 punch and a punch in rows 2-9. Format characters use other combinations.

Punched paper tape is a common input/output media for microprocessors. Paper tape is available for widths of 5, 7, and 8 channels, where a channel is a single binary digit position. (See Fig. 9-2 for an example of 8-channel tape having ASCII characters). A timing reference must be available on the tape to tell the tape reader that a digit is being processed. This timing signal is generated by *sprocket holes*, which are the small holes near the center of the tape. Photo readers are the most commonly used tape input devices, and they take advantage of the smaller sprocket hole to insure that if a data hole is present, it is squarely on the sensing element at the time the sprocket hole says "read." Paper tape is slow, cumbersome, and error prone, but the readers and punches are simple devices and hence relatively inexpensive, which accounts for the continuing use of this media. Paper tape is normally read at a rate of 500 to 2000 characters per second and punched at 200–300 characters per second.

PARITY CHECK

Errors are more likely to occur during data transmission than during internal computation, so it is generally a prudent step to provide a means of determining, within reasonable probability, if a data error has occurred during transmission. We could, for instance, exercise the option of asking for a retransmission of data so that we could compare it with the received data, bit by bit. This is an example of redundant transmission on a comparitively large scale, but some type of redundant information must be transmitted for some sort of comparison to be made.

Parity checks provide a lower redundancy (fewer extra bits required) and simply involve counting the number of ones (or zeros) in a fixed-length data group, determining if this count is odd or even, and then forcing the count to be either odd or even by appending one more digit (the parity bit) to the data

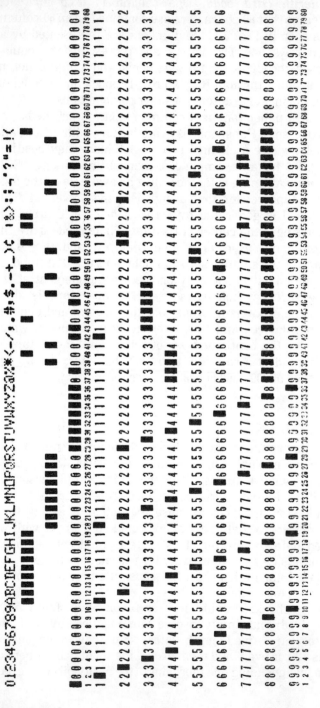

Fig. 9-1. Eighty-column punched card with interpreted Hollerith characters.

1234567890
:-QWERTYUIOP
ASDFGHJKL;P
ZXCVBNM,./
!"#$%&'()*=
_@[\+-]<>?

PUNCH CHARACTERS, READ
FROM LEFT TO RIGHT ON
THE TAPE.

Fig. 9-2. Eight-channel punched paper tape using even parity. The parity column is nearest the bottom of the page. The "carriage return" and "line feed" characters also appear on the tape.

153

group. If we expect an odd number of ones, this is termed *odd parity*; and even number of ones is *even parity*.

Example: A data group consists of 8 bits of useful data and 1 bit for parity. Odd parity is the rule. The data group to be transmitted is $4A_{16} = 01001010_2$. Since there are an odd number of ones already in the group, the parity bit is set to zero to *maintain* odd parity.

Clearly a simple parity check does not guarantee proper transmission since compensating errors can occur that would permit data to pass the parity check, but still be in error. If the data line is noisy enough to exhibit more than an occasional transmission data error, then multiple parity errors will likely occur.

Parity is quite often set and checked by hardware such as the M6800 ACIA device. A few processors have an instruction that simply sets or tests parity, as in the Intel 8080. The following parity check (PCK) program demonstrates a technique to determine if the number of ones in a byte in the AMP memory are odd or even.

LABEL	OP CODE	OPERAND	COMMENTS
PCK	LDI	INI	Initial counter value
	LBI*	CTR	Counter address
	EX	0	Initialize counter
	LBI*	BTE	Byte address
	LD	0	Byte→A
	XAX		Byte→X
	LBI*	PAR	Parity address
	LDI	0	0→A
	EX	0	0→PAR
STR	XAX		Byte→A
	ARS		Byte shifted right one place, LSB→C
	XAX		Byte→X
	LDI	0	0→A
	ADC		[C] + [PAR]→A
	EX	1	"1" count→PAR, CTR address→BM
	LD		Load counter
	A		Add [CTR] + [CTR]
	EX	1	[A]→CTR, PAR address→BM
	SKC		If C = 1, skip
	T	STR	Transfer back
INE	RTN		Exit
	EQU	( )	
CTR	EQU	( )	Initial conditions
BTE	EQU	( )	
PAR	EQU	( )	

*The LBI's could equally well be LB's.

154

At the completion of PCK the binary count of the number of ones in the byte in question is continued in PAR. All that need be done by the main program is to load (PAR) and shift right to load C with the least significant digit (LSD). If this is a one, then there were an odd number of ones in the original byte; if C = 0 then there were an even number.

CHECK SUM

Although the PCK routine may not be the cleverest subroutine ever written, it demonstrates that a bit of manipulation is necessary to determine the value of the parity bit in the absence of specific hardware checks. A checking technique which is more easily implemented in most processors is that of the *check sum*. Here all the transmitted words or bytes are simply added together, without regard to overflows. The resulting characteristic sum is then transmitted along with the good data.

The program at the receiving end adds everything up in the same way and compares the new check sum with the transmitted one. Often it is found to be convenient to transmit the 2's complement of the check sum so that the receiving processor can simply add up everything, including the check sum, and compare the result to zero.

The check sum is not as positive an indicator of good or bad transmission as a parity bit in every word or byte, but it is easier to use and is fairly effective. The check sum suffers to a greater degree from the possibility of occurrence of compensating errors than does the parity check.

KEYBOARD INTERFACE

Keyboards used as input devices are wired as matrixes in which a depressed key completes a circuit between a row line and a column line, as shown in Fig. 9-3. In actual operation, these lines are referred to as the *keyboard lines* and the *strobe lines*. The strobe lines are driven sequentially by the CPU, while the keyboard lines are sampled to determine if any key has been depressed. A depressed key will carry the strobe signal from one of the strobe lines when it is energized and route the pulse to one of the keyboard lines, where the combination of strobe line and keyboard line is used to determine precisely which key was depressed.

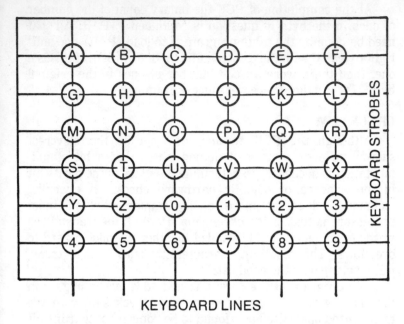

Fig. 9-3. Simple keyboard schematic diagram.

The strobe lines are often time-shared with those of the display for economy of hardware and software, since this technique reduces the number of conductors required and simplifies the decoding to a simple time-division multiplexing process.

The keyboard lines, on the other hand, are normally dedicated to keyboard sampling because the keys are depressed and released erratically, making it necessary to employ some kind of sampling scheme to determine if the key has just been depressed or if it is still being held down. This sampling process is essential to prevent repetitive entries of the same key each time the strobe line is pulsed. The sampling process is then used to establish valid key entries. Most people hold a key down for about 200 to 300 milliseconds, though much longer times are possible. And it is very difficult to make a key closure on any keyboard for less than 35 to 45 milliseconds. Allowing about 5 milliseconds for opening and closure noise of the contacts, a sampling interval of 10 to 15 milliseconds is suggested. This interval is long enough to avoid sampling a noise pulse more than once, and short enough to insure two successive samples of good information for all but intentionally shortened key strokes.

The logic of a typical keyboard sampling routine is shown in the flow chart of Fig. 9-5. The subroutine defined by this flow chart issues strobes and immediately samples the set of keyboard lines, storing the state of each set of keyboard inputs as each strobe (discrete output) is issued. It then examines each of the stored inputs to see if any response occurred. Failing to receive a positive return, the subroutine resets the *sample* and *flag-1* registers, clearing the slate to begin sampling the next input. Logic is provided to insure that the two successive samples were from the same key closure, and that the input is accepted only once (flag-1 is set when the data is found to be valid). In addition to the two successive samples, this routine requires that the key show open for at least one sample before another input will be accepted (flag-1 is reset only upon an error or upon finding all keys up). The location labeled *valid* holds the valid keyboard input data, and is loaded only once by the KBS subroutine for each accepted input. The processing routine must zero this location before reentering KBS to avoid accepting the same datum twice. It may be necessary to provide for a stack of valid key data if the processing routine cannot get around fast enough to be sure that *valid* is unloaded before it can be loaded a second time by KBS.

DISPLAY DRIVE

Microprocessor output display devices range from the simple seven-segment LED (light-emitting diode) display to sophisticated CRTs. Included in this list are gas discharge (orange-colored) and flourescent (blue-green) displays. All segmented displays (Fig. 9-6) are controlled by the same general logic, although the gas discharge units utilize an initial

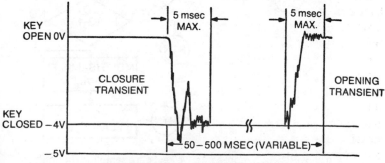

Fig. 9-4. Typical keystroke waveform.

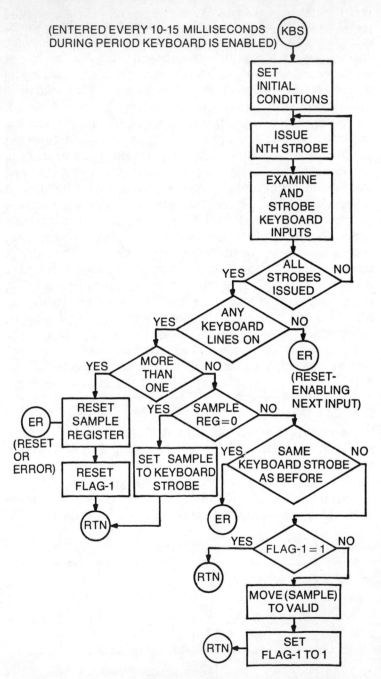

Fig. 9-5. Flow of a representative keyboard sampling routine.

starting pulse and require a cutoff pulse to prevent unwanted segment glow. Digits are usually selected by the same discrete outputs from the microprocessor that are used for the keyboard strobes (Fig. 9-7). When these outputs are used to drive a display, the keyboard lines should not be sampled, and when the keyboard is driven, the segment control should be turned off to avoid unwanted display flicker.

A display program should first select the digit to be driven, then output 3 bits of data to the segment decoder, which will provide a seven-or eight-line output (depending if decimal point is used) to directly drive the correct segments. (An example of this type circuit is the Rockwell display controller.) A table look-up scheme normally provides the conversion between the BCD digit representation in the CPU and the segments to be driven. In the usual scanning-type display it is desirable to refresh the display units at least 10 times per second, though a refresh rate of less than 20 times per second will cause an LED display to appear to flicker when it is moved rapidly from side to side. Other display types exhibit longer persistence and continue to emit light for up to 100 milliseconds, thus reducing the flicker effect.

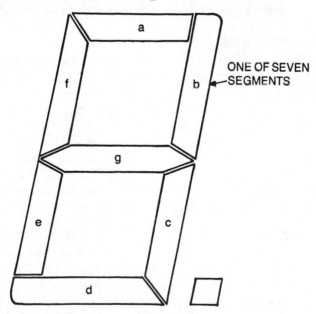

Fig. 9-6. Configuration of a standard seven-segment display with decimal point.

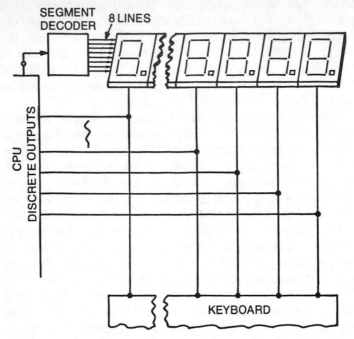

Fig. 9-7. Typical display-drive schematic using CPU discrete outputs.

AUXILIARY STORAGE MEDIA

While punched cards and paper tape are the more popular storage elements for microcomputer programs and data, they do not normally suffice for on-line storage because of handling and access difficulties. Neither media can be used for unattended auxiliary storage where data is temporarily transferred to the outside to make room in internal RAM for more recent data, with the expectation that information held outside can be recalled at any time under CPU control. Magnetic tapes and magnetic disks are the favorite elements used for temporary bulk external storage.

Magnetic Tape

Magnetic tape is a very adequate, reasonably reliable storage media where high-speed data storage and retrieval is not an important factor. The *latency* time to find the desired block of data is variable, depending on whether the beginning of the block is just under the read head or buried deeply in the tape reel. As bulk storage, magnetic tape has no present-day peer since there is no upper bound to the number of tape reels

160

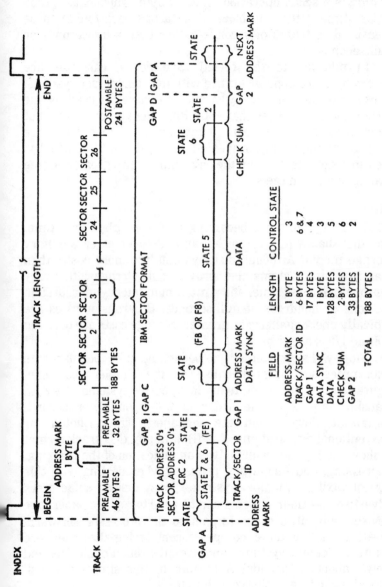

Fig. 9-8. IBM floppy disk track and sector formats. (Courtesy Rockwell International)

FIELD	LENGTH	CONTROL STATE
ADDRESS MARK	1 BYTE	3
TRACK/SECTOR ID	6 BYTES	6 & 7
GAP 1	17 BYTES	4
DATA SYNC	1 BYTE	3
DATA	128 BYTES	5
CHECK SUM	2 BYTES	6
GAP 2	33 BYTES	2
TOTAL	188 BYTES	

161

that can be kept in inventory. The capacity of a 7-track 2400-foot tape reel can be as much as 20 megabytes, with the cost per byte well below any competitive system. Reading and writing is a serial operation, byte by byte, which causes tape *access* time (after the block of data has been found) to be measured in tenths of seconds rather than microseconds or milliseconds.

In addition to the reeled tape decks, cassettes are becoming more popular for use with microprocessor systems. These units are physically similar to cassettes used by the music industry. They have limited storage capacity, but microprocessors seldom need megabyte volumes. They are easy to handle, of very convenient size and, most importantly, the tape is protected from the environment to a greater degree than tape on open reels.

Disks

These systems are becoming more prevalent with time. The disk has a number of advantages over other auxiliary storage media. Although disk systems are more costly than magnetic tape systems, they provide bulk storage with a very reasonable access time, and a maximum latency measured in the tens or hundreds of milliseconds. Bit transfer rates are typically one megahertz or greater. Storage costs are between 1/8 and 1/2 cent per bit.

Floppy disk systems are becoming quite popular with microprocessor users because of the simpler disk configuration, and hence relatively inexpensive systems. The data transfer rate is of the order of 250 kilobits per second, somewhat slower than the megahertz rates quoted for conventional disk systems. The IBM floppy disk track format is shown in Fig. 9-8, which gives an indication of the indexing, addressing, and formatting required when dealing with this type of auxiliary memory system. Floppy disk manufacturers advertise that their systems can be used to replace paper tape devices with little or no impact to the processor software. These units are quite compact, considering that they are rotating memory systems, and occupy about 3 cubic feet and weigh about 50 pounds. A system of this size has a disk capacity of perhaps 250,000 8-bit bytes.

Chapter 10

Compilers

It is apparent that there are significant gains to be made by constructing microprocessor programs in as natural a manner as possible. Perhaps the ideal situation will occur some day when the programmer can shout commands at a processor and have those verbal instructions properly interpreted, stored, and executed. (This is not as far-fetched as it appears on the surface. Considerable effort has been expended on developing pattern recognition techniques for "training" an input device to recognize a set of words or phrases.) However, until such a system is available, precise written instructions form the basis for communicating with computing systems.

Assemblers are a partial answer, for as we have seen, they suffer from the fact that they are constructed to satisfy the machine, not the man. With few exceptions, assemblers translate input statements one-for-one into machine language. Some rather clever assemblers exist, but by and large, they are created from relatively unsophisticated blocks of code.

Interpreters represented another major step forward in allowing the programmers to create code in a more acceptable format to him. The interpreter program examines the source code, picks it apart, and executes it on the spot by converting the program line-by-line to machine language. This permits the interpreter's problem to be bounded to the most complex single statement that can be formed in the interpreter language (with some added data storage control). The fundamental problem with interpreters is that they don't do anything until the program is to be executed, then use many machine instructions to decipher and sequentially execute each operation, thus significantly slowing down the computation.

Simulators, as in the simulation routines mentioned in Chapter 8, are virtually all interpretive. Speed is not normally critical for simulators except when the simulated microprocessor is expected to work in real time handling inputs and outputs in the same fashion as the real processor.

Compilers, however, work on source code before execution. They generate several machine language instructions from each source *statement*. The compiler is then out of the way, its job completed, and the resulting program runs at machine speed.

BASIC COMPILER CONFIGURATION

Compilers are composed of a complex code, with the number of instructions used to implement a compiler of ten numbering in the thousands. A compiler can be thought of as existing in two parts, together with an extensive library of utility routines. The first part is a *discriminator* that determines the sense of each statement of the source code. The second part is composed of a set of *generators* that produce assembly code, based on information in each of the source statements.

Compilers either work from the "top down" where a statement form is assumed and tests are made on the scanned input data to determine the validity of the assumption, or from the "bottom up" where nothing is assumed. The statement is scanned a character at a time, testing against the rules until a valid statement type is determined. Compilers available at this writing for microprocessors are FORTRAN IV, MPL, and PL/M. FORTRAN and MPL will be briefly described here.

FORTRAN

Probably the most common scientific programming language used in the Free World is FORTRAN. The general acceptance of FORTRAN is almost entirely due to the fact that IBM dominated the computer market at the time FORTRAN was introduced (ca. 1959) to an even greater degree than it dominates it today. In addition, the FORTRAN source language is easy to use and efficient.

A word of caution is necessary at this point. There are many versions of the FORTRAN language. The differences among them are often subtle, but unintentional programming errors can arise from relying on general FORTRAN descriptions (even the one here) instead of the specific rules associated with the version at hand.

The name FORTRAN is derived from FORmula TRANslation. FORTRAN is a truly near-algebraic language using algebraic symbols whenever the communications media permits. As with most compilers, the FORTRAN compiler works into an assembler. Your source code is compiled into a standard assembly code, which in turn is converted into machine language. This means that to modify a version of FORTRAN for a particular microprocessor, it is not necessary to reprogram the compiler, but rather to recode the assembler output to fit the idiosyncrasies of the microprocessor.

The FORTRAN compiler will not run on the microprocessor, but rather on one of the larger computer systems. Often, access to the compiler will be by means of a terminal working into a large Mach-2 computer with the main frame time-shared with many other users.

Basic FORTRAN

Unfamiliarity with FORTRAN is becoming rare, but a quick review may prove to be useful.

The FORTRAN source language is composed of *statements*. The format is generally one statement per input line. A simple FORTRAN program composed of four statements is:

READ, I, J
PRINT, I, J
STOP
END

This program causes data to be read into the microprocessor and printed out in a standard print format, where one is available. (Format statements will likely be needed to provide format control for most FORTRAN versions encountered.)

Because input media for FORTRAN are normally 80-column IBM cards (Fig. 9-1), one input line is composed of 80 or less characters, with the meanings dependent upon the columns used. FORTRAN coding forms normally have the column designators printed on them:

Columns 1–5 contain the *statement number field* (label). Any valid unsigned non-zero character can be used, and these include capital letters A–Z, decimal numbers 0–9 blanks, and special characters: ( ), . * + − = /

Column 6 contains a *continuation designator* (other than 0 or blank), indicating that the input line is not a new statement but rather part of the preceding statement. Usually no more than 10 continuations are permitted in a single statement.

Columns 7–72 contain the statement.

Columns 73–80 contain an *identification* or *sequence* field. Decks of any size or importance should always be sequenced. (Too often a deck is dropped, and having to manually reorder a deck of any size tends to ruin an otherwise good day).

Every FORTRAN statement contains at least one *keyword*. This is a word or symbol that clues the compiler to what the statement is about. Other data forms used are *constants* and *variables*. (Blanks have meaning when used with character strings or *literal constants*, but blanks should not occur within a variable name; otherwise they can be rather freely used to improve readability.)

Comments are designated by a C in column 1. They are not part of the program; they are ignored by the compiler and printed out on the listing unchanged.

Arithmetic assignment statements used in FORTRAN look like equalities, but as in AMP assembler code and in other computer code forms, the equal sign means "is replaced by." As an example, a valid FORTRAN statement is: ALPHA = BETA + DELTA. Execution of this statement causes the values in locations BETA and DELTA to be added together. The sum is then placed in location ALPHA. The statement BETA + DELTA = ALPHA is meaningless in FORTRAN since there is no way the compiler can decide where to put ALPHA. If we wish to increment a counter, we may write: CTR = CTR + 1, which has meaning only when the equal sign means "is replaced by."

Arithmetic operations are

+	Addition
−	Subtraction
*	Multiplication
/	Division
**	Exponentiation

As in algebra, the value of the result often depends on the order of execution of the various arithmetic operations. FORTRAN utilizes algebraic hierarchy rules: Exponentiation is performed first, multiplication and division next, addition and subtraction last. When two operations at the same level are encountered, the operations are performed from left to right, except for exponentiation, which is performed from right to left. The FORTRAN Statement, $B = A/C*D$ is evaluated as $(A/C)D$, not $A/(CD)$. In the FORTRAN statement $B = A**C**D$, the C^D term is evaluated first since it is the exponent of A.

Parentheses are invaluable in FORTRAN; they bind sets of arithmetic operations together. Again, the operations are performed in algebraic order, with the innermost parenthetical expression evaluated first. In the statement

$$A = (((B*C + D) + (E/F + G)) - B**2)$$

$(B*C + D)$ is evaluated, then $(E/F + G)$, then the sum, and finally $B**2$ is subtracted, forming A.

As an example of a simple FORTRAN program, recall the Newton iteration in Chapter 5. The defining equation is

$$x_{N+1} = x_N - (2x_N{}^2 - 1)/4x_N$$

This process to continue until $2x_N{}^2 - 1 = y_N$, differs from zero by no more than $1/256$, or 0.0039. A FORTRAN program to accomplish this is as follows:

LABEL	STATEMENT
1	XN = 1
2	YN = 2*XN**2 − 1
	IF (.0039 − YN) 3,3,4
3	XN = XN − YN (4*XN)
	GO TO 2
4	WRITE (6, 5) XN
5	FORMAT (F 10.5)
	END

A sample coding sheet for the program is shown in Fig. 10-1, and the FORTRAN output is given in Fig. 10-2 with the answer 0.70833. This program generally follows the logic of the flow chart of Fig. 5-7, but because Fig. 5-7 was prepared with the more involved coding rules of the AMP in mind, there is not a one-to-one correspondence.

FORTRAN WORK SHEET

DECK NO. _____ PROGRAMMER _____ DATE _____

FOR PROGRAM NO. _____ TITLE _____

CARD NO.	TYPE			10					20					30					40					50		
C		NEWTON RAPHSON SQUARE ROOT ROUTINE																								
1		XN = 1																								
2		YN = 2. * XN ** 2 - 1																								
		IF (.0039 - YN) 3,3,4																								
3		XN = XN - YN / (4. * XN)																								
		GO TO 2																								
4		WRITE (,6,,5,) XN																								
5		FORMAT (F 10.5)																								
		END																								

Fig. 10-1. FORTRAN source code.

Transfer Statements

The preceding example also used both *conditional*(IF) and *unconditional* transfer statements, not previously discussed. The IF conditional transfer statement is a powerful tool of FORTRAN. There are two forms: the *arithmetic* IF and the *logical* IF.

The arithmetic IF is of the form: IF (arithmetic expression) L_1 , L_2 , L_3 , where the L's are labels of program statements. The IF statement causes the program to branch to L_1 if the current value of the statement within the parentheses is less than zero, to L_2 if it equals zero, and to L_3 if it is greater than zero.

The logical IF form is: IF (logical expression) single statement. If the logical expression is true, the single statement is executed. If the expression is false, control passes to the next instruction in sequence.

GO TO Statement

The GO TO statement is most often used as in the preceding example, which illustrates an unconditional transfer statement. The general form is: GO TO (or GOTO) label. This form causes program control to be transferred to the statement associated with the GO TO label. There are two other forms of GO TO: the *computed* GO TO and the *assigned* GO TO.

In the computed GO TO, the general statement form is: GO TO (L_1 , L_2 ,...L_N) integer. The L's are statement labels, and the integer is a variable which, when it assumes a value between 1 and N, causes control to be transferred to the

```
FORTRAN IV G1   RELEASE 2.0              MAIN DATE = 76243

                 C  NEWTON RAPHSON SQUARE ROOT ROUTINE
 0001            1 XN = 1
 0002            2 YN = 2 * XN ** 2 - 1
 0003              IF (.0039 - YN ) 3,3,4
 0004            3 XN = XN - YN / (4 * XN)
 0005              GO TO 2
 0006            4 WRITE ( 6 , 5 ) XN
 0007            5 FORMAT ( F 10.5 )
 0008              END


0.70833

0
```

Fig. 10-2. FORTRAN output for Newton-Raphson routine.

corresponding statement label. That is, when the GO TO statement is executed, the value of the integer at that time is used to effect the appropriate transfer.

The assigned GO TO statement is of the general form: GO TO integer (L_1, L_2 ...L_N). The integer in this statement is also a variable, but it is used in conjunction with a separate assignment statement that must precede the GO TO statement. The assignment statement is of the form: ASSIGN L TO I, where L is the label and I is an integer. The purpose of the assigned GO TO is to provide a method by which branches from several different points in the program may be established. When the GO TO is executed, control goes to the labeled statement last assigned to the integer variable. For example, ASSIGN 10 TO KALL means that integer variable KALL is now assigned to label 10, so if the statement GO TO KALL (7, 10, 25) appears later in the program, control is immediately transferred to label 10, provided 10 is the most recent assignment to KALL.

DO Statements

The general form of the DO statement is: DO label variable = starting value, ending value, increment. Where the starting, ending, and increment values can be constants or integer variables.

Examples:

$$DO\ 80\ I = 1, 100, 3$$
$$A (I) = C (I) + B (I)$$
$$80\ CONTINUE$$

In this case, the arithmetic statement will be executed with variable values for A(I) = A(1), A(4), A(7), ... A(100). Once the limit of I = 100 is exceeded, the program exits from the loop. The label 80 specified in the DO statement defines the *last* statement executed in the DO loop. The statements following the DO and continuing until the final statement are the *range* of the DO, and the value of the variable may not be respecified within this range. The final statement must follow (on the coding sheet) the DO statement.

DO loops can also be *nested*; that is, one or more DO loops can be contained within another DO loop. However, if a DO loop is contained within another, it must be wholly contained—all statements within the range of an *inner* DO must be within the range of the *outer* DO. In most versions of FORTRAN, the last statement in a DO loop cannot be another DO, or a STOP, PAUSE, GO TO, or arithmetic IF. Consult the manual for the particular version you are using for the rules of your game. The CONTINUE statement in our example may be used as insurance against ending a DO loop with a forbidden statement.

Dimension Statement

In dealing with arrays of numbers, it is often convenient to be able to label the entire array. Arrays may represent matrixes of coefficients of simultaneous equations, elements of vectors, or any other kind of ordered data. The DIMENSION statement provides a means of naming the array, and of limiting the number of elements contained.

Example: DIMENSION A(35), B(64), C(3,16). Here, arrays A and B are one-dimensional arrays having a maximum of 35 and 64 elements, respectively. Array C is two-dimensional, having no more than 3 rows and 16 columns.

When referring to an array element, indexes must be used; for example, $A(35) = ALPH + 1$, where the index (35) indicates the 35th element of array A. The power of the DIMENSION statement comes from the use of variables rather than constants as the indexes. For example, $A(I + 2*J) = ALPH + 1$, where arithmetic can be done on I and J. This suggests a rather powerful tool for matrix operations.

Input/Output Data Forms

FORTRAN has very flexible input/output, but not all these capabilities are needed for most programs generated for microprocessors. Integer and floating-point data is used most often. FORTRAN has two input/output types: formatted and *unformatted*. Formatted data makes possible a conversion between the data as it is held in memory and the more familiar characters, letters, and numerals used for communication with the outside world. Record or unformatted data is transferred between memory and external hardware in unchanged (and generally unreadable) form.

Formatted information transfer is controlled by WRITE and FORMAT statements.

The FORMAT Statement

Consider the data to be handled as a continuous character stream. The FORMAT statement causes this stream to be broken into lines, often called *records*. For example,

Line 1	A B C D E 1 7 6 2
Line 2	F G H I J K L 9 5 4
Line 3	M N O P Q R 1 0 0

And the lines are further broken into *fields*, or columns of characters.

Data characteristics must also be specified:

1 0 3 7 5	5-digit integer
T	Logical
9 . 1 2 4	Floating point
MICRO	Character

The general FORMAT statement is: LABEL FORMAT (scale factor, repetition factor, format code, number of character positions in the field, number of character positions to the right of the decimal point). The *scale factor* is optional and identifies the power of 10 by which the value in machine units should be multiplied to yield the value in problem units. The *repetition factor* is also optional and is used to denote the number of identical consecutive fields on a line. The *format code* specifies the data type and includes the following letter codes:

- I   Integer
- F   Floating point
- E   Floating point (exponential form)
- D   Floating point (double precision)
- G   General
- L   Logical
- A   Character
- Z   Hexadecimal
- H   Literal data
- X   Skip
- T   Fixed position

(These may or may not all be available in the particular version of FORTRAN you are using.)

As an example, consider the F (floating point) format code. In our Newton-Raphson example, we chose a floating-point format, FORMAT (F 10.5), which indicates 10 characters in the field, with 5 characters to the right of the decimal point. The general form is: (F T . R), where T is the total number of characters in the field, and R is the number of characters to the right of the decimal point.

Read and Write Statements

These statements identify the values to be transmitted, where they come from or go to, and the controlling FORMAT statement (declared separately). The general forms are: READ (unit, format, END = label 1, ERR = label 2) list; and WROTE (unit, format) list. Here, *unit* identifies the *file* or *logical unit* that data comes from or goes to, *format* is the label of the controlling FORMAT statement, and *list* is the list of data to be operated upon. END and ERR are options, where label 1 is associated with END and is the label of the statement to which control is transferred when there is no more data to read, while label 2 is the statement to which control should be transferred if an input error occurs.

Summary

Though much more could be said about the FORTRAN compiler, it is the main objective of this book to acquaint you with a few of its main features so that you will investigate its use in creating a microprocessor code. The conveniences offered by such a compiler can do much to alleviate the chores involved in generating lengthy and involved assembly language codes for any microprocessor system.

MPL COMPILER LANGUAGE

Both Intel and Motorola have introduced compilers structured specifically for microprocessor applications, and most notably for use with their 8080 and 6800 microprocessors. The Intel language is known as PL/M, the Motorola as MPL. MPL has been chosen for discussion as a representative higher order language having both bit and character manipulation capability. The following is based on preliminary data available at the time of writing.

The MPL compiler, like the FORTRAN compiler, develops assembly language code. In the case of MPL, the compiler output is compatible with the M6800 macro assembler, which creates the machine language program for the 6800 system.

MPL source programs are made up of *statement sets* and these statements fall into the following classes.

Specification Statements. Statements in this category are used to declare characteristics of variables and arrays.

Procedure Statements. These define operating procedures.

Arithmetic Statements. These statements cause useful work to be done. Computations performed as a result of these statements will replace the current value of a labeled or indexed variable.

Control Statements. These permit the programmer to control program flow and to terminate execution.

Procedural, arithmetic, and control statements are considered *executable*, while specification statements are not. The normal order of an MPL program entity is: (1) procedure statement, (2) specification statement, (3) at least one executable statement, and (4) the END statement. As with FORTRAN, the 80-column card is considered the basic input medium. MPL statements are written within columns 1 through 72, with continuations possible except when dealing with constants.

Statement Labels. Labels consist from one to six alphabetic or numeric characters, with the first character constrained to be alphabetic. Labels must be followed by a colon. Provision is made within MPL to accept raw assembler code, which is identified as such by a dollar sign in the first column. When assembler code statements are encountered by the compiler, the contents are passed unaltered to the input to the assembler. (This is a very handy option when dealing with microprocessor code.)

Comments. A comment string as long as needed can be used in MPL. Identification of a comment may be either by (A) enclosing the comment within /* and */, or (B) closing a preceding statement by an exclamation point and following the exclamation point by the comment.

Data Formats

MPL handles several data classes. Since we are dealing here with a compiler tailored for use with a microprocessor, binary representations are quite evident. The data classes are:

Bit String. Seven bits, BIT (7) through BIT(1), are identified as single-bit fields. These may be set or tested individually. BIT(8) is used for an 8-bit field that can be manipulated with Boolean operators, cycled, and tested.

Binary Integer. BINARY(1) identifies one-byte (single precision) operations. BINARY (2) identifies two-byte (double precision) operations. Tests, arithmetic operations including shifts, and logical operations may be performed on binary integers.

ASCII Numeric. DECIMAL(1) through DECIMAL(12), SIGNED DECIMAL(1) through SIGNED DECIMAL(12), and DECIMAL(I, J) or SIGNED DECIMAL (I, J) identify decimal data presented in ASCII format (see Table 9-1). Index I is the *total* digit count in the word and index J is the digit count *after* the decimal point. This data is packed one digit per byte plus one byte for the sign, where needed. Addition, subtraction, test, and replacement are operations that may be performed upon this class of data.

ASCII Alphanumeric. CHARACTER (M) defines an ASCII character set (Table 9-1) that occupies M bytes, one byte per character, where M ranges from 1 through 255.

Variable Data

The meaning and use of MPL variables is sufficiently similar to FORTRAN that the details need not be discussed here. MPL variable types may be binary bit string, numeric ASCII, or literal string (alphanumeric ASCII). The variable type must be declared by a DECLARE statement before the variable can be legally used.

Constant Data

MPL constants are of five types: binary, hexadecimal, integer, string, and address constants.

Binary Constants. These are represented by a string of bits followed by the letter B. Binary constants occupy one or two bytes.

Hexadecimal Constants. These are represented by a hexadecimal number either enclosed in double quotes or in no quotes at all, and followed by the letter H. If no quotes are used, the first character must be numeric (0—9). Hexadecimal data occupies either one or two bytes.

Integer Constants. Binary integers occupy either one or two bytes. Numeric ASCII constants occupy from 1 to 12 bytes. Integer constants may be positive, negative, or zero.

String Constants. These are a set of ASCII characters enclosed in single quotes. String constants are packed 1 ASCII character per byte and may be between 1 and 255 bytes in length. Example: 'SUM OF'.

Address Constants. These are a set of ASCII characters enclosed in single quotes and which denote the value of an address.

Symbolics. Symbolics identify an array and its associated elements, a variable, a procedure name, and of course a statement label. Symbolic names must be uniquely defined within a program. Further, MPL has reserved some symbolic configurations as key words, and they may not be used otherwise. (Four character sets with the letter Z as the first character are off limits.)

Arrays

As in FORTRAN, array notation provides a compact means of addressing ordered data sets by first identifying the dimension and type of the array, then identifying the row and column of the desired array element.

Example: A 4-row by 3-column MATRIX labelled MATX can be identified to MPL by the statement: DECLARE MATX (4, 3).

A reference to the array element at row 4, column 2 would be made as MATX (4, 2). The array elements can also be identified by variable indexes.

Indexing. Index units (sometimes called subscripts) are sets of integers separated by commas that are used to identify array elements. Index values must be greater than zero and less than 256, and they must be positive. Indexed arrays can be of the form ABC (I), DIAG (I − 2), or ZED (I − 1, J, K + 4), but three indexes are the maximum that MPL will accept.

Pointers. Because the M6800 does not have hardware multiplication, indexed operations will likely use more machine cycles than this alternate scheme of array addressing. A data set is addressed by pointers using a 2-byte binary integer. A pointer is established by one of two formats, either V:P or P→V, where V is the variable label and P is the pointer.

Arithmetic and Logic Expressions

MPL expressions are composed of *primaries* (operands) and *operators*. A primary can be composed of data declared as

BIT, BINARY, CHARACTER, or DECIMAL. The operators are:

SYMBOL	OPERATION
+	Addition
−	Subtraction, also can be used as a "unary minus"
*	Multiplication
'	Division
SHIFT	Shift
IAND	Logical AND
IOR	Logic OR
IEOR	Logic exclusive OR (or EOR)

If more than one primary appears in an expression, as it usually will, the primaries must be separated by an operator. For example, the shift operation is written as A SHIFT B, where A is the primary to be shifted, and B is a constant (either positive or negative) that defines the direction and number of places the operand is to be shifted. A positive value of B commands a left shift, while a negative value commands a right shift. The order of operations is what one should expect, and the MPL precedence rank is:

1. Unary minus (used to denote a negative number)
2. SHIFT
3. Logic AND, OR, EOR
4. Multiplication, division
5. Addition, subtraction

The first operation on the list is performed before the second, and so on, when several operations are encountered in the same arithmetic expression.

The unary minus is treated as zero minus the primary; for example, A = −B is considered A = 0 − B. Parentheses are used here as they are used in FORTRAN, to bind operations in a manner acceptable to the programmer when the MPL order of operation is awkward to use.

Statements

The statement types used in MPL are:

Origin. This statement has an input format of ORIGIN "Hex". This is really an instruction to the assembler to reinitialize the origin address. If no origin statement appears, the first address will be 00.

Declare. The format of a DECLARE statement is rather complex. Rather than discuss it in detail here, we will observe that DECLARE is used to define and identify a data structure. To this end DECLARE may be used to set down the level (matrix, row, column), name, data type, and dimension. DECLARE may also be used to initialize variables.

Arithmetic Assignment. This statement takes the form: variable = arithmetic expression. (Again note that the equal sign is used to mean "is replaced by.") As an example of an MPL operation, consider that the following variables have been specified: I is a BINARY (1) variable, C and D are DECIMAL (5) variables, and A(2,2) is BINARY (2) array. The arithmetic assignment C = D causes the value of D to replace the current value of C; I = C causes the value of C to be converted to pure binary and then to replace the current value of I; C = A(1,2) causes the content of row 1, column 2 of array A to be converted to a numeric ASCII character that then replaces the current value of C; and A(2,1) = C causes the current value of C to be converted to double-precision binary which then replaces the current value of row 2, column 1 of array A.

Control Statements. GO TO , IF, DO, and END are dealt with by MPL in the same fashion as in FORTRAN.

Procedures

A program in MPL vernacular is a *procedure*. A *main procedure* is a main program and is identified either by the statement PROCEDURE OPTIONS (main), where MPL compiles the entire program into RAM, or by PROCEDURE OPTIONS (main, stack name), with the identification of a stack name. The stack name causes the compiler to compile the program into both ROM and RAM, using the general rule of compiling declared addresses into RAM and declared procedures into ROM.

Subroutine Procedures. A subroutine procedure has the general form PROCEDURE label $(A_1, A_2, ... A_N)$, where the A's are a list of arguments associated with the procedure. The subroutine is called by a CALL statement in the form CALL SUB (A, B, C), where SUB in this example is the label of the subroutine procedure, and A, B, and C are its arguments.

Summary

MPL is available on the Xerox Sigma 9 and the GE MK III time-sharing systems. MPL programs appear similar to FORTRAN in arithmetic structure, but are significantly different in input format. Again, the best procedure is to carefully examine the idiosyncracies of the specific compiler system you plan to use.

PL/M COMPILER LANGUAGE

The PL/M language is a higher order language originally designed for use with the Intel 8008 microprocessor, which is compatible with the more recent 8080 system. The PL/M compiler is also a cross-compiler built to run on a larger machine. (It is not possible today to execute any PL/M version on either the 8008 or the 8080.)

PL/M includes a complete symbolic addressing capability and a number of basic statements directing character, arithmetic, and logic operations on 8- and 16-bit bytes. The arithmetic and logic statements are nearly algebraic. A set of conditional statements are built around IF A, THEN B, ELSE C, where A is a conditional relationship, which if true, then B occurs; but if A is not true, then C is executed.

Due to its more restricted usage, we will not further explore PL/M, but if an 8008 or an 8080 system is envisioned, PL/M will deserve your consideration. There are sufficient similarities to the preceding compiler languages, though, that you should be able to quickly grasp the major operating features.

SUMMARY

The objective of the limited discussions in this chapter has been to alert the user of microprocessor hardware to the features and structures of higher level languages, some of which are tailored to the unique problems associated with creating reasonably-efficient microprocessor codes, while offering the programming advantages of these languages. However, the prospective user should also be aware that compiler code will not, in general, be as efficient as hand-created assembler code when considering either execution times or amount of memory used.

But compilers are getting better. In fact, HAL, a high-level language compiler used for developing control programs for the Space Shuttle, actually did better than the programmer using a machine language assembler on a few benchmark programs.

Even so, it is prudent to expect at least a 25% increase in execution time and about a 20% increase in required memory when using a compiler instead of an assembler. At the same time, the program development cycle, using a compiler, can be almost cut in half for programs not involving a lot of bit handling. Where the choice exists, and the program is significant, a rather careful consideration of the prospective advantages and disadvantages should be made before deciding on the source language.

Chapter 11

Microprocessor Configurations

There are a myriad of microprocessor systems on the market today—each one having unique characteristics, but all possessing some elements in common. Rather than dwelling on the differences, it is probably better to examine the common features and similarities of today's systems.

All microprocessors use parallel digital arithmetic. All operate in binary. Although some advertise BCD operation, deep down inside, their arithmetic is binary. BCD is handled in a manner similar, if not identical, to the discussion of BCD in Chapter 2.

All microprocessors have some kind of a data bus structure. The information transfer among devices is via this data bus. (New systems such as the Rockwell PPS-4-1 integrate the entire microprocessor on a single chip.) And all have internally stored programs.

The instruction sets range from at least 40 unique instructions to over 100. For example, the Intersil 6100 has over 40 instructions, as does the National IMP 8, while the Intel 8080 has 110.

To date, all systems in quantity production use MOS or TTL technology, with the exception of the TI SBP0400 that uses

I ^{2} L. The MOS systems use either PMOS or NMOS, with the NMOS units being inherently faster (see Chapter 12). The PMOS systems tend to make up for their slower clock rates by using clever logic, exemplified by the multifaceted instruction repertoire of AMP. PMOS systems range in cycle time from about 0.7 to 4 microseconds, while NMOs systems operate in the region of 0.3 to 2 microseconds.

Power supplies are characteristically ±5 and ±12 volts, with the newer designs requiring only a single supply, usually 5 volts.

All competitive microprocessor systems have ROMs, PROMS, and RAMs available in various configurations. These are identical in use to the AMP RAMs and ROMs. Salient information concerning some of the more popular microprocessors available today is given in Table 11-1 (with thanks to A.O. Williman and H. Jelenek).

Because of the general acceptance of the Motorola M6800, Intel 8080, and the Rockwell PPS-8 systems, these three have been chosen from among those systems in Table 11-1 for more detailed discussion.

MOTOROLA M6800 MICROPROCESSOR

The M6800 is an NMOS microprocessor system built around a bus-oriented 8-bit parallel CPU called a microprocessing unit (MPU). The minor cycle (basic) clock is 1 megahertz as compared with the 200 kilohertz of AMP. The M6800 has a minimum instruction execution time of 2 microseconds. Unlike the AMP, the M6800 has two accumulators. A 16-bit index register is available for memory addressing. In addition, the M6800 has a 16-bit stack pointer containing the next available address in the push-down/pop-up stack. The program counter is also a 16-bit register containing the program address. A flag or *condition code* register stores the results of ALU operation.

A typical M6800 device configuration and bus structure is shown in Fig. 11-1. The MPU communicates with the other devices via the 8-bit data bus, the 12-bit address bus, and the 4-bit chip select bus (for memory paging). Bus control, read/write control, and system timing are provided by five signal lines. Finally, control of the MPU itself is provided via five inputs to the MPU and one output, which are termed the *processor control* lines. The devices shown in addition to the

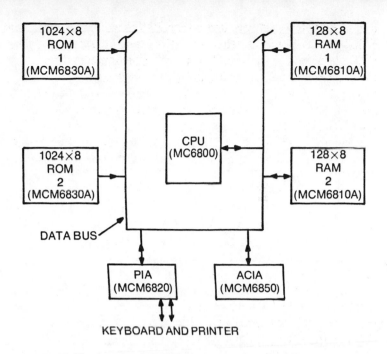

Fig. 11-1. M6800 system configuration.

CPU are the RAM; the ROM; the asynchronous communications interface adapter (ACIA), which performs data error checking, control, and formatting of serial asynchronous information transmitted and received by the M6800 system; and the peripheral interface adapter (PIA), which provides control of information interchange between the M6800 and peripheral equipment using two 8-bit bidirectional data buses for peripheral communication and four control lines. A clock, consisting of a one megahertz oscillator, driver, and buffer, provides basic system timing (the M6800 system uses a 2-phase clock). A 5 volt DC, switched power supply completes the electrical components.

The M6800 has the ability to communicate with peripherals through the PIA and ACIA. Almost any configuration can be accommodated that does not exceed the maximum data rate. A 0 to 600 bit per second *modem* (modulator-demodulator) is available from Motorola to be used with equipment having a serial data transmission requirement.

We will now briefly examine some of the characteristics of the principal M6800 component devices.

Table 11-1. Existing General-Purpose Microprocessors

PARAMETER	INTEL 4004	INTEL 4040	INTEL 8008-1	INTEL 8080	MOTOROLA M6800	NATIONAL IMP-8
Word length	4-bit	4-bit	8-bit	9-bit	8-bit	8-bit
Technology	PMOS	PMOS.	PMOS	NMOS	NMOS	PMOS
Cycle time (μs)	1 3	1 35	4	0.5	1	1.4
Instruction time (μs)	10.8	10.8	20	2	2	4.6
Number of instructions	46	60	48	110	72	40+
Power supply (volts)	15	+5, -10	+5, -9	+5, +12 -5	+5	+5, -12
CPU configuration	16-pin single chip	24-pin single chip	18-pin single chip	40-pin single chip	40-pin single chip	24-pin 3 chips
Chip family	RAM. IO. ROM. PROM	ROM. IO RAM. PROM	RAM. ROM PROM	RAM. ROM. PROM	RAM. ROM. I/O	RAM. CROM. PROM
CPU price and quantities	$18 65 (1-24)	$20 70 (unit)	$35(1-24)	$75(1-24)	$35(1-9) $32.50(10-49) $29.95(50-99)	$130(1-24) 140(25-99)
Software support	Simulator. assembler. cross-assembler	Assembler simulator. utilities	Assembler. Simulator cross-assembler. PLM compiler	Assembler. simulator. cross-assembler. PL M compiler	Assembler simulator. EXOR-assembler. text editor. full monitor program	Assembler. utility programs. diagnostic programs. loaders. debug aids

PARAMETER	NATIONAL IMP-16	NATIONAL PACE	ROCKWELL PPS-4	ROCKWELL PPS-8
Word length	16-bit	16-bit	4-bit	8-bit
Technology	PMOS	PMOS	PMOS	PMOS
Cycle time (µs)	1.4	4	2.5	2
Instruction time (µs)	4.6	8	5	4
Number of instructions	40+	45	50	90+
Power supply (volts)	+5, −12	+5, −12	+5, −12	+5, −12
CPU configuration	24-pin 5–6 chips	40-pin single chip	42-pin single chip	42-pin single chip
Chip family	RAM, CROM, PROM	RAM, ROM, I/O, PROM	RAM, ROM, CLOCK, RAMROM I/O	RAM, ROM, CLOCK, I/O, DMA
CPU price and quantities	$160 (1–24) $128 (25–99)	$75.	$39.50 (1–24) $30 (25–99)	$67.50 (1–24) $50 (25–99)
Software support	Assembler, utility programs, diagnostic program, loaders, debug aids.	Resident assembler, compiler debugger editor, relocating loader linking loader	Assembler, simulator, hardware emulator, GE Tymshare, TSO	Assembler, simulator, hardware emulator, GE Tymshare

185

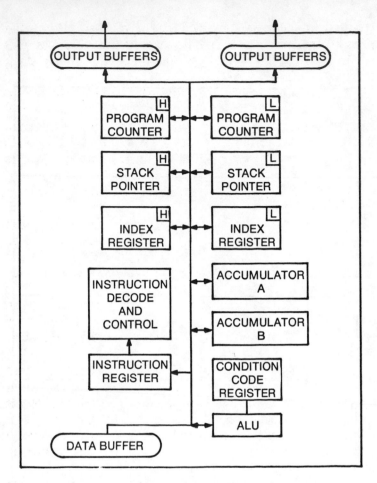

Fig. 11-2. M6800 CPU block diagram. To provide for 16-bit operation, the program counter, stack pointer, and index register each consist of two 8-bit registers, with the H portion holding the higher 8 bits and the L portion holding the lower.

The MPU

Figure 11-2 is a block diagram of the MPU, showing principal functional elements. The MC6800 has seven address modes, selectable by instruction type. These are:

Implied Addressing. This is performed by 1-byte instructions. Some instructions in the set do not require a defined address. For example, the ABA instruction causes the content of accumulator A to be added to accumulator B, and the sum stored in accumulator A. Another class of instructions

186

requires an address, but identifies a register holding the address information. Examples are push (PSH) and pull (PUL), which derive address information from the stack pointer register (Fig. 11-2).

Accumulator Addressing. This address class consists of 1-byte (8-bit) instructions. Either the A or B accumulator is selected as the operand address (really an *implied* address, but specified separately).

Immediate Addressing. The operand is contained in the second byte of a 2-byte instruction, or in the second and third bytes of the LDS (load stack pointer) and LDX (load index register) instructions.

Direct Addressing. These are all 2-byte instructions with the address contained in the second byte, permitting the selection of one of 256 addresses, beginning at location 0 and ending at location 255. Execution times are reduced when accessing information stored in these locations.

Extended Addressing. Here the address contained in the second byte of a 3-byte instruction addresses the 8 high-order operand bits while the third byte addresses the 8 low-order bits.

Relative Addressing requires 2-byte instructions, where the address contained in the second byte is added to the 8 least significant bits of the program counter. (An offset of +2 is automatically added to the counter by the hardware, permitting the next instruction to be selected from −126 bytes to +129 bytes away from the present instruction). Instructions in this class are *conditional* transfers.

Indexed Addressing is performed by a set of 2-byte instructions, where the second byte is added to the content of the index register. This sum is used to address the operand, but is held in temporary storage so the content of the index register is unchanged unless intentionally incremented, decremented, or reloaded.

MPU REGISTER COMPLEMENT

The Program Counter is a 2-byte register (H and L) containing the current instruction address. The program counter is incremented by one at each instruction execution time, permitting sequential program flow unless modified by a transfer instruction.

Stack Pointer is a 2-byte register containing the RAM address of the next available location in the stack.

The Index Register is a 2-byte register used to store a 16-bit memory address to provide a means of temporary address modification when in the indexed addressing mode. The index register can also be used as a data storage register.

Accumulators A and B are each 8-bit registers used to hold the results of the arithmetic and logic operations.

The Condition Code Register is an 8-bit register that holds the results of arithmetic operations for testing and program branch control. (The two high-order bits are not presently used and are arbitrarily set to one). The condition code register configuration is

7	6	5	4	3	2	1	0
1	1	H	I	N	Z	V	C

where C holds the carry-out of bit number 7 (really the eighth bit) unless reset.

V holds the overflow state as a result of a test of the latest addition operation.

Z is one-set if the addressed accumulator content is zero.

N is one-set if the addressed accumulator content is less than zero.

I indicates the persence of an interrupt.

H holds the value of the intermediate carry for BCD operation.

The Arithmetic and Logic Unit (ALU) performs the basic arithmetic and logic manipulations in conjunction with the accumulators. (In short, it does what all ALUs do.)

The Buffers provide the necessary drive, shaping, matching, and time delays to provide for orderly data transmission on and off the MPU chip.

Instruction Set

Table 11-2 gives an overview of the M6800 instruction set. The actions of most of the op codes are self-explanatory, although access to an M6800 programming manual is mandatory before any serious programming should be done.

The RAM

The MCM 6810A read/write memory is a 128×8-bit RAM (Fig. 11-3). This RAM has six chip-select inputs and seven

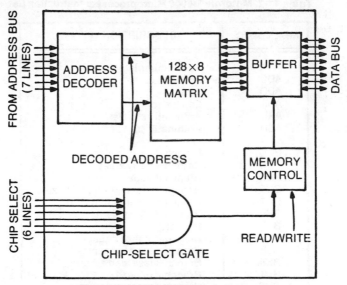

Fig. 11-3. M6800 RAM block diagram.

address inputs interfacing directly to the address bus. The RAM is addressed by information on the chip-select lines, which are decoded in straight-forward fashion by the chip-select gate. A byte within the RAM is selected by decoding information on the seven address lines. Two-way data transfer between the RAM and the MPU is performed via the data bus. An external read/write control is provided, telling the RAM when to transmit or to accept and store information.

The ROM

The MCM 6830A ROM is a 1024 × 8-bit fixed, static memory with a 500 nanosecond access time (Fig. 11-4). Its configuration closely resembles that of the RAM. Salient differences are the three additional address lines needed to address 1024 bytes rather than the RAM's 128, the four chip-select lines, and the absence of a read/write signal, which of course is not needed by the ROM. The ROM has a significantly higher memory storage capacity than that of the RAM.

Peripheral Interface Adapter

Each MC 6820 PIA (Fig. 11-5) provides for a bidirectional 8-bit data bus communication with the MPU, and two similarly configured 8-bit buses are used for data transfer with the

Table 11-2. Motorola M6800 Microprocessor Instruction Set

MNENOMIC	DESCRIPTION
ABA	Add accumulators
ADC	Add with carry
ADD	Add
AND	Logic and
ASL	Arithmetic shift left
ASR	Arithmetic shift right
BCC	Branch if carry is clear
BCS	Branch if carry is set
BEQ	Branch if equal to zero
BGE	Branch if greater or equal to zero
BGT	Branch if greater than zero
BHI	Branch if higher
BIT	Bit test
BLE	Branch if less or equal
BLS	Branch if lower or same
BLT	Branch if less than zero
BMI	Branch if minus
BNE	Branch if not equal to zero
BPL	Branch if plus
BRA	Branch always
BSR	Branch to subroutine
BVC	Branch if overflow is clear
BVS	Branch if overflow is set
CBA	Compare accumulators
CLC	Clear carry
CLI	Clear interrupt mask
CLR	Clear
CLV	Clear overflow
CMP	Compare
COM	Complement
CPX	Compare index register
DAA	Decimal adjust
DEC	Decrement
DES	Decrement stack pointer
DEX	Decrement index register
EOR	Exclusive OR
INC	Increment
INS	Increment stack pointer

outside world. The two peripheral buses can be programmed as either inputs or outputs. Three chip-select inputs are used for device addressing. In addition, two programmable control

Table 11-2. (con't.)

MNEMONIC	DESCRIPTION
INX	Increment index register
JMP	Jump
JSR	Jump to subroutine
LDA	Load accumulator
LDS	Load stack pointer
LDX	Load index register
LSR	Logical shift right
NEG	Negate
NOP	No operation
ORA	Inclusive OR
PSH	Push Data
PUL	Pull data
ROL	Rotate left
ROR	Rotate right
RTI	Return from interrupt
RTS	Return from subroutine
SBA	Subtract accumulators
SBC	Subtract with carry
SEC	Set carry
SEI	Set interrupt mask
SEV	Set overflow
STA	Store accumulator
STS	Store stack register
STX	Store index register
SUB	Subtract
SWI	Software interrupt
TAB	Transfer accumulators
TAP	Transfer accumulators to condition code register
TBA	Transfer accumulators
TAP	Transfer condition code register to accumulator
TST	Test
TSX	Transfer stack pointer to index register
TXS	Transfer index register to stack pointer
WAI	Wait for interrupt

registers are available to provide command signals to the peripherals. The PIA will normally be programmed by the MPU during execution of the system initialization routines.

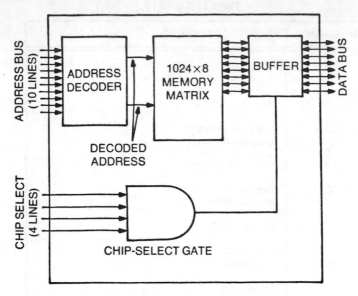

Fig. 11-4. M6800 ROM block diagram.

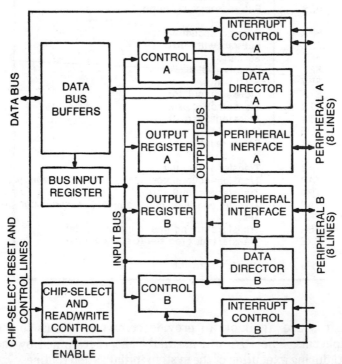

Fig. 11-5. M6800 peripheral interface adapter (PIA) block diagram.

Asynchronous Communications Interface Adapter

This is a rather complex interface device (Fig. 11-6). It provides for data transfer between the M6800 and peripherals over two serial data lines by converting the parallel 8-bit data on the data bus to a serial bit stream, and adding the necessary clocking for transmission data control. Serial data is received, together with its associated clock, parity (see Chapter 9) is checked (either odd or even, selected by the MPU), and the serial data is assembled in the parallel buffer for transmission to the MPU via the data bus.

INTEL 8080 MICROPROCESSOR

It is probably today's most commonly used micropro-cessor configuration. The Intel 8080 is an 8-bit parallel microprocessor (microcomputer) using NMOS technology

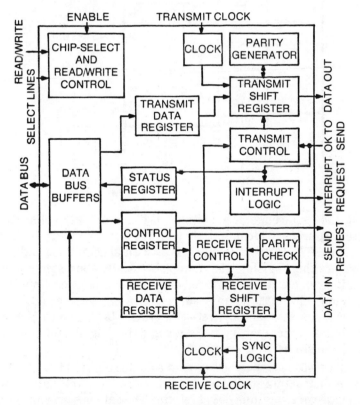

Fig. 11-6. M6800 asynchronous communications interface adapter (ACIA) block diagram.

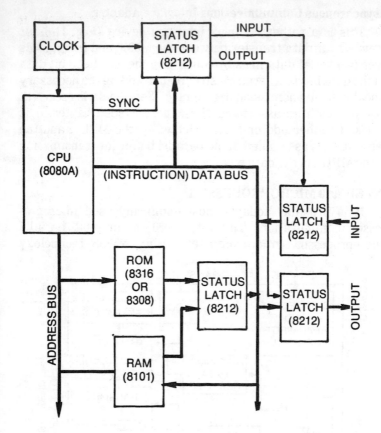

Fig. 11-7. Minimal 8080 system configuration.

and, the required supply voltages are ±5 and +12 volts. The 8080 is source-code compatible with the Intel 8008 CPU (MCS-8 system). The 8080A CPU utilizes an 8-bit accumulator and six 8-bit working registers that can be optionally addressed either singly or in paris for single- or double-precision operations. In addition, the 8080A may address RAMs without address restrictions as a last-in/first-out (LIFO) stack. The CPU also has four 8-bit temporary registers and five flag bits for storing program status.

The 8080 is structured around a 16-line address bus and an 8-line instruction data bus. (See Fig. 11-7 for the data flow structure of a minimal 8080 system.) The data bus provides for 8-bit bidirectional communication among the CPU, ROM, RAM, and input/output devices. The 16-bit address bus is unidirectional, carrying information to the memories and to the input/output devices and providing for a maximum for 65,536 unique addresses. Up to 256 input devices and 256 output devices can be addressed via this bus.

An interlock is provided via the *hold* signal under CPU control. When *hold* is commanded true by the CPU, the address and data buses are *floated*. These lines are then, in effect, disconnected and may be tied to peripheral interface devices and direct memory access (DMA) channels.

8080A CPU

Referring to Fig. 11-8, we see that the 8080 has a number of internal Registers, separated by function into three categories: general registers, program control registers and internal registers. The general and program control registers and their functions are:

NAME	DESIGNA-TOR	USED FOR	LENGTH (BYTES)
Accumulator	A	General-purpose arithmetic and logic operations	1
B Register	B	General storage or most significant half of 2-byte register BC	1
C Register	C	General storage or least significant half of BC	1
D Register	D	General storage or most significant half of 2-byte register DE	1
E Register	E	General storage or least significant half of DE	1
H Register	H	General storage or most significant half of 2-byte register HL	1
L Register	L	General storage or least significant half of HL	2

NAME	DESIGNA-TOR	USED FOR	LENGTH (BYTES)
Program Counter	PC	Contains the address of the instruction to be executed. The content of PC drives the address bus lines during an instruction read or "fetch."	2
Stack Pointer	SP	Contains the address of the latest data byte to be placed in the stack.	2
Flag Register	F	Contains five 1-bit stack registers, which are as follows:	
	C	Carry/borrow out of the most significant bit of the ALU	
	C_1	Intermediate carry out of the fourth bit of the ALU. Used for BCD operations. (C_1 is identical in function to AMP's Q.)	
	Z	Contains a 1 when [A] is equal to zero, otherwise [Z] = 0	
	S	Contains a 1 when the MSB of (A) is a 1, otherwise [S] = 0	
	P	Contains a 1 when [A] has an even number of one's; contains a 0 when [A] has an odd number of one's. Thus, P can be used to generate a natural odd parity.	

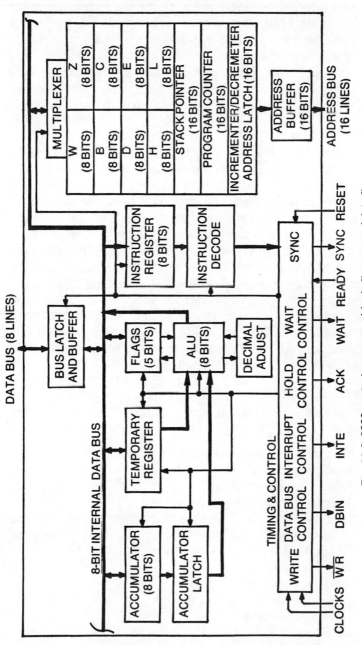

Fig. 11-8. 8080 central processor block diagram and data flow.

The internal registers are not directly accessible by the programmer. They are the 8-bit instruction register, the accumulator latch, the temporary register, the increment/decrement address latch, the bus latch and buffer, and the address buffer. These registers are used for intermediate or temporary storage of data, for holding input information, and for holding addresses and data for off-chip transmission.

8080 Instructions

The basic 8080 clock rate is 2 megahertz. The time required to execute an instruction varies, depending upon the operation and the number of memory references used. As a reference point, 8080 add time is 2 microseconds. An instruction requires from one to five machine (or memory) cycles for fetch and execute. Each machine cycle requires 3 to 5 of the basic 0.5 microsecond clock periods. (The idle states *wait*, *hold*, and *halt* continue for an indefinite time, depending upon external controls). The 8080 instruction execution uses a minimum of four clock periods for non-memory referencing operations of register exchanges and accumulator arithmetic operations, and a maximum of 18 periods for the most complex instructions. At the 2 megahertz clock rate, the range of execution times is then 2 to 9μsec.

8080 Instruction Set

The 8080A instruction set is composed of the following groups:

Transfers, data registers, and memory
Branches and subroutine calls
Load/store accumulator
Save/restore data registers
Double-length data register operations: increment, decrement, direct load/store H&L, load immediate, and index register operations
Indirect transfer
Stack pointer modifications
Logic operations
Binary Arithmetic
Decimal Arithmetic
Set/reset enable flip-flop
Increment/decrement memory of data registers

The instruction list summary is contained in Table 11-3, indicating the mnemonic operation code commonly used, a brief description of the instruction operation, and the number of bytes of memory occupied. (Subroutine calls and returns may use additional cycles, depending upon the state of the condition flags).

The instructions are 1, 2, or 3 bytes long and are stored as:

1 byte	$D_7 \ldots \ldots D_0$	Op code
2 bytes	$D_7 \quad \ldots . D_0$	Op code
	$D_7 \quad \ldots . D_0$	Operand
3 bytes	$D_7 \quad \ldots . D_0$	Op code
	$D_7 \quad \ldots . D_0$	Operand 1 or low-order address
	$D_7 \quad \ldots . D_0$	Operand 2 or high-order address

Read-Only Memories

The 8316A ROM (Fig. 11-9) contains 16,384 bits of permanent storage, organized in 2048 8-bit bytes. The access time is 850 nanoseconds. The 8316A operates from a single

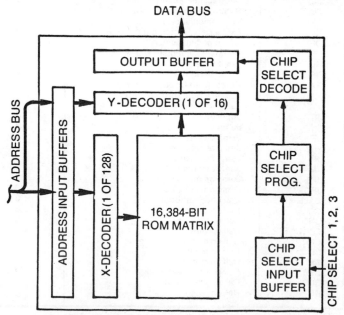

Fig. 11-9. Intel 8316 ROM block diagram.

Table 11-3. Intel 8080 Instruction Set

MNEMONIC	DESCRIPTION	INSTRUCTION LENGTH (BYTES)
MOV r1, r2	Move register to register	1
MOV M,r	Move register to memory	1
MOV r,M	Move memory to register	1
HLT	Halt	1
MVI r	Move immediate register	2
MVI M	Move immediate register	2
INR r	Increment register	1
DCR r	Decremet register	1
INR M	Increment memory	1
DCR M	Decrement memory	1
ADD r	Add register to A	1
ADC r	Add register to A with carry	1
SUB r	Subtract register from A	1
SBB r	Subtract register from A with borrow	1
ANA r	And register with A	1
XRA r	Exclusive-OR register with A	1
ORA r	OR register with A	1
CMP r	Compare register with A	1
ADD M	Add memory to A	1
ADC M	Add memory to A with carry	1
SUB M	Subtract memory from A	1
SBB M	Subtract memory from A with borrow	1
ANA M	And memory with A	1
XRA M	Exclusive -OR memory with A	1
ORA M	OR memory with A	1
CMP M	Compare memory with A	1
ADI	Add immediate to A	2
ACI	Add immediate to A with carry	2
SUI	Subtract immediate from A	2
SBI	Subtract immediate from A with borrow	2
ANI	And immediate with A	2
XRI	Exclusive-OR immediate with A	2
ORI	OR immediate with A	2
CPI	Compare immediate with A	2
RLC	Rotate A left	1
RRC	Rotate A right	1
RAL	Rotate A left through carry	1
RAR	Rotate A right through carry	1
JMP	Jump unconditional	3
JC	Jump on carry	3
JNC	Jump on no carry	3
JZ	Jump on zero	3
JNZ	Jump on no zero	3
JP	Jump on positive	3
JM	Jump on minus	3
JPE	Jump on parity even	3
JPO	Jump on parity odd	3
CALL	Call unconditional	3
CC	Call on carry	3
CNC	Call on no carry	3
CZ	Call on zero	3
CNZ	Call on no zero	3
CP	Call on positive	3
CM	Call on minus	3
CPE	Call on parity even	3
CPO	Call on parity odd	3
RET	Return	1

Table 11-3 (con't.)

MNEMONIC	DESCRIPTION	INSTRUCTION LENGTH (BYTES)
RC	Return on carry	1
RNC	Return on no carry	1
RZ	Return on zero	1
RNZ	Return on no zero	1
RP	Return on positive	1
RM	Return on minus	1
RPE	Return on parity even	1
RPO	Return on parity odd	1
RST	Restart	1
IN	Input	2
OUT	Output	2
LXI B	Load immediate register pair B & C	3
LXI D	Load immediate register pair D & E	3
LXI H	Load immediate register pair H & L	3
LXI SP	Load immediate stack pointer	3
PUSH B	Push register pair B & C on stack	1
PUSH D	Push register pair D & E on stack	1
PUSH H	Push register pair H & L on stack	1
PUSH PSW	Push A and flags on stack	1
POP B	Pop register pair B & C off stack	1
POP D	Pop register pair D & E off stack	1
POP H	Pop register pair H & L off stack	1
POP PSW	Pop A and flags off stack	1
STA	Store A direct	3
LDA	Load A direct	3
XCHG	Exahange D & E, H & L registers	1
XTHL	Exhange top of stack, H&L	1
SPHL	H &L to stack pointer	1
PCHL	H &L to program counter	1
DAD B	Add B & C to H & L	1
DAD D	Add C & E to H & L	1
DAD H	Add H & L to H & L	1
DAD SP	Add stack pointer to H & L	1
STAX D	Store A indirect	1
STAX D	Store A indirect	1
LDAX B	Load A indirect	1
LDZX D	Load A indirect	1
INX B	Increment B & C registers	1
INX D	Increment D & E registers	1
INX H	Increment H & L registers	1
INX SP	Increment stack pointer	1
DCX B	Decrement B & C	1
DCX D	Decrement D & E	1
DCX H	Decrement H & L	1
DCX SP	Decrement stack pointer	1
CMA	Compliment A	1
STC	Set carry	1
CMC	Complement carry	1
DAA	Decimal adjust A	1
SHLD	Store H & L direct	3
LHLD	Load H & L direct	3
EI	Enable interrupts	1
DI	Disable interrupt	1
NOP	No operation	1

+5-volt power supply. The 8308 ROM is also available, having one-half the storage capacity of the 8316 (8192 bits organized as 1024 8-bit words). The access time of the 8308 is almost one-half that of the 8316 (450 nanoseconds). Both ROM are TTL compatible on input and output.

As in other systems, chip-select logic permits the selective addressing of multiple ROM within an 8080 system. Address decoding in the 8316A is performed by X-Y decoders, where 7 address lines drive the X-decoder, and 4 drive the Y. The X-decoder selects 16 bytes for presentation to the Y-decoder which then, using the information on 4 address lines, selects 1 of the 16 bytes for presentation to the output register. The ROM's output goes to the 8212 input/output port, rather than directly to the data bus.

Random-Access Memory

The 8101 RAM (Fig. 11-10) is a 1024-bit memory organized in 256 4-bit bytes. The RAM organization is not directly compatible with an 8-bit processor, so 2 RAMs must be used, one supplying the low-order 4 bits of the 8080 byte to the data bus, and the other supplying the 4 high-order bits.

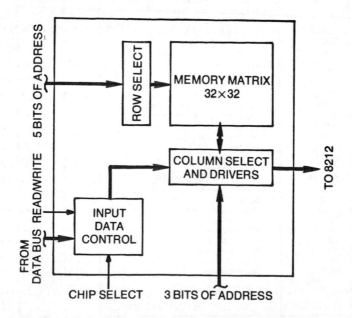

Fig. 11-10. Intel 8101 RAM block diagram.

The RAM's output goes to the data bus via the 8212 input/output port. Address information is received directly from the address bus. The 8101 access time is 1300 nanoseconds. Another version, functionally identical to the 8101, the 8101-2, is a faster memory having an 850 nanosecond access delay. The RAM is composed of static logic and therefore needs no clock or refresh to retain memory. Readout is nondestructive; outputs are TTL compatible.

Input/Output Port

The 8212 is a bipolar input/output interface device that is also used as an 8080 system component. It is logically a simple device, so no functional block diagram is shown. The 8212 is a parallel 8-bit latch/buffer, providing 8 tristate outputs driven by 8 inputs. Once set, the 8212 can hold information in its register until modified or cleared. A clear input control is provided. The device can accept low-level ROM and RAM signals, providing sufficient amplification to interface with the 8080 CPU.

ROCKWELL PPS-8 MICROPROCESSOR

The PPS-8 is an 8-bit parallel microprocessor system. It is the successor to the PPS-4 on which AMP is based. The PPS-8 architecture is built around a bus-oriented structure, implemented with PMOS technology, and using a 4-phase clock. Because multiple operations are available as the result of single instruction execution, the effective computational rate is higher than the 200−256 kilohertz clock rate would indicate.

The PPS-8 organization is distributed to a degree since the various LSI integrated circuits making up the system have built-in intelligence. This further adds to the system throughput by permitting simultaneous execution of several normally serial operations during each minor clock cycle.

A typical system block diagram and data flow is shown in Fig. 11-11. The PPS-8 instruction and operand access time is 2 microseconds, with 4 to 5 μsec required for a complete processor cycle (one-byte instruction read, data access, and execution). Decimal (BCD) addition and subtraction take 12 μsec per digit. The PPS-8 has over 90 instructions (Table 11-4), and they include the use of pooled data, instructions, and indirect addresses.

Table 11-4. Rockwell PPS-8 Instruction Set

MNEMONIC	DESCRIPTION	TIMING CYCLES (BYTES)
Register Instructions		
LY	Load Y from data memory	2 cycle (1 or 2)
LX	Load X from data memory	2 cycle (1 or 2)
LZ	Load Z from data memory	2 cycle (1 or 2)
XAX	Exchange A and X	1 cycle (1)
XAY	Exchange A and Y	1 cycle (1)
XAZ	Exchange A and Z	1 cycle (1)
XY	Exchange X and Y	1 cycle (1)
LXA	Load X from A	1 cycle (1)
LYA	Load Y from A	1 cycle (1)
LZA	Load Z from A	1 cycle (1)
XAL	Exchange A and L upper	1 cycle (1)
LLA	Load L upper from A	1 cycle (1)
XL	Exchange L with Z and X	1 cycle (1)
LAI	Load A immediate	3 cycle (1, 2, or 3)
LXI	Load X immediate	3 cycle (1, 2, or 3)
LYI	Load Y immediate	3 cycle (1, 2 or 3)
LZI	Load Z immediate	3 cycle (1, 2 or 3)
LAL	Load accumulator through link register; address to program memory	3 cycle (1 or 2)
LXL	Load X through link register; address to program memory	3 cycle (1 or 2)
LYL	Load Y through link register; address to program memory	3 cycle (1 or 2)
LZL	Load Z through link register; address to program memory	3 cycle (1 or 2)
Data Transfer Instructions		
L	Load A	1 cycle, 1 byte
LN	Load A; increment and test data address	1 cycle, 1 byte
LD	Load A; decrement and test data address	1 cycle, 1 byte
LDXL	Load A; decrement test; and exchange data address with L	1 cycle, 1 byte
LNXL	Load A; increment test; and exchange data address with L	1 cycle, 1 byte
LNCX	Load A; increment test and compare exchange data address with L	1 cycle, 1 byte
LDCX	Load A; decrement test and compare data address; exchange data address with L	1 cycle, 1 byte
LNXY	Load A; increment and test data address; exchange X and Y	1 cycle, 1 byte
S	Store A	1 cycle, 1 byte
SN	Store A; increment and test data address	1 cycle, 1 byte
SD	Store A; decrement and test data address	1 cycle, 1 byte
SNXL	Store A; increment and test data address; exchange with L	1 cycle, 1 byte

Table 11-4 (con't.)

MNEMONIC	DESCRIPTION	TIMING CYCLES (BYTES)
Data Transfer Instructions		
SDXL	Store A: decrement and test data address: exchange with L	1 cycle, 1 byte
SNCX	Store A: increment test: compare data address exchange with L	1 cycle, 1 byte
SDCX	Store A: decrement test: compare data address: exchange with L	1 cycle, 1 byte
SNXY	Store A: increment and test data address: exchange X and Y	1 cycle, 1 byte
X	Exchange	2 cycles, 2 bytes
XN	Exchange A and M: increment and test data address	2 cycles, 2 bytes
XD	Exchange A and M: decrement and test data address	2 cycles, 2 bytes
XNXL	Exchange A and M: increment and test data address: exchange with L	2 cycles, 2 bytes
Data Transfer Instructions		
XDXL	Exchange A and M: decrement and test data address: exchange with L	2 cycles, 2 bytes
XNCX	Exchange A and M: increment test and compare data address: exchange with L	2 cycles, 2 bytes
XDCX	Exchange A and M: decrement test and compare data address: exchange with L	2 cycles, 2 bytes
XNXY	Exchange A and M: increment and test address: exchange X and Y	2 cycles, 2 bytes
Increment Decrement Instructions		
INXY	Increment X: test and exchange with Y	1 cycle, 1 byte
DEXY	Decrement X: test and exchange with Y	1 cycle, 1 byte
INCX	Increment and test X	1 cycle, 1 byte
DECX	Decrement and test Y	1 cycle, 1 byte
INCA	Increment A	1 cycle, 1 byte
INCY	Increment and test Y. Note: this instruction may not be preceded by a skip as it is a combination of XY and INXY	2 cycles, 2 bytes
DECY	Decrement and test Y. Note: this instruction may not be preceded by a skip as it is a combination of XY and DEXY	2 cycles, 2 bytes
Bit Manipulation Instructions		
RAR	Rotate accumulator right one bit through carry	1 cycle, 1 byte with no branch

Table 11-4 (con't.)

MNEMONIC	DESCRIPTION	TIMING CYCLES (BYTES)
Bit Manipulation Instructions		
RAL	Rotate accumulator left one bit through carry	1 cycle, 1 byte with no branch
MDR	Move digit right: shift four bits right	1 cycle, 1 byte with no branch
MDL	Move digit left: shift four bits left	1 cycle, 1 byte with no branch
SC	Set carry to one	1 cycle, 1 byte
RC	Reset carry to zero	1 cycle, 1 byte
SB	Set bit N in memory to one	2 cycles, 1 or 2 bytes
AN	Logic AND of memory with accumulator	1 cycle, 1 byte
OR	Logic OR of memory with accumulator	1 cycle, 1 byte
EOR	Logic exclusive—OR or memory with accumulator	1 cycle, 1 byte
COM	complement accumulator	1 cycle, 1 byte
ANI	Logic AND of immediate value with accumulator	3 cycles 1, 2 or 3 bytes
Arithmetic Instructions		
A	Add	1 cycle 1 byte
AC	Add with carry	1 cycle 1 byte
ASK	Add and skip if carry is set	1 cycle 1 byte
ACSK	Add with carry and skip if carry is set	1 cycle 1 byte
DC	Decimal correct 1	1 cycle 1 byte
DCC	Decimal correct 2	1 cycle 1 byte
AISK	Add immediate and skip if flop is not used or changed	3 cycles- 1, 2 or 3 bytes
Skip/Branch Instructions		
B	Branch unconditionally. Branch tag set on prior instruction	1 or 2 cycles- 1 or 2 bytes
NOP	No operation	1 cycle-1 byte
BDI	Branch and disable interrupts. Branch tag set on prior instuction	2 cycles-2 bytes
SKZ or BNZ	Skip next instruction if accumulator is zero	1 cycle-1byte plus any branch
SKNZ or BZ	Skip next instruction accumulator is not zero	1 cycle-1byte plus any branch
SKC or BNC	Skip next instruction if carry is one	1 cycle-1byte plus any branch
SKNC or BC	Skip next instruction if carry is not one	1 cycle-1byte plus any branch
SKP or BN	Skip next instruction if positive	1 cycle-1 byte plus any branch
SKN or BP	Skip next instruction if negative	1 cycle-1 byte plus any branch
SKE or BNE	Skip next instruction if A equals memory addressed by Z, X	2 cycle-1 byte plus any branch
BBT	Branch if bit true	2 or 3 cycles- 2 or 3 bytes
BBF	Branch if bit false	2 or 3 cycles- 2 or 3 bytes
Subroutine Instructions		
BL	Branch and link to subroutine	3 cycles-1 or 2 bytes
RT	Return	3 cycles-1 byte

Table 11-4 (con't.)

MNEMONIC	DESCRIPTION	TIMING CYCLES (BYTES)
Subroutine Instructions		
RSK	Return and skip next instruction	3 cycles-1byte
RTI	Return and enable interrupts	3 cycles-1 byte
Stack Instructions		
PSHA	Push accumulator into memory addressed by stack register	2 cycles 1 or 2 bytes
PSHX	Push X into memory addressed by stack register	2 cycles-1 or 2 bytes
PSHY	Push Y into memory addressed by stack register	2 cycles-1 or 2 bytes
PSHZ	Push Z into memory addressed by stack register	2 cycles-1 or 2 bytes
POPA	Pop data into accumulator from memory addressed by decremented stack register: then test	2 cycles-1 or 2 bytes
POPX	Pop data into X from memory addressed by decremented stack register: then test	2 cycles-1 or 2 bytes
POPY	Pop data into Y from memory addressed by decremented stack register: then test	2 cycles-1 or 2 bytes
POPZ	Pop data into Z from memory addressed by decremented stack register: then test	2 cycles-1 or 2 bytes
PSHL	Push L into memory addressed by stack register: and load A and W into L	3 cycles-1 byte
POPL	Pop data into L from memory addressed by decremented stack register	3 cycles-1 byte
Input/Output Instructions		
IN	Input 8 bits	2 cycles-2 bytes
OUT	Output 8 bits	2 cycles-2 bytes
IO4	Input and output 4 bits	2 cycles-2 bytes
RIS	Read interrupt status	2 cycles- 2 bytes

Figure 11-12 is a block diagram illustrating the basic features of the 11806 CPU. The CPU has:

The necessary logic to obtain and decode instructions from the ROMs,

A 14-bit P register for controlling the ROM addresses.

An 8-bit parallel arithmetic/logic unit (ALU).

Three 8-bit registers (X, Y, Z) for RAM operand addressing.

A 16-bit L register for subroutine linking, RAM operand addressing, and ROM indirect addressing.

A 5-bit stack pointer (S).

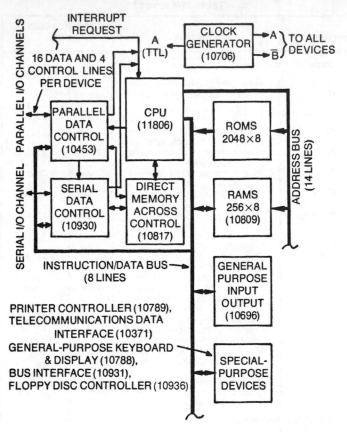

Fig. 11-11. Rockwell PPS-8 system configuration and data flow.

Multiplexed drivers and receivers to provide the proper electrical interface with the address and instruction/data bus.

Logic for priority interrupts, and for a direct memory access (DMA) mode.

Instruction Decode. The logic identified by this box in Fig. 11-12 takes in the instruction bit pattern, determines the required operation(s) and controls the execution. PPS-8 instructions can be one, two, or three bytes long, requiring one major clock cycle per byte for execution.

P Register. This program, or instruction address register, contains the address of the instruction currently being executed. Its function is identical to that of the AMP P

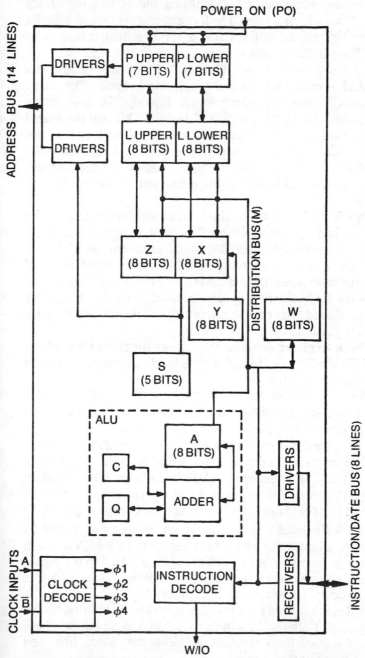

POWER ON (PO)

ADDRESS BUS (14 LINES)

DRIVERS

P UPPER (7 BITS) | P LOWER (7 BITS)

DRIVERS

L UPPER (8 BITS) | L LOWER (8 BITS)

DISTRIBUTION BUS (M)

Z (8 BITS) | X (8 BITS)

Y (8 BITS)

W (8 BITS)

S (5 BITS)

ALU

A (8 BITS)

C

Q

ADDER

DRIVERS

INSTRUCTION/DATE BUS (8 LINES)

CLOCK INPUTS

A

B̄

CLOCK DECODE

φ1
φ2
φ3
φ4

INSTRUCTION DECODE

RECEIVERS

W/IO

Fig. 11-12. PPS-8 central processor block diagram and data flow.

register, however the least significant 7 bits of the PPS-8 register are incremented, permitting the addressing of 128 instructions within a page. The P register is set to zero with the "power on" signal (PO), causing the first instruction to be taken from ROM-0, page-0, word-0.

Arithmetic/Logic Unit. The ALU's 8-bit adder generates a sum and a carry within one major clock cycle. The carry flip-flop (C) and the intermediate flip-flop (Q) hold carry information out of the position of the eight bit and the fourth bit, respectively, to facilitate multi-byte operations and packed BCD arithmetic (see Chapter 2). The A register is the primary data register in the CPU and, like other accumulators in other microprocessors, is the prime source and destination of data.

The X Register holds the 7 least significant bits of the 14-bit operand (RAM) address. The most significant bit of the 8-bit X register is an upper RAM address control bit. If this bit is one, the Z register content controls the most significant half of the RAM address field; if the bit is zero, the most significant half of the RAM address field is set to all zeros. The X register may be loaded, stored, incremented, and decremented under program control.

The Z Register contains the 7 most significant bits of the 14-bit RAM address. It may also be used as a general-purpose 8-bit storage register.

The Y Register is an alternate least-significant-RAM-address register (alternate to X). It may be used as a counter, or as a general-purpose 8-bit storage registers.

The L Register contains a return address after a transfer to a subroutine or receiving an interrupt. It functions similarly to the SA and SB registers of AMP. In addition, L is used as an address register for indirect ROM operands, an alternate RAM address register, or as a pair of 8-bit storage registers.

The S Register is a 5-bit up/down counter and is used as the address pointer to a 32-byte stack in the PPS-8 RAM. The S register is incremented each time data is added to the stack, and decremented each time data is retrieved. (See discussion on push-down/pop-up stacks in Chapter 12.)

W Register. This 8-bit register serves as an internal buffer and storage register. In addition it is used as an intermediate register during the execution of load-accumulator, link, and push-A-into-L instructions.

Clock Decode. This logic takes the A and $\overline{B}$ clock signals transmitted from the clock generator and derives the 4-phase MOS clock needed by the CPU's internal logic.

Drivers and Receivers. These elements properly condition the electrical signals for off-chip data transmission and reception.

Read-Only Memory

This is a PMOS memory having twice the storage capacity of the AMP ROM, but being functionally identical to it. The PPS-8 ROM is a 16,384-bit memory organized in 2048 8-bit bytes. Memory access time is 1.8 μsec. For the ROM functional configuration see Fig. 1-3. The ROM part number is A52XX, where the last two digits are used to identify specific ROMs having customer-dependent patterns.

The ROM is addressed using the 14-bit CPU address outputs for a maximum of 2^{14} or 16,384 bytes. An extension is available by use of a separate address-select line that permits 32,768 bytes to be addressed in two banks of eight ROMs each.

Random-Access Memory

The PPS-8 RAM (No. 10809) is a 2048-bit memory organized in 256 8-bit bytes. It is logically identical with the AMP RAM, whose block diagram can be seen in Fig. 1-4. The PPS-8 RAM is a dynamic memory with internal refresh logic. Access time is the same as that for the ROM (1.8 μsec). As with the ROM, the CPU can directly address a maximum of 16,384 data bytes on 64 RAMs. Expansions beyond this are accommodated by utilizing an Input-Output Control Signal in conjunction with a minor wiring change to select additional bands.

Clock Generator and
General-Purpose Input/Output Controller

These devices are identical in function to the AMP clock and AMP IOC respectively. Simplified block diagrams are shown in Figs. 1-5 and 1-6.

Serial Data Controller

This device is a digital transmitter/receiver used to interface the PPS-8 system to a serial data channel. The SDC can handle full duplex (simultaneous transmission and re-

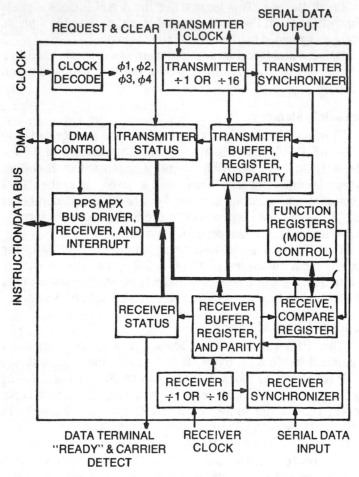

REQUEST & CLEAR

TRANSMITTER CLOCK

SERIAL DATA OUTPUT

CLOCK

CLOCK DECODE — φ1, φ2, φ3, φ4

TRANSMITTER ÷1 OR ÷16

TRANSMITTER SYNCHRONIZER

DMA

DMA CONTROL

TRANSMITTER STATUS

TRANSMITTER BUFFER, REGISTER, AND PARITY

INSTRUCTION/DATA BUS

PPS MPX BUS DRIVER, RECEIVER, AND INTERRUPT

FUNCTION REGISTERS (MODE CONTROL)

RECEIVER STATUS

RECEIVER BUFFER, REGISTER, AND PARITY

RECEIVE, COMPARE REGISTER

RECEIVER ÷1 OR ÷16

RECEIVER SYNCHRONIZER

DATA TERMINAL "READY" & CARRIER DETECT

RECEIVER CLOCK

SERIAL DATA INPUT

Fig. 11-13. PPS-8 serial data controller (SDC) block diagram.

ception) operation at synchronous rates up to 256,000 bits per second, or asynchronous rates up to 18,000. Figure 11-13 is the SDC block diagram showing signal flow onto, within, and off of the chip. Features of primary interest are:

The availability of direct memory load or read (DMA) in conjunction with the direct memory access control device

Error detection capability (even or odd parity, framing, and dropout)

Simultaneous transmission and reception at different data rates

Programmable transmission modes: Asynchronous characters of 5, 6, 7, or 8 bits; synchronous character of 8 bits

Buffered data handling

Programmable character search mode

The reception data flow is from the serial data input line, through the synchronizer, to the parity check (if required), then to the receiver buffer, and on to the instruction/data bus. The receiver clock provides the necessary timing. For asynchronous reception, the clock rate is established at 16 times the expected reception rate to permit the incoming data to be sampled at a frequency high enough to insure that all transitions are sampled at least once.

Transmitted data is received on the instruction/data bus, flows to the transmitter buffer. Parity is then added if required. The formatted message is sent to the transmitter synchronizer and put out on the serial data output line, which is timed by the transmitter clock.

The function registers are two 8-bit registers which are loaded with control words to establish the operating modes. The three status registers are each 4 bits long and hold information concerning the quality of reception. The receive compare register is used in conjunction with a search feature that permits PPS-8 to receive selected data on a serial party line, by serially looking for predetermined characters to determine validity of incoming data.

Parallel Data Controller

The PDC interfaces the PPS-8 with two 8-bit parallel data channels, A and B, with each channel having 8 lines of data and 2 control lines. Each channel has a dedicated 8-bit data buffer and function register. The two channels utilize a common 5-bit device status register and a 4-bit interrupt status register. The control of each channel is under CPU program control. Functional elements and data flow are depicted in Fig. 11-14.

The contents of the input data lines are copied into the appropriate data buffer during phase two of the basic clock cycle. The CPU reads the resulting data at any time. During output the data lines are driven continuously and directly from the data buffers, which can be loaded by the CPU at any time.

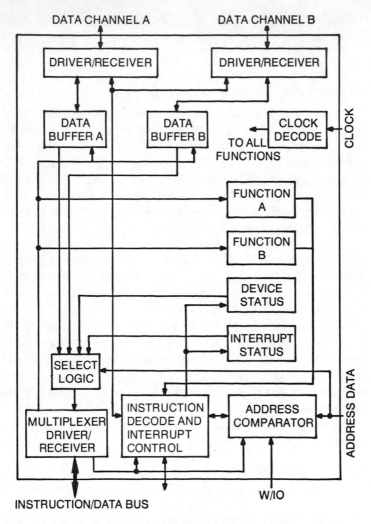

DATA CHANNEL A   DATA CHANNEL B

DRIVER/RECEIVER   DRIVER/RECEIVER

CLOCK

DATA BUFFER A   DATA BUFFER B   CLOCK DECODE

TO ALL FUNCTIONS

FUNCTION A

FUNCTION B

DEVICE STATUS

INTERRUPT STATUS

SELECT LOGIC

ADDRESS DATA

MULTIPLEXER DRIVER/ RECEIVER   INSTRUCTION DECODE AND INTERRUPT CONTROL   ADDRESS COMPARATOR

INSTRUCTION/DATA BUS   W/IO

Fig. 11-14. PPS-8 parallel data controller block diagram.

Data transmission can be either clocked or unclocked. A "handshake" input and output is also available; in this mode two control lines are used to provide a *ready* signal and to acknowledge receipt of data from the peripheral hardware.

Direct Memory Access Controller

This device allows PPS-8 input/output peripherals to access RAM without interrupting normal program execution (see Chapter 12). This is accomplished by utilizing memory access time termed, *cycle stealing*, but otherwise it leaves the program flow unchanged.

The DMAC controls the address bus and commands two memory control signals during direct memory access operations. One DMAC controls eight distinct channels, with two-way communications possible through time multiplexing. A priority system insures that requests will be honored sequentially, in order of the predetermined priority sequence.

Figure 11-15 is the DMAC block diagram. The DMAC has eight 14-bit address registers, and eight 8-bit record length registers to service the eight DMA channels. The data hold register enables sampling the content of a record length register by the CPU. As can be seen from Fig. 11-11 the DMAC interfaces with either the parallel data control or the serial data control.

As an example of DMAC operation, consider a single I/O device connected to a DMAC. At the time the device desires memory access, it transmits a request over DMA channel 0. The DMAC forwards the request to the CPU which acknowledges the request at the time of completion of execution of the first non-input/output instruction after receipt of the inquiry. The CPU then waits while the DMA accesses RAM by:

1. Acknowledging the CPU response.
2. Placing on the address bus the address of the RAM location sought.
3. Driving the read inhibit (RIH) and write I/O (W/IO) false or true, depending upon whether data is to be read from or written into the RAM.
4. The I/O device then placed data on the instruction/data bus or accepts data from it.

The DMAC increments the appropriate address register from the selected counter and then repeats the preceding operation until:

1. The I/O device is satisfied.
2. The record length register cycles from 255 to zero.
3. The lower address register cycles from all ones to all zeros.
4. Interrupt 0 (high priority) goes true.
5. The DMAC is asked to service a higher priority channel.

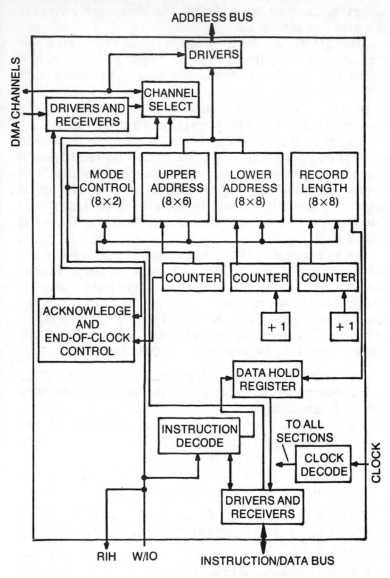

Fig. 11-15. PPS-8 direct memory access controller (DMAC) block diagram.

Specific available system configurations and programming data concerning the PPS-8 can be obtained from Rockwell International, Microelectronics Device Division, Anaheim, California.

Chapter 12
Special Programming Techniques

As the programmer gains familiarity with the microprocessor structure and the supporting software packages, he will find that his programs will become more efficient, both in memory used and in execution time required. In this chapter, we explore some techniques that have been found useful in creating real-time data handling and process control programs, in the hope that they may stimulate the reader in determining new and more efficient solutions for his microprocessor programs.

NON-INTEGRAL POWER-OF-TWO SCALING

In Chapter 4 we discussed the use of the *binary scale* for keeping track of the numerical values of variables, while permitting the microprocessor to perform arithmetic in groups of binary digits. Although the scaling rules provide a well-structured way of maintaining values of variables, the restriction that the scale factor be an *integral* power of two is unnecessary and may adversely affect the problem solution.

The placement of a binary point at the left-hand end of the register is unchanged from the discussion of Chapter 4, and it is still required that we deal only with binary fractions when expressing data in machine units. This means that we must select an appropriate scale factor, which we will use to *divide* the input number (given in problem units) such that the resulting quotient magnitude (in machine units) is always less than one. In order to reconstruct the output answers so that they appear in the proper units, it is then necessary to carry this scale factor as an implied *multiplier* externally to the microprocessor.

The binary fraction held in the microprocessor is equal the number (in problem units) divided by the maximum register value (a power of two). To reverse the procedure, the number (in problem units) is then equal to the product of the binary fraction in the microprocessor and the maximum register value.

An equivalent scale factor may also be stated as being equal to the value of a bit appearing in a particular position, usually the least significant. Thus it is possible to refer the scale factor to either the maximum register value or to the least significant bit, with the choice being left up to the programmer.

Microprocessor Example

To illustrate these scaling methods, assume that our microprocessor is sampling a varying voltage that is proportional to an angular error signal. The voltage is converted to a binary signal by an 8-bit analog-to-digital converter. The input to the converter varies over a range of ± 5 volts and yields an angular indication of 10^{-4} radians per volt. The processor is expected to establish a recent time history of this voltage from eight samples, determine the short-term average, and send out a control signal to drive the error toward zero. The control signal is of opposite sign and is proportional to the average error. In general, the faster the voltage can be sampled and the control signal computed, the better control is achieved. Error excursions will then be less and the system's stability will be enhanced.

Examining specifications in this problem, we see that the actual error angle is quite small: $(\pm 5V)$ $(10^{-4}$ rad/V$)$ $= \pm 5 \times 10^{-4}$ radian (actually 4.98×10^{-4} since the most significant bit would have a value of 2.5×10^{-4}). The value of the least significant bit in the 8-bit register is then $(5 \times 10^{-4})/2^8 = 1.95 \times 10^{-6}$ radian. Working with the least significant bit then, we can derive an appropriate scale factor by dividing by the factor 2^Y, selecting the smallest value of Y such that the quotient is less than one. In this case, however, it is necessary to use a negative value of exponent since the number is much less than one to begin with. Thus if $Y = -18$, the quotient will be about 0.51. The scaling is now manageable, and the averaging can be performed. To simplify conversion arithmetic, it is easier to perform multiplication rather than division, so division by the factor 2^Y can be replaced with multiplication by 2^{-Y}. Upon output, a second multiplication can then be used to rescale the result in the output register to develop the proper magnitude of the output voltage for control.

One, or perhaps both, of these multiplications may be unnecessary. Arithmetic can clearly be performed at a scale of 1.95×10^{-6} radians (using as reference the value of the least significant digit), in which case no scaling is required to change the 8-bit input data. And in the example, if the output and input scale factors were the same, no multiplications would be needed. Thus it might only be necessary to accept the raw 8-bit input data, process it, and then correct the output scale if it has changed. In simple cases of addition and sub-traction the scale is not likely to change as drastically as in multiplication or division (where scale factors are added and subtracted).

Since we selected a power of two ($2^3 = 8$) for the sample size, the averaging is most efficiently performed by shifting the input data right three places before addition, regardless of the scale factor used, and then adding the new datum to the sum of the previous seven digits. The averaging process then reduces to that of adding a new datum and subtracting an old one. In most similar problems the averaging period is selectable within reasonable bounds, and because of the convenience associated with shifting, powers of two are clearly preferred.

Additon and Subtraction

The scaling rules for addition and subtraction of non-integral powers of two can be stated as follows: *The scale factors must be equal, and the use of the maximum register values is preferred. If the scale factor is referred to the least significant bit (LSB), then the largest quantity (maximum value) that can be contained in the word is equal to $B\,2^N - 1$, where B is the scale factor and N is the register length excluding the sign bit.* An addition or subtraction operation that leads to a result exceeding this maximum value will, of course, result in an overflow.

Multiplication

In multiplication the scale factor is truly a *factor*, so multiplication in the processor implies the associated multiplication of external scale factors. The general form of the maximum register value after multiplication is: (LSB_1) (LSB_2) (2^{N1}) (2^{N2}), where we are neglecting the small difference between 2^N and $2^N - 1$, and N represents the register length excluding the sign bit. Thus if register lengths N_1 and N_2 are equal, the expression reduces to (LSB_1) (LSB_2) (2^{2N}).

Example: A 15-bit memory register contains the number 0.39562 stored at an LSB scale of 0.0000245 radian. A second 15-bit register contains 0.6152 at an LSB scale of $0.001831 \, sec^{-1}$. The product, 0.2434, is a measure of angular velocity in radians per second. Now the maximum values of the registers are

$$(2^{15}) \, (0.0000245) = 0.8028$$
$$(2^{15}) \, (0.001831) = 60$$

The maximum value of the product register is then

$$(0.8028) \, (60) = 48.17$$

and the numerical value of the LSB is

$$(48.17)/2^N = 0.001470$$

for a 15-bit register $(N = 15)$.

Division

The scaling for division is similar to the procedure followed for multiplication, with the exception that the scale of the denominator is divided into the scale of the numerator to determine the scale of the quotient. Division can produce an overflow, but if the maximum value of the quotient register is selected to contain the scaled quotient, no overflow will result.

Example: Register A contains the value 5 scaled with a maximum register value of 6.283. Register B contains the value 8.4 scaled with a maximum register value of 16. The resulting quotient (A/B) is 0.595, which is scaled at the value 0.3927 for a full register. But since 0.595 is clearly larger than 0.3927, an overflow will occur. The difficulty here is that the denominator is significantly smaller than the maximum register value, leading to a larger quotient than can be contained under the given scalings. To obtain a correct result, the numbers held in either register A, or register B, or both must be rescaled to provide for a maximum product value that is greater than 0.3927.

PUSH-DOWN/POP-UP STACKS

Several of today's processors have facilities for handling data in stack form. The continual updating of data is often unwieldy, particularly when the data storage and retrieval are interleaved. Perhaps the best analogy is an inventory system in which bins are initially stocked with material having a limited shelf life. Material extraction proceeds according to either a first-in/first-out (FIFO) system or to a last-in/first-out (LIFO) system. New material is added to the bins as it arrives from the suppliers at unpredictable intervals. This new material must be identified, and its time of entry into the inventory system noted, to maintain the FIFO or LIFO record systems.

The relation to data handling is rather precise, for by replacing *material* with *data*, the analogy describes a common problem encountered when the microprocessor is expected to manage and manipulate data arriving from an asynchronous source. Stack manipulations make this handling more straightforward. Microprocessors available at this writing do not mechanize FIFO systems because of the more complex data handling required.

A brute-force (and not too bright) approach to the LIFO stack problem is to define a block of RAM to hold the stacked data. Each time a word of information is added to the stack, move the entire stack "down" in memory, though at the cost of at least two machine cycles per datum move. If a word is then extracted, all other data in the stack is moved up, once again at the same cost in execution time.

But clearly the same LIFO stack effect can be achieved by simply manipulating addresses, rather than the actual data. All microprocessors having this feature operate in the same general fashion (see Intel 8080 and Rockwell PPS-8 Chapter 11). A special address register holds the address of the next element to be stored in the stack. This pointer can be thought of as running up and down as the size of the stack increases and decreases. Where LIFO is used, it is only necessary to maintain a running account of the top data element. Since data will not be removed from or added to the "bottom" of the stack (except, of course, the first piece of data entered), the initial address remains fixed. The stack is therefore empty if the address pointer is equal to the address location at the bottom of the stack.

INTERRUPT HANDLING

When coupled to any set of peripheral devices that demand attention from the CPU on short notice, some means of interrupting the normal program flow without affecting the program sequence is required. Most commercial microprocessors have the capability of handling one or more of these *interrupts*. Characteristically, the interrupt, when received, causes program control (after completing execution of the current instruction) to be transferred to the first instruction of a service and data-handling sequence, with the address of the next instruction of the normal program flow stored as a return. This service sequence normally ignores further interrupts, saves register data for restoration of the normal program flow upon completion of the interrupt handling, identifies the interrupt (if more than one is possible), identifies the peripheral unit that caused the interrupt to be issued, and transfers to the proper routine to service that particular unit. Upon completion, register contents are restored, the interrupts enabled once again, and control transferred to the mainstream routine via execution of the *return* instruction.

Interrupts are then nothing more than unexpected transfers under control of an outside source, normally those devices that handle input/output data. However, interrupts are also used for timing control when a program is intended to operate in real time, relying on a precise external timer. Here, the entire routine, not just the present instruction, must be completed before the interrupt can take over control. Program control then ties up in a loop (usually a one-word transfer to itself) until restated by the presence of the interrupt, thus maintaining precise execution timing at the beginning of each computational cycle.

Several interrupts may be available, each of them used to control ultimate entry to a specific service program. There is, however, the possibility of interrupts occurring nearly simultaneously, or continually modifying program control, with the net effect that the processor either becomes confused or is tied up servicing interrupts. Thus, a priority system is usually established in which priority designations are assigned to each interrupt line. The occurrence of a priority-1 interrupt then masks out all other interrupts of priority 2, 3, 4, etc. The occurrence of a priority-2 interrupt masks out priority 3, 4, etc. Such priorities can normally be established under CPU control and changed as the program functions require.

DIRECT MEMORY ACCESS

Input/output operations rob time from the CPU's normal computational cycle. Very often all that is required of the processor is to transfer data between an input or output buffer and processor memory, so no reformatting or arithmetic is needed. Under these circumstances, a direct memory access (DMA) function can save vital machine cycles and program storage.

Most DMA operations still steal time from the mainstream program by using clock time normally devoted to RAM access. (ROM readout is not usually subject to DMA operation.) At the completion of execution of most instructions (input/output instructions are common exceptions), the CPU acknowledges the receipt of a DMA inquiry, enters an "idle" mode by releasing control of both the address and data buses (or their equivalents), and allows the DMA controlling device to read from or write into RAM as it desires. Depending upon the configuration, one or more bytes may be accessed before control is transferred back to the CPU. DMA is particularly useful where rapid response to the peripheral device is required, such as the use of DMA access to drive and refresh CRT displays. (See Chapter 11, Intel 8080 and Rockwell PPS-8).

POOLED DATA

Where the microprocessor has an instruction format requiring the frequent use of multibyte instructions or long constant data strings, the opportunity exists to store this information only once, and then reference it, using single-byte commands, thus saving memory. Using the Rockwell PPS-8 as an example, three data pools are used: the *command pool* (instructions), the *literal pool* (data bytes), and the *subroutine entry pool* (branch instruction address bytes). These pools occupy specific locations in pages 0 and 1 of the PPS-8 ROM.

As an example of the memory efficiency gained, a 3-byte PPS-8 instruction, if used 25 times in a program, would occupy 75 bytes of memory. But when identified in a data pool, the instruction would occupy only one byte in the program flow each time the instruction is used (a total of 25 bytes) and two bytes in the data pool, for a total of 27 bytes instead of 75. The instruction requires only two bytes stored in the pool since the instruction type has already been identified by the address specified by the main program; it does not then need to be re-specified.

The use of data pools is not mandatory—they are established primarily to save memory. If you are certain that such memory savings are not necessary, the use of these pools with their attendent complications can be avoided.

NON-BINARY COUNTERS

The positional-notation binary system satisfies all the requirements for general calculations. But for purposes of simply counting, any unique sequence of stable states is sufficient. The use of systems other than binary is motivated by hardware or software simplicity, or by the need to form a sequence having a desirable property that binary does not.

Shift Counters

Perhaps the simplest form of a shift counter is to place a 1-bit somewhere in a word and shift it until it reaches the end, noting the different states or counts.

Example 1: A left shift (or binary addition) inserts zeros at the right.

$$
\begin{array}{c}
0....01 \\
0...010 \\
0..0100 \\
\bullet \\
\bullet \\
\bullet \\
0010..0 \\
010...0 \\
10....0 \\
0.....0
\end{array}
$$

Example 2: A logic right shift inserts zeros at the high-order end.

```
        10....0
       010...0
      0010..0
          •
          •
          •
       0...010
       0....01
       0.....0
```

Example: 3 An arithmetic right shift copies the sign bit into the next lower order bit.

```
    1000...000
    1100...000
    1110...000
        •
        •
        •
    1111...100
    1111...110
    1111...111
```

All of the preceding counters will count only the same number of stable states as there are bits in the word, making them relatively inefficient. But for programming purposes, no separate incrementation is required, initialization is simple, and the count termination can be determined by either a zero test or sign test.

Gray-Code Counters

In many transmission applications of ordered data, it is desirable to have as few state changes in the transmitted values as is possible. But binary-represented data does not satisfy this criterium. For example, the addition of one count to 01111111 creates the new value 10000000, in which all the ones have been changed to zeros and the zero to a one—the maximum possible number of state changes.

In contrast, the Gray code produces a count sequence in which there is exactly one state change per count, a zero may change to a one, or a one to a zero, but both changes cannot occur at the same time. The changes occurring in the Gray code as the count progresses are fully predictable and therefore decodable.

Table 12-1. Four-Bit Binary and Gray Code Equivalence

BINARY	GRAY CODE
0000	0000
0001	0001
p010	0011
0011	0010
0100	0110
0101	0111
0110	0101
0111	0100
1000	1100
1001	1101
1010	1111
1011	1110
1100	1010
1101	1011
1110	1001
1111	1000

Table 12-1 lists the binary and Gray code equivalences, and such a look-up table could be incorporated into the microprocessor system to facilitate conversion. But for direct counting the look-up table can be replaced by simple conversion algorithms that operate directly upon the stored data.

Gray Code to Binary. The starting condition is that the high-order bits of both number systems must be equal; that is $B_N = G_N$. Binary and Gray code always use the same number of digits to represent equivalent numbers. Proceeding from the high-order bits to the low-order bits, the conversion takes place bit by bit, applying the formula

$$G_K = B_K \oplus B_{K+1}$$

Therefore, to convert 1011_2 to Gray code, we first set the fourth, or MSD, of the Gray code number equal to the binary number; in this case $G_4 = B_4 = 1$. The next bits are converted as follows:

$$G_3 = B_3 \oplus B_4 = 0 \oplus 1 = 1$$
$$G_2 = B_2 \oplus B_3 = 1 \oplus 0 = 1$$
$$G_1 = B_1 \oplus B_2 = 1 \oplus 1 = 0$$

So the Gray code is 1110.

Gray Code to Binary. The conversion procedure follows the formulas:

226

$$B_N = G_N$$
$$B_K = G_K \oplus B_{K+1}$$

If we then wish to convert 1110 in Gray code back to binary, we proceed as follows:

$$B_4 = G_4 = 1$$
$$B_3 = G_3 \oplus B_4 = 1 \oplus 1 = 0$$
$$B_2 = G_2 \oplus B_3 = 1 \oplus 0 = 1$$
$$B_1 = G_1 \oplus B_2 = 0 \oplus 1 = 1$$

So we once again have 1011_2.

Counting. The Gray-code counting sequence is started by setting the initial conditions to all zeros. Counting is conducted by setting the least significant bit to one; that is, $G_1 = 1$. At the second count, the next higher order bit is set to one. For the third count, the low-order bit is set to zero. The counting pattern continues as illustrated in Table 12-1. The bit configuration from one count to the next then varies by only one bit change, which is the salient characteristic of Gray-code counters.

Polynomial Counters

A predictable, recursive count can be generated using simple exclusive-OR logic, similar to that used in the Gray-code counter. For this we take an N-bit register holding bits numbered in the sequence A_{N-1}, A_{N-2} ...A_2, A_1, A_0. The counting proceeds by calculating $A_1 \oplus A_0$, then right-shifting the N-bit number and inserting the newly calculated bit at the left so that it becomes the new A_{N-1}. The old A_0 is shifted out of the register and is lost.

Two special cases must be considered when starting the polynomial counter. First, if the counter is initially set to all zeros, the counter would never get started because $0 \oplus 0 = 0$. Second, if the counter is set to any value other than all zeros, the counter will cycle through all possible combinatorial values except zero. Thus, if the counter is initially set to all zeros, it will remain in that state until deliberately set to another state; and when set to another state, it will then cycle through all $2^N - 1$ unique number combinations before repeating. For example, if a 4-bit counter is preset to binary 1000, it will cycle through the number sequence shown in Table 12-2, repeating the sequence again at step 16. Whatever the counter length, if the counter is preset with a one in its most

Table 12-2. Four-Bit Polynomial Counter Sequence

SEQUENCE NUMBER	POLYNOMIAL BINARY	HEX
1	1000	8
2	0100	4
3	0010	2
4	1001	9
5	1100	C
6	0110	6
7	1011	B
8	0101	5
9	1010	A
10	1101	D
11	1110	E
12	1111	F
13	0111	7
14	0011	3
15	0001	1
16	1000	8

significant bit, the cycle will end with only a one in its least significant bit before repeating the sequence, which indicates that a test for one could be used to check for completion.

Because of the relative simplicity of mechanizing such a counter, program sequencers and other internal processor counters may operate according to the polynomial algorithm. Since all possible binary combinations are used during the count, with none repeated, this is an efficient counting system.

Chapter 13

Characteristics and Fabrication of Microprocessors

The technology that has made possible the small size and low cost of today's microprocessors is of more than passing interest to the engineers, scientists, and laymen who are configuring and creating the software for these systems. The fabrication techniques give insight into the structures and, to a degree, the functions of the various devices that comprise a microprocessor chip set.

PMOS AND NMOS DEVICES

The starting material used is a single crystal silicon wafer having a precisely controlled orientation of the crystal lattice with respect to the silicon surface. This control is important to obtain the desired electrical parameters, particularly due to phenomena that occur very near the silicon surface.

Patterns are applied to the silicon and subsequent layers with the aid of *photoresist*—an organic material that changes character when light (usually ultraviolet)) impinges upon it, permitting a precise pattern to be retained by the resist when it is exposed through a mask. (Figure 13-5, discussed later, shows the use of the photoresist and the resulting patterns.) Masks are made in a precision optical facility capable of resolving lines to the order of 1 micron (10^{-6} meter). Precision is paramount to obtain the dense patterns needed.

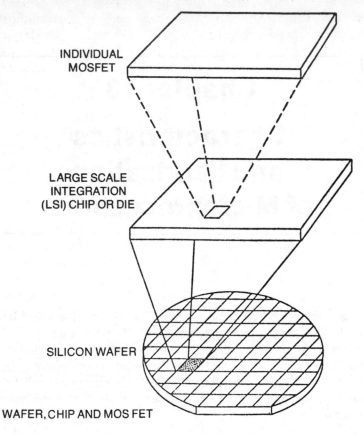

INDIVIDUAL MOSFET

LARGE SCALE
INTEGRATION
(LSI) CHIP OR DIE

SILICON WAFER

WAFER, CHIP AND MOS FET

Fig. 13-1. Silicon wafer, chip, and MOSFET. (Courtesy Rockwell International)

About 100 devices, all identical, are fabricated at one time on a single wafer. Figure 13-1 shows a wafer approximately two inches in diameter, containing a complement of those devices, also called *chips* or *die*. Figure 13-2 shows two photographs taken at different magnifications of the surface of a PMOS die, showing the oxide steps and metal conductor lines.

PMOS devices have been available since 1964, with the process maturing in the intervening years. Initially, most manufacturers used a "high voltage" process, requiring supply voltages on the order of −30 volts. More recently, manufacturers have produced "low voltage" devices operating in the range of 17 volts (+5, −12). Low-voltage

P-channel MOS requires about half the operating power used by devices made by the high-voltage process. Low-voltage devices are also compatible with TTL voltages, allowing a microprocessor built from low-voltage PMOS to be more easily integrated into a system where common TTL bipolar logic is used.

MOS logic is made using field-effect transistors (FETs), with perhaps a few resistors, capacitors, and diodes. An FET is symmetric and hence *unipolar* (bidirectional). We will briefly discuss the *enhancement-type P- and N-channel devices*. To understand their operation, the construction should be understood. Looking at the N-channel device of Fig. 13-3, we observe that the channels of N material are separated by ₁P-type material. N-type material has an excess of free electrons; hence the conduction mechanism is one of electron flow. The P material has a deficiency of free electrons such that a barrier exists, impeding current flow from *source* to *drain* even though a source—drain potential exists.

However, if we apply a positive potential to the *gate*, the available electrons in the P material are swept into the area underneath the gate, creating a conductive path, since there are now free electrons available between the N regions. The more positive the potential applied to the gate, the stronger the potential field and the more electrons attracted into the region. The P material under the gate is said to be *enhanced* with electrons, so this configuration is known as an *enhancement-type* FET. The metal gate is isolated from the source and drain by silicon dioxide (SiO_2) insulator, so no gate current flows.

The switching mechanism is entirely due to the field established. A gate bias voltage of about one volt (relative to the potential of the P substrate) will start conduction. Saturation then occurs at a gate bias of about +4 volts, and this corresponds to a condition in which no further increase in source—drain curent occurs for a further increase in positive potential applied to the gate.

The AMP P-channel devices operate in the same fashion as the N-channel, except that the N and P materials are interchanged, the charge carriers are *holes* (absence of electrons), and the potentials are reversed. It turns out that N-channel devices operate at higher speeds than correspondingly designed P-channel devices because electrons have a higher mobility in silicon than do holes.

A

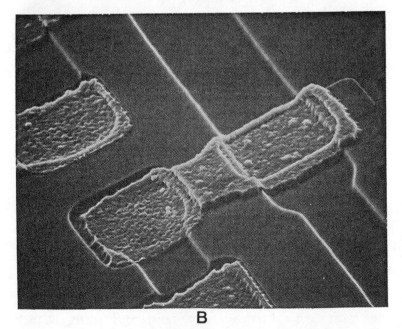

B

Fig. 13-2. Photograph of PMOS LIS. (A) at 85-times magnification. (B) at a magnification of 1700 times, showing oxide steps and metal. (Courtesy Rockwell International)

The creation of N and P materials is accomplished by *doping* the silicon by adding minute quantities of electron *donor* and *acceptor* impurities, or by forcibly implanting ions, using an electron beam gun or by a combination of both processes. The ion implantation method is a newer technique and has rapidly matured. Virtually all manufacturers today are using some form of ion implantation to fabricate MOS microprocessor parts. The impurity quantities are much easier to control and the depth distribution desired by the designer is much easier to achieve.

Figure 13-4 is a pictorial outline of the process steps required to fabricate the PMOS low-voltage enhancement FETs used in AMP. The starting material is a silicon wafer about 10 mils (0.01 inches) thick, lightly doped with an N-type material. The dimensions shown for the thicknesses of various layers are given in microns, where $1\mu = 1 \times 10^{-6}$ meter.

Step 1 is the growth of a silicon dioxide layer over the entire surface. This is normally done in a furnace by passing superheated steam past the wafer.

Steps 2—3 are the application and development of the photoresist to define the P regions.

Steps 4—5 show the surface configuration after etching the oxide where the P regions are to be formed, and removing the

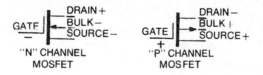

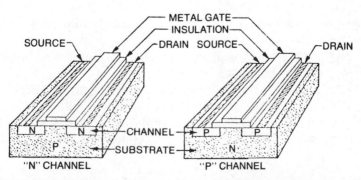

Fig. 13-3. Cross section of P- and N-channel MOSFET configurations with schematics.

protective photoresist. (Note that the etch stops at the silicon surface). Also, for clarity, steps 5 and those subsequent show the FET cut through the center, comparable to the FETs in Fig. 13-3.

Steps 6—10 configure the gate oxide by first growing a thicker oxide layer to accommodate the required gate oxide thickness, etching everything but the gate area. This also removes the oxide once again from the potential P regions.

Step 11 adds the acceptor impurity to the P region by passing boron bromide gas across the wafer. The boron diffuses somewhat into the unprotected silicon surface. This process physically adds the impurity to the silicon rather than doping by ion implantation. (If implantation were to be used, it would likely be done at this point, before the oxide growth and replacing both the boron addition and "drive.")

Step 12 accomplishes two things at once. First, the boron deposited in step 11 is not of sufficient depth to provide the needed P region, so the boron is "driven in" at high temperatures. (Actually, boron atoms diffuse into the silicon at high temperature.) At the same time, oxide is grown over the top of the P material.

Steps 13—14 provide for precise definition of the gate area and prepare for establishing the source and drain contacts.

Steps 15—16 define a further growth of oxide and the growth of a silicon nitride layer. Silicon nitride is a very tenacious, dense material with a high dielectric constant. The presence of sodium is deadly to MOS devices. Sodium ions are highly mobile and hence carry charge where it isn't wanted. Silicon nitride is a very effective barrier against sodium so it is the use of silicon nitride that has permitted the packaging of these devices in plastic, allowing the prices to come down one more notch.

Step 17 frees the areas where the source and drain contacts are to be made.

Steps 18—19 provide the metal conductive pattern, first by evaporating a thin layer of aluminum over the entire surface, then by masking those areas where the metal is to be retained and etching away all unwanted aluminum through the mask. At this point, the FET is electrically complete.

Steps 21—22 provide a protective overcoat of *silox* (silicon dioxide), similar to the oxide layer that was grown in Step 1. This time, however, the silicon dioxide layer is not grown, but

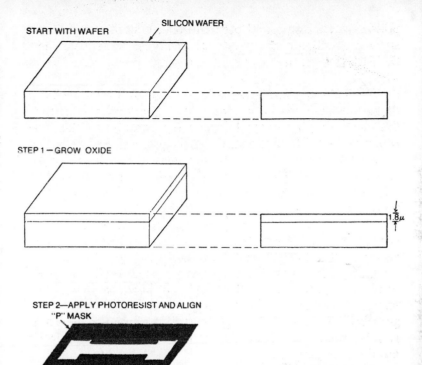

START WITH WAFER — SILICON WAFER

STEP 1 — GROW OXIDE

1.8μ

STEP 2—APPLY PHOTORESIST AND ALIGN
"P" MASK

OXIDE

STEP 3—DEVELOP PHOTORESIST
PHOTORESIST   DEVELOPED AREA
OXIDE
SILICON

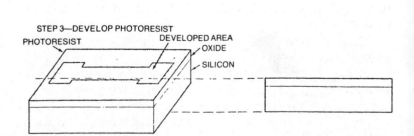

Fig. 13-4. The processing steps involved in fabricating a typical PMOS low-voltage FET such as found in many PMOS microprocessors. (Courtesy Rockwell International)

235

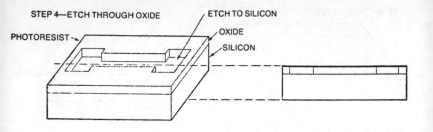

STEP 4—ETCH THROUGH OXIDE

ETCH TO SILICON

PHOTORESIST

OXIDE

SILICON

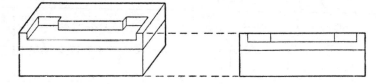

STEP 5—STRIP PHOTORESIST

OXIDE

SILICON

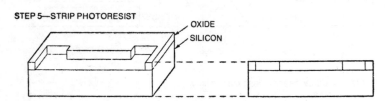

STEP 6—REGROW P REGION

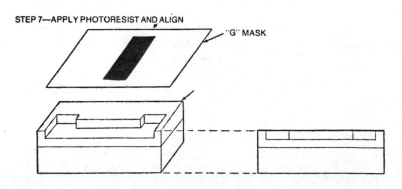

STEP 7—APPLY PHOTORESIST AND ALIGN

"G" MASK

Fig. 13-4. continued

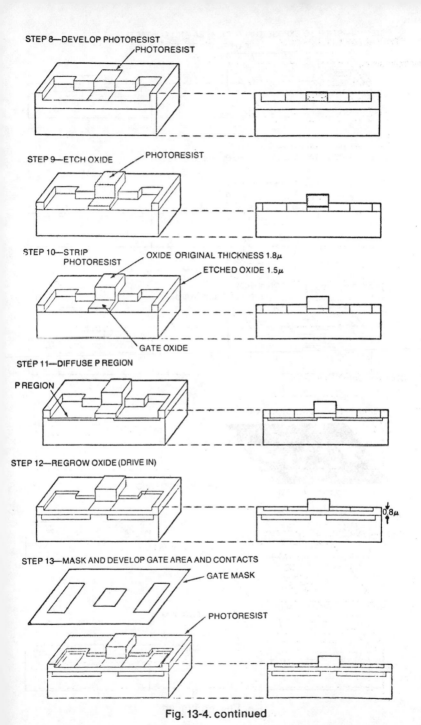

STEP 8—DEVELOP PHOTORESIST

PHOTORESIST

STEP 9—ETCH OXIDE

PHOTORESIST

STEP 10—STRIP PHOTORESIST

OXIDE ORIGINAL THICKNESS 1.8μ

ETCHED OXIDE 1.5μ

GATE OXIDE

STEP 11—DIFFUSE P REGION

P REGION

STEP 12—REGROW OXIDE (DRIVE IN)

0.8μ

STEP 13—MASK AND DEVELOP GATE AREA AND CONTACTS

GATE MASK

PHOTORESIST

Fig. 13-4. continued

STEP 14—STRIP TO EXPOSE THIN GATE AREA AND CONTACTS

P-DIFFUSED REGION

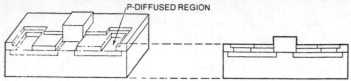

STEP 15—REGROW GATE OXIDE TO REQUIRED THICKNESS

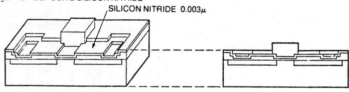

STEP 16—DEPOSITE SILICON NITRIDE

SILICON NITRIDE 0.003μ

STEP 17—APPLY CONTACT MASK AND ETCH

CONTACT MASK

NITRIDE

ETCH NITRIDE AND GATE OXIDE
DOWN TO SILICON (P-REGION)

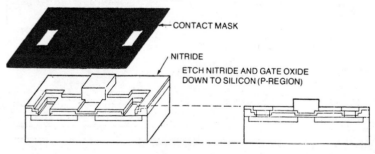

STEP 18—EVAPORATE ALUMINUM

ALUMINUM 1μ

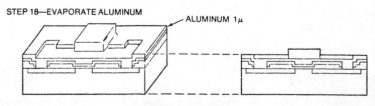

Fig. 13-4. continued

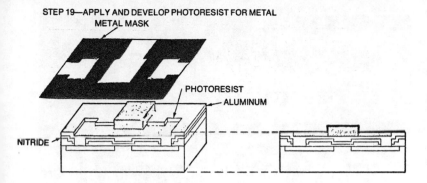

STEP 19—APPLY AND DEVELOP PHOTORESIST FOR METAL

METAL MASK

PHOTORESIST
ALUMINUM
NITRIDE

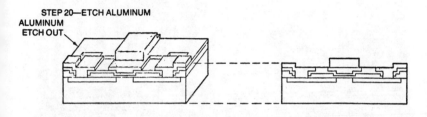

STEP 20—ETCH ALUMINUM
ALUMINUM
ETCH OUT

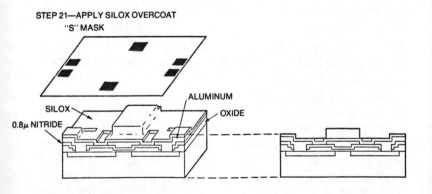

STEP 21—APPLY SILOX OVERCOAT
"S" MASK

SILOX
0.8μ NITRIDE
ALUMINUM
OXIDE

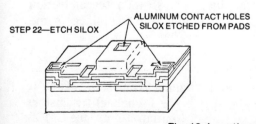

ALUMINUM CONTACT HOLES
SILOX ETCHED FROM PADS
STEP 22—ETCH SILOX

Fig. 13-4 continued

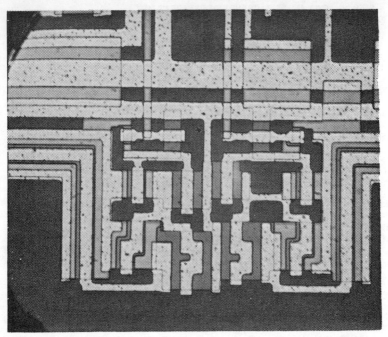

Fig. 13-5. CMOS-SOS structure with magnification of about 250 times. (Courtesy Rockwell International).

deposited directly on the wafer from *silane* (SiO_2 + methane). The deposited layer of silox is not as dense or continuous a film as the thermally grown oxide, but it is still more than adequate to protect the device from mechanical damage. Holes are then cut through the silox layer to expose the contact pads, and 1-mil diameter wires are attached to make contact to the outside world. The conductive paths of the MOS device are formed either by the P (or N) channels, or by the top metal layer, or both. To provide crossings the path goes from the metal down to a P region, then crosses other metal lines, and emerges again on the other side. Even so, the interconnection problem on a MOS chip is not trivial, and this places some restrictions on the designs.

COMPLEMENTARY MOS (CMOS)

CMOS combines N- and P-channel transistors. The N-channel transistor normally drives the P-channel transistor. (See Fig. 13-5 for a typical CMOS configuration.) One CMOS transistor is always turned on and the other turned off. The primary advantages of CMOS are low power and high speed relative to N- and P-channel MOS processes. The prime disadvantage lies in the more complex fabrication process. CMOS circuits can operate at 20 MHz with a power consumption of only a few microwatts. Consequently, more and more CMOS devices will be seen as the requirements for high speed and low power toughen, particularly for military applications.

A variation of CMOS, offering even higher speeds and lower power, is CMOS-SOS (CMOS on silicon on sapphire, or just CMOS on sapphire.) The use of a sapphire substrate provides almost perfect isolation between adjacent devices, thus reducing the unwanted coupling capacitance that adversely affects speed. The isolating substrate also further reduces the required power. Such devices are becoming available at this writing as microprocessor components and should help push processor clock speeds into the 10 MHz range.

INTEGRATED INJECTION LOGIC (I^2L)

A debate concerning the superiority of MOS vs bipolar integration has been going on for about the last ten years. Until recently, the argument has been academic, since the two technologies did not directly clash in the marketplace. MOS had a clear superiority in unit cost and in functional density, while bipolar devices had a clear edge in speed. However, MOS—particularly CMOS—has been increasingly invading the high-speed bipolar market, while bipolar devices have been achieving even higher densities at lower costs.

The primary speed limitation in both bipolar and MOS large-scale integration (LSI) is the ability to charge and discharge internal capacitances. In the case of bipolar devices, any significant improvement must be made by decreasing capacitances. This decrease is tied directly to decreasing device area, which in turn is dependent upon the quality of the photolithographic process. MOS speeds have been increased by several means—use of high-dielectric insulators, insulating with sapphire substrates, employing N-channel devices, etc. Meanwhile, the bipolar designers have achieved excellent densities while maintaining high speeds using integrated-injection logic (I^2L), also called merged transistor logic (MTL).

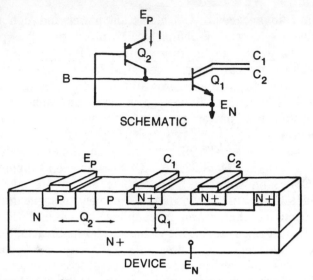

Fig. 13-6. I^2L device cross section and associated schematic.

The improvements of I^2L over more conventional bipolar devices come principally from shrinking the direct-coupled transistor logic into a single equivalent complementary transistor. A schematic and corresponding I^2L device structure is shown in Fig. 13-6. The vertical NPN transistor (Q_1) has multiple collectors and operates as an inverter. The lateral PNP transistor (Q_2) is used as a current source and load. Several I^2L microprocessor devices are now available with others to be introduced. For example, a 4-bit slice chip, the SBP-0400, contains over 1400 gates and includes most of the functions required for 4-bit parallel processing.

The user can expect a great deal from these newer technologies and should not be disappointed. Microprocessor devices should be available soon with speeds in the range of 0.4−0.5 million operations per second, fully parallel, with built-in floating-point arithmetic and hardware multiply and divide. Such devices will be easier to use and will be supported by continually advancing software packages, thus making unnecessary much of the bookkeeping required when using today's processors. At the same time, I suspect that some of the fun of communicating directly with a microprocessor in its own language will be lost.

Bibliography

Operator's Manual for PPS-4MP Assemulator, Rockwell International Document 29400 N30.

Electronics Magazine, "Technical Articles," February 6, 1975.

FORTRAN Programming and WATFIV, James L. Parker, Marilyn Bohl, SRA (IBM) 1973.

M6800 Microcomputer System Design Data, Motorola, Inc., 1976.

An Introduction to Microcomputers, Adam Osborne, Osborne and Associates, Berkeley, CA, 1975.

PPS-8 Microcomputer Programming Manual, Rockwell International, August 1975.

M6800 Macro Assembler Manual, Motorola Microsystems, Phoenix, Arizona.

MPL Language Reference Manual, Motorola Microsystems, 3102 N. 56th Street, Phoenix, Arizona, 1976.

Intel 8080 Microcomputer System Manual, January 1975.

PPS-4-1 Single Circuit Microcomputer Series Programming Manual, July 1976

Intel Data Catalog, Intel Corporation, 1975.

User Manual for the COSMAC Microprocessor, RCA Corporation, 1975.

PPS-4 Microcomputer Program Library, Rockwell International, 1974.

Operators Manual for PPS-4MP Assemulator, Rockwell International, 1975.

Microprocessor/Microprogramming Handbook, Brice Ward, TAB BOOKS, Blue Ridge Summit, PA, 1975 (No. 785)

Appendices

Appendix A

Single-Digit Hexadecimal (Hex) Multiplication Table

	1	2	3	4	5	6	7	8	9	A	B	C	D	E	F
1	1	2	3	4	5	6	7	8	9	A	B	C	D	E	F
2		4	6	8	A	C	E	10	12	14	16	18	1A	1C	1E
3			9	C	F	12	15	18	1B	1E	21	24	27	2A	2D
4				10	14	18	1C	20	24	28	2C	30	34	38	3C
5					19	1E	23	28	2D	32	37	3C	41	46	4B
6						24	2A	30	36	3C	42	48	4E	54	5A
7							31	38	3F	46	4D	54	5B	62	69
8								40	48	50	58	60	68	70	78
9									51	5A	63	6C	75	7E	87
A										64	6E	78	82	8C	96
B											79	84	8F	9A	A5
C												90	9C	A8	B4
D													A9	B6	C3
E														C4	D2
F															E1

(Courtesy Rockwell International)

Appendix B

A Proof of the Hartmann Conversion System

Any integer N expressed in a positional notation system is of the form

$$N_1 = a_n b^n + a_{n-1} b^{n-1} + \ldots$$

$$+ a_1 b + a_0 = \Sigma^K_{i=1} a_i b^i + a_0$$

where b is the base and the a_1 the coefficients.

We wish to find a new set of coefficients such that

$$\Sigma^K_{i=1} a_i b^i + a_0 = \Sigma^R_{i=1} A$$

$$_i B^i + A_0$$

where B is the new base. If we are looking for the new number (N_2), then

$$N_1 = N_2 = a_0 + \Sigma^K_{i=1} a_1$$

$$[B^i + (b^i - B^i)]$$

where B^i is added and subtracted term by term and expressed as a summation.

We can express $(b^i - B^i)$ as

$$(b - B)(b^{i-1} B^0 +$$

$$b^{i-2} B + \ldots + b^0 B^{i-1})$$

by dividing $(b^i - B^i)$ by $(b - B)$.

If we now substitute equation (4) into (3), we have

$$N_2 = a_0 + \Sigma^K_1 \, a_i \, [B^i + M(b^{i-1} + $$

$$b^{i-2} B + \ldots + b B^{i-2} + B^{i-1})]$$

where $M = (b - B)$.

If we now refer to the example of Table 2-10 and apply equation (5), we have

$$b = 2$$
$$B = 10$$
$$M = (b - B) = 2 - 10 = 8$$
$$a_0 = 1$$
$$a_1 = 1$$
$$a_2 = 0$$
$$a_3 = 1$$
$$K = 3$$

So:

$$1011_2 = 1 + 1[10 + (-8)(1)] + 0[100 + (-8)(10 + 2)]$$

$$+ 1[(1000) + (-8)(100 + 20 + 4)]$$

$$= 1 + 0 + 2 + 8$$

$$= 11_{10}$$

(Courtesy Rockwell International)

Appendix C
Powers and Conversions

POWERS OF TWO

2^n	n	2^{-n}
1	0	1.01
2	1	0.5
4	2	0.25
8	3	0.125
16	4	0.062 5
32	5	0.031 25
64	6	0.015 625
128	7	0.007 812 5
256	8	0.003 906 25
512	9	0.001 953 125
1 024	10	0.000 976 562 5
2 048	11	0.000 483 281 25
4 096	12	0.000 244 140 625
8 192	13	0.000 122 070 312 5
16 384	14	0.000 061 035 156 25
32 768	15	0.000 030 517 578 125
65 536	16	0.000 015 258 789 062 5
131 072	17	0.000 007 629 394 531 25
262 144	18	0.000 003 814 697 265 625
524 288	19	0.000 001 907 348 632 812 5
1 048	20	0.000 000 953 674 316 406 25
2 097 152	21	0.000 000 476 837 158 203 125
4 194 304	22	0.000 000 238 418 579 101 562 5
8 388 608	23	0.000 000 119 209 289 550 731 25
16 777 216	24	0.000 000 059 604 644 775 390 625
33 554 432	25	0.000 000 029 802 322 387 695 312 5
67 108 864	26	0.000 000 014 901 161 193 847 656 25
134 217 728	27	0.000 000 007 450 580 596 923 823 125
268 435 456	28	0.000 000 003 725 290 298 461 914 062 5
536 870 912	29	0.000 000 001 862 645 149 230 957 031 25
1 073 741 824	30	0.000 000 000 931 322 574 615 478 515 625
2 147 483 648	31	0.000 000 000 465 661 287 307 739 257 **812** 5

(This data courtesy of Rockwell International)

TABLE OF POWERS OF SIXTEEN$_{10}$

16^n	n	16^{-n}
1	0	$0.10000\ 00000\ 00000\ 00000 \times 10$
16	1	$0.62500\ 00000\ 00000\ 00000 \times 10^{-1}$
256	2	$0.39062\ 50000\ 00000\ 00000 \times 10^{-2}$
4 096	3	$0.24414\ 06250\ 00000\ 00000 \times 10^{-3}$
65 536	4	$0.15258\ 78906\ 25000\ 00000 \times 10^{-4}$
1 048 576	5	$0.95367\ 43164\ 06250\ 00000 \times 10^{-6}$
16 777 216	6	$0.59604\ 64477\ 53906\ 25000 \times 10^{-7}$
268 435 456	7	$0.37252\ 90298\ 46191\ 40625 \times 10^{-8}$
4 294 967 296	8	$0.23283\ 06436\ 53869\ 62891 \times 10^{-9}$
68 719 476 736	9	$0.14551\ 91522\ 83668\ 51807 \times 10^{-10}$
1 099 511 627 776	10	$0.90949\ 47017\ 72928\ 23792 \times 10^{-12}$
17 592 186 044 416	11	$0.56843\ 41886\ 08080\ 14870 \times 10^{-13}$
281 474 976 710 656	12	$0.35527\ 13678\ 80050\ 09294 \times 10^{-14}$
4 503 599 627 370 496	13	$0.22204\ 46049\ 25031\ 30808 \times 10^{-15}$
72 057 594 037 927 936	14	$0.13877\ 78780\ 78144\ 56755 \times 10^{-16}$
1 152 921 504 606 846 976	15	$0.86736\ 17379\ 88403\ 54721 \times 10^{-18}$

TABLE OF POWERS OF TEN$_{16}$

10^n	n	10^{-n}
1	0	$1.0000\ 0000\ 0000\ 0000$
A	1	$0.1999\ 9999\ 9999\ 999A$
64	2	$0.28F5\ C28F\ 5C28\ F5C3 \times 16^{-1}$
3E8	3	$0.4189\ 374B\ C6A7\ EF9E \times 16^{-2}$
2710	4	$0.68DB\ 8BAC\ 710C\ B296 \times 16^{-3}$
1 86A0	5	$0.A7C5\ AC47\ 1B47\ 8423 \times 16^{-4}$
F 4240	6	$0.10C6\ F7A0\ B5ED\ 8D37 \times 16^{-4}$
98 9680	7	$0.1AD7\ F29A\ BCAF\ 4858 \times 16^{-5}$
5F5 E100	8	$0.2AF3\ 1DC4\ 6118\ 73BF \times 16^{-6}$
3B9A CA00	9	$0.44B8\ 2FA0\ 9B5A\ 52CC \times 16^{-7}$
2 540B E400	10	$0.6DF3\ 7F67\ 5EF6\ EADF \times 16^{-8}$
17 4876 E800	11	$0.AFEB\ FF0B\ CB24\ AAFF \times 16^{-9}$
E8 D4A5 1000	12	$0.1197\ 9981\ 2DEA\ 1119 \times 16^{-9}$
918 4E72 A000	13	$0.1C25\ C268\ 4976\ 81C2 \times 16^{-10}$
5AF3 107A 4000	14	$0.2D09\ 370D\ 4257\ 3604 \times 16^{-11}$
3 8D7E A4C6 8000	15	$0.480E\ BE7B\ 9D58\ 566D \times 16^{-12}$
23 86F2 6FC1 0000	16	$0.734A\ CA5F\ 6226\ F0AE \times 16^{-13}$
163 4578 5D8A 0000	17	$0.B877\ AA32\ 36A4\ B449 \times 16^{-14}$
DE0 B6B3 A764 0000	18	$0.1272\ 5DD1\ D243\ ABA1 \times 16^{-14}$
8AC7 2304 89E8 0000	19	$0.1D83\ C94F\ B6D2\ AC35 \times 16^{-15}$

HEXADECIMAL-DECIMAL INTEGER CONVERSION

The following table provides for direct conversions between hexadecimal integers in the range 0−FFF and decimal integers in the range 0−4095. For conversion of larger integers, the table values may be added to the following figures:

Hexadecimal	Decimal	Hexadecimal	Decimal
01 000	4 096	20 000	131 072
02 000	8 192	30 000	196 608
03 000	12 288	40 000	262 144
04 000	16 384	50 000	327 680
05 000	20 480	60 000	393 216
06 000	24 576	70 000	458 752
07 000	28 672	80 000	524 288
08 000	32 768	90 000	589 824
09 000	36 864	A0 000	655 360
0A 000	40 960	B0 000	720 896
0B 000	45 056	C0 000	786 432
0C 000	49 152	D0 000	851 968
0D 000	53 248	E0 000	917 504
0E 000	57 344	F0 000	983 040
0F 000	61 440	100 000	1 048 576
10 000	65 536	200 000	2 097 152
11 000	69 632	300 000	3 145 728
12 000	73 728	400 000	4 194 304
13 000	77 824	500 000	5 242 880
14 000	81 920	600 000	6 291 456
15 000	86 016	700 000	7 340 032
16 000	90 112	800 000	8 388 608
17 000	94 208	900 000	9 437 184
18 000	98 304	A00 000	10 485 760
19 000	102 400	B00 000	11 534 336
1A 000	106 496	C00 000	12 582 912
1B 000	110 592	D00 000	13 631 488
1C 000	114 688	E00 000	14 680 064
1D 000	118 784	F00 000	15 728 640
1E 000	122 880	1 000 000	16 777 216
1F 000	126 976	2 000 000	33 554 432

HEXADECIMAL-DECIMAL INTEGER CONVERSION (continued)

	0	1	2	3	4	5	6	7	8	9	A	B	C	D	E	F
000	0000	0001	0002	0003	0004	0005	0006	0007	0008	0009	0010	0011	0012	0013	0014	0015
010	0016	0017	0018	0019	0020	0021	0022	0023	0024	0025	0026	0027	0028	0029	0030	0031
020	0032	0033	0034	0035	0036	0037	0038	0039	0040	0041	0042	0043	0044	0045	0046	0047
030	0048	0049	0050	0051	0052	0053	0054	0055	0056	0057	0058	0059	0060	0061	0062	0063
040	0064	0065	0066	0067	0068	0069	0070	0071	0072	0073	0074	0075	0076	0077	0078	0079
050	0080	0081	0082	0083	0084	0085	0086	0087	0088	0089	0090	0091	0092	0093	0094	0095
060	0096	0097	0098	0099	0100	0101	0102	0103	0104	0105	0106	0107	0108	0109	0110	0111
070	0112	0113	0114	0115	0116	0117	0118	0119	0120	0121	0122	0123	0124	0125	0126	0127
080	0128	0129	0130	0131	0132	0133	0134	0135	0136	0137	0138	0139	0140	0141	0142	0143
090	0144	0145	0146	0147	0148	0149	0150	0151	0152	0153	0154	0155	0156	0157	0158	0159
0A0	0160	0161	0162	0163	0164	0165	0166	0167	0168	0169	0170	0171	0172	0173	0174	0175
0B0	0176	0177	0178	0179	0180	0181	0182	0183	0184	0185	0186	0187	0188	0189	0190	0191
0C0	0192	0193	0194	0195	0196	0197	0198	0199	0200	0201	0202	0203	0204	0205	0206	0207
0D0	0208	0209	0210	0211	0212	0213	0214	0215	0216	0217	0218	0219	0220	0221	0222	0223
0E0	0224	0225	0226	0227	0228	0229	0230	0231	0232	0233	0234	0235	0236	0237	0238	0239
0F0	0240	0241	0242	0243	0244	0245	0246	0247	0248	0249	0250	0251	0252	0253	0254	0255

HEXADECIMAL-DECIMAL INTEGER CONVERSION (continued)

	0	1	2	3	4	5	6	7	8	9	A	B	C	D	E	F
100	0256	0257	0258	0259	0260	0261	0262	0263	0264	0265	0266	0267	0268	0269	0270	0271
110	0272	0273	0274	0275	0276	0277	0278	0279	0280	0281	0282	0283	0284	0285	0286	0287
120	0288	0289	0290	0291	0292	0293	0294	0295	0296	0297	0298	0299	0300	0301	0302	0303
130	0304	0305	0306	0307	0308	0309	0310	0311	0312	0313	0314	0315	0316	0317	0318	0319
140	0320	0321	0322	0323	0324	0325	0326	0327	0328	0329	0330	0331	0332	0333	0334	0335
150	0336	0337	0338	0339	0340	0341	0342	0343	0344	0345	0346	0347	0348	0349	0350	0351
160	0352	0353	0354	0355	0356	0357	0358	0359	0360	0361	0362	0363	0364	0365	0366	0367
170	0368	0369	0370	0371	0372	0373	0374	0375	0376	0377	0378	0379	0380	0381	0382	0383
180	0384	0385	0386	0387	0388	0389	0390	0391	0392	0393	0394	0395	0396	0397	0398	0399
190	0400	0401	0402	0403	0404	0405	0406	0407	0408	0409	0410	0411	0412	0413	0414	0415
1A0	0416	0417	0418	0419	0420	0421	0422	0423	0424	0425	0426	0427	0428	0429	0430	0431
1B0	0432	0433	0434	0435	0436	0437	0438	0439	0440	0441	0442	0443	0444	0445	0446	0447
1C0	0448	0449	0450	0451	0452	0453	0454	0455	0456	0457	0458	0459	0460	0461	0462	0463
1D0	0464	0465	0466	0467	0468	0469	0470	0471	0472	0473	0474	0475	0476	0477	0478	0479
1E0	0480	0481	0482	0483	0484	0485	0486	0487	0488	0489	0490	0491	0492	0493	0494	0495
1F0	0496	0497	0498	0499	0500	0501	0502	0503	0504	0505	0506	0507	0508	0509	0510	0511
200	0512	0513	0514	0515	0516	0517	0518	0519	0520	0521	0522	0523	0524	0525	0526	0527
210	0528	0529	0530	0531	0532	0533	0534	0535	0536	0537	0538	0539	0540	0541	0542	0543
220	0544	0545	0546	0547	0548	0549	0550	0551	0552	0553	0554	0555	0556	0557	0558	0559
230	0560	0561	0562	0563	0564	0565	0566	0567	0568	0569	0570	0571	0572	0573	0574	0575
240	0576	0577	0578	0579	0580	0581	0582	0583	0584	0585	0586	0587	0588	0589	0590	0591
250	0592	0593	0594	0595	0596	0597	0598	0599	0600	0601	0602	0603	0604	0605	0606	0607
260	0608	0609	0610	0611	0612	0613	0614	0615	0616	0617	0618	0619	0620	0621	0622	0623
270	0624	0625	0626	0627	0628	0629	0630	0631	0632	0633	0634	0635	0636	0637	0638	0639

	0	1	2	3	4	5	6	7	8	9	A	B	C	D	E	F
280	0640	0641	0642	0643	0644	0645	0646	0647	0648	0649	0650	0651	0652	0653	0654	0655
290	0656	0657	0658	0659	0660	0661	0662	0663	0664	0665	0666	0667	0668	0669	0670	0671
2A0	0672	0673	0674	0675	0676	0677	0678	0679	0680	0681	0682	0683	0684	0685	0686	0687
2B0	0688	0689	0690	0691	0692	0693	0694	0695	0696	0697	0698	0699	0700	0701	0702	0703
2C0	0704	0705	0706	0707	0708	0709	0710	0711	0712	0713	0714	0715	0716	0717	0718	0719
2D0	0720	0721	0722	0723	0724	0725	0726	0727	0728	0729	0730	0731	0732	0733	0734	0735
2E0	0736	0737	0738	0739	0740	0741	0742	0743	0744	0745	0746	0747	0748	0749	0750	0751
2F0	0752	0753	0754	0755	0756	0757	0758	0759	0760	0761	0762	0763	0764	0765	0766	0767
300	0768	0769	0770	0771	0772	0773	0774	0775	0776	0777	0778	0779	0780	0781	0782	0783
310	0784	0785	0786	0787	0788	0789	0790	0791	0792	0793	0794	0795	0796	0797	0798	0799
320	0800	0801	0802	0803	0804	0805	0806	0807	0808	0809	0810	0811	0812	0813	0814	0815
330	0816	0817	0818	0819	0820	0821	0822	0823	0824	0825	0826	0827	0828	0829	0830	0831
340	0832	0833	0834	0835	0836	0837	0838	0839	0840	0841	0842	0843	0844	0845	0846	0847
350	0848	0849	0850	0851	0852	0853	0854	0855	0856	0857	0858	0859	0860	0861	0862	0863
360	0864	0865	0866	0867	0868	0869	0870	0871	0872	0873	0874	0875	0876	0877	0878	0879
370	0880	0881	0882	0883	0884	0885	0886	0887	0888	0889	0890	0891	0892	0893	0894	0895
380	0896	0897	0898	0899	0900	0901	0902	0903	0904	0905	0906	0907	0908	0909	0910	0911
390	0912	0913	0914	0915	0916	0917	0918	0919	0920	0921	0922	0923	0924	0925	0926	0927
3A0	0928	0929	0930	0931	0932	0933	0934	0935	0936	0937	0938	0939	0940	0941	0942	0943
3B0	0944	0945	0946	0947	0948	0949	0950	0951	0952	0953	0954	0955	0956	0957	0958	0959
3C0	0960	0961	0962	0963	0964	0965	0966	0967	0968	0969	0970	0971	0972	0973	0974	0975
3D0	0976	0977	0978	0979	0980	0981	0982	0983	0984	0985	0986	0987	0988	0989	0990	0991
3E0	0992	0993	0994	0995	0996	0997	0998	0999	1000	1001	1002	1003	1004	1005	1006	1007
3F0	1008	1009	1010	1011	1012	1013	1014	1015	1016	1017	1018	1019	1020	1021	1022	1023

HEXADECIMAL-DECIMAL INTEGER CONVERSION (continued)

	0	1	2	3	4	5	6	7	8	9	A	B	C	D	E	F
400	1024	1025	1026	1027	1028	1029	1030	1031	1032	1033	1034	1035	1036	1037	1038	1039
410	1040	1041	1042	1043	1044	1045	1046	1047	1048	1049	1050	1051	1052	1053	1054	1055
420	1056	1057	1058	1059	1060	1061	1062	1063	1064	1065	1066	1067	1068	1069	1070	1071
430	1072	1073	1074	1075	1076	1077	1078	1079	1080	1081	1082	1083	1084	1085	1086	1087
440	1088	1089	1090	1091	1092	1093	1094	1095	1096	1097	1098	1099	1100	1101	1102	1103
450	1104	1105	1106	1107	1108	1109	1110	1111	1112	1113	1114	1115	1116	1117	1118	1119
460	1120	1121	1122	1123	1124	1125	1126	1127	1128	1129	1130	1131	1132	1133	1134	1135
470	1136	1137	1138	1139	1140	1141	1142	1143	1144	1145	1146	1147	1148	1149	1150	1151
480	1152	1153	1154	1155	1156	1157	1158	1159	1160	1161	1162	1163	1164	1165	1166	1167
490	1168	1169	1170	1171	1172	1173	1174	1175	1176	1177	1178	1179	1180	1181	1182	1183
4A0	1184	1185	1186	1187	1188	1189	1190	1191	1192	1193	1194	1195	1196	1197	1198	1199
4B0	1200	1201	1202	1203	1204	1205	1206	1207	1208	1209	1210	1211	1212	1213	1214	1215
4C0	1216	1217	1218	1219	1220	1221	1222	1223	1224	1225	1226	1227	1228	1229	1230	1231
4D0	1232	1233	1234	1235	1236	1237	1238	1239	1240	1241	1242	1243	1244	1245	1246	1247
4E0	1248	1249	1250	1251	1252	1253	1254	1255	1256	1257	1258	1259	1260	1261	1262	1263
4F0	1264	1265	1266	1267	1268	1269	1270	1271	1272	1273	1274	1275	1276	1277	1278	1279
500	1280	1281	1282	1283	1284	1285	1286	1287	1288	1289	1290	1291	1292	1293	1294	1295
510	1296	1297	1298	1299	1300	1301	1302	1303	1304	1305	1306	1307	1308	1309	1310	1311
520	1312	1313	1314	1315	1316	1317	1318	1319	1320	1321	1322	1323	1324	1325	1326	1327
530	1328	1329	1330	1331	1332	1333	1334	1335	1336	1337	1338	1339	1340	1341	1342	1343
540	1344	1345	1346	1347	1348	1349	1350	1351	1352	1353	1354	1355	1356	1357	1358	1359
550	1360	1361	1362	1363	1364	1365	1366	1367	1368	1369	1370	1371	1372	1373	1374	1375
560	1376	1377	1378	1379	1380	1381	1382	1383	1384	1385	1386	1387	1388	1389	1390	1391

	0	1	2	3	4	5	6	7	8	9	A	B	C	D	E	F
580	1408	1409	1410	1411	1412	1413	1414	1415	1416	1417	1418	1419	1420	1421	1422	1423
590	1424	1425	1426	1427	1428	1429	1430	1431	1432	1433	1434	1435	1436	1437	1438	1439
5A0	1440	1441	1442	1443	1444	1445	1446	1447	1448	1449	1450	1451	1452	1453	1454	1455
5B0	1456	1457	1458	1459	1460	1461	1462	1463	1464	1465	1466	1467	1468	1469	1470	1471
5C0	1472	1473	1474	1475	1476	1477	1478	1479	1480	1481	1482	1483	1484	1485	1486	1487
5D0	1488	1489	1490	1491	1492	1493	1494	1495	1496	1497	1498	1499	1500	1501	1502	1503
5E0	1504	1505	1506	1507	1508	1509	1510	1511	1512	1513	1514	1515	1516	1517	1518	1519
5F0	1520	1521	1522	1523	1524	1525	1526	1527	1528	1529	1530	1531	1532	1533	1534	1535
600	1536	1537	1538	1539	1540	1541	1542	1543	1544	1545	1546	1547	1548	1549	1550	1551
610	1552	1553	1554	1555	1556	1557	1558	1559	1560	1561	1562	1563	1564	1565	1566	1567
620	1568	1569	1570	1571	1572	1573	1574	1575	1576	1577	1578	1579	1580	1581	1582	1583
630	1584	1585	1586	1587	1588	1589	1590	1591	1592	1593	1594	1595	1596	1597	1593	1599
640	1600	1601	1602	1603	1604	1605	1606	1607	1608	1609	1610	1611	1612	1613	1614	1615
650	1616	1617	1618	1619	1620	1621	1622	1623	1624	1625	1626	1627	1628	1629	1630	1631
660	1632	1633	1634	1635	1636	1637	1638	1639	1640	1641	1642	1643	1644	1645	1646	1647
670	1648	1649	1650	1651	1652	1653	1654	1655	1656	1657	1658	1659	1660	1661	1662	1663
680	1664	1665	1666	1667	1668	1669	1670	1671	1672	1673	1674	1675	1676	1677	1678	1679
690	1680	1681	1682	1683	1684	1685	1686	1687	1688	1689	1690	1691	1692	1693	1694	1695
6A0	1696	1697	1698	1699	1700	1701	1702	1703	1704	1705	1706	1707	1708	1709	1710	1711
6B0	1712	1713	1714	1715	1716	1717	1718	1719	1720	1721	1722	1723	1724	1725	1726	1727
6C0	1728	1729	1730	1731	1732	1733	1734	1735	1736	1737	1738	1739	1740	1741	1742	1743
6D0	1744	1745	1746	1747	1748	1749	1750	1751	1752	1753	1754	1755	1756	1757	1758	1759
6E0	1760	1761	1762	1763	1764	1765	1766	1767	1768	1769	1770	1771	1772	1773	1774	1775
6F0	1776	1777	1778	1779	1780	1781	1782	1783	1784	1785	1786	1787	1788	1789	1790	1791

HEXADECIMAL-DECIMAL INTEGER CONVERSION (continued)

	0	1	2	3	4	5	6	7	8	9	A	B	C	D	E	F
700	1792	1793	1794	1795	1796	1797	1798	1799	1800	1801	1802	1803	1804	1805	1806	1807
710	1808	1809	1810	1811	1812	1813	1814	1815	1816	1817	1818	1819	1820	1821	1822	1823
720	1824	1825	1826	1827	1828	1829	1830	1831	1832	1833	1834	1835	1836	1837	1838	1839
730	1840	1841	1842	1843	1844	1845	1846	1847	1848	1849	1850	1851	1852	1853	1854	1855
740	1856	1857	1858	1859	1860	1861	1862	1863	1864	1865	1866	1867	1868	1869	1870	1871
750	1872	1873	1874	1875	1876	1877	1878	1879	1880	1881	1882	1883	1884	1885	1886	1887
760	1888	1889	1890	1891	1892	1893	1894	1895	1896	1897	1898	1899	1900	1901	1902	1903
770	1904	1905	1906	1907	1908	1909	1910	1911	1912	1913	1914	1915	1916	1917	1918	1919
780	1920	1921	1922	1923	1924	1925	1926	1927	1928	1929	1930	1931	1932	1933	1934	1935
790	1936	1937	1938	1939	1940	1941	1942	1943	1944	1945	1946	1947	1948	1949	1950	1951
7A0	1952	1953	1954	1955	1956	1957	1958	1959	1960	1961	1962	1963	1964	1965	1966	1967
7B0	1968	1969	1970	1971	1972	1973	1974	1975	1976	1977	1978	1979	1980	1981	1982	1983
7C0	1984	1985	1986	1987	1988	1989	1990	1991	1992	1993	1994	1995	1996	1997	1998	1999
7D0	2000	2001	2002	2003	2004	2005	2006	2007	2008	2009	2010	2011	2012	2013	2014	2015
7E0	2016	2017	2018	2019	2020	2021	2022	2023	2024	2025	2026	2027	2028	2029	2030	2031
7F0	2032	2033	2034	2035	2036	2037	2038	2039	2040	2041	2042	2043	2044	2045	2046	2047
800	2048	2049	2050	2051	2052	2053	2054	2055	2056	2057	2058	2059	2060	2061	2062	2063
810	2064	2065	2066	2067	2068	2069	2070	2071	2072	2073	2074	2075	2076	2077	2078	2079
820	2080	2081	2082	2083	2084	2085	2086	2087	2088	2089	2090	2091	2092	2093	2094	2095
830	2096	2097	2098	2099	2100	2101	2102	2103	2104	2105	2106	2107	2108	2109	2110	2111
840	2112	2113	2114	2115	2116	2117	2118	2119	2120	2121	2122	2123	2124	2125	2126	2127
850	2128	2129	2130	2131	2132	2133	2134	2135	2136	2137	2138	2139	2140	2141	2142	2143
860	2144	2145	2146	2147	2148	2149	2150	2151	2152	2153	2154	2155	2156	2157	2158	2159
870	2160	2161	2162	2163	2164	2165	2166	2167	2168	2169	2170	2171	2172	2173	2174	2175

	2176	2177	2178	2179	2180	2181	2182	2183	2184	2185	2186	2187	2188	2189	2190	2191
880	2176	2177	2178	2179	2180	2181	2182	2183	2184	2185	2186	2187	2188	2189	2190	2191
890	2192	2193	2194	2195	2196	2197	2198	2199	2200	2201	2202	2203	2204	2205	2206	2207
8A0	2208	2209	2210	2211	2212	2213	2214	2215	2216	2217	2218	2219	2220	2221	2222	2223
8B0	2224	2225	2226	2227	2228	2229	2230	2231	2232	2233	2234	2235	2236	2237	2238	2239
8C0	2240	2241	2242	2243	2244	2245	2246	2247	2248	2249	2250	2251	2252	2253	2254	2255
8D0	2256	2257	2258	2259	2260	2261	2262	2263	2264	2265	2266	2267	2268	2269	2270	2271
8E0	2272	2273	2274	2275	2276	2277	2278	2279	2280	2281	2282	2283	2284	2285	2286	2287
8F0	2288	2289	2290	2291	2292	2293	2294	2295	2296	2297	2298	2299	2300	2301	2302	2303
900	2304	2305	2306	2307	2308	2309	2310	2311	2312	2313	2314	2315	2316	2317	2318	2319
910	2320	2321	2322	2323	2324	2325	2326	2327	2328	2329	2330	2331	2332	2333	2334	2335
920	2336	2337	2338	2339	2340	2341	2342	2343	2344	2345	2346	2347	2348	2349	2350	2351
930	2352	2353	2354	2355	2356	2357	2358	2359	2360	2361	2362	2363	2364	2365	2366	2367
940	2368	2369	2370	2371	2372	2373	2374	2375	2376	2377	2378	2379	2380	2381	2382	2383
950	2384	2385	2386	2387	2388	2389	2390	2391	2392	2393	2394	2395	2396	2397	2398	2399
960	2400	2401	2402	2403	2404	2405	2406	2407	2408	2409	2410	2411	2412	2413	2414	2415
970	2416	2417	2418	2419	2420	2421	2422	2423	2424	2425	2426	2427	2428	2429	2430	2431
980	2432	2433	2434	2435	2436	2437	2438	2439	2440	2441	2442	2443	2444	2445	2446	2447
990	2448	2449	2450	2451	2452	2453	2454	2455	2456	2457	2458	2459	2460	2461	2462	2463
9A0	2464	2465	2466	2467	2468	2469	2470	2471	2472	2473	2474	2475	2476	2477	2478	2479
9B0	2480	2481	2482	2483	2484	2485	2486	2487	2488	2489	2490	2491	2492	2493	2494	2495
9C0	2496	2497	2498	2499	2500	2501	2502	2503	2504	2505	2506	2507	2508	2509	2510	2511
9D0	2512	2513	2514	2515	2516	2517	2518	2519	2520	2521	2522	2523	2524	2525	2526	2527
9E0	2528	2529	2530	2531	2532	2533	2534	2535	2536	2537	2538	2539	2540	2541	2542	2543
9F0	2544	2545	2546	2547	2548	2549	2550	2551	2552	2553	2554	2555	2556	2557	2558	2559

HEXADECIMAL-DECIMAL INTEGER CONVERSION (continued)

	0	1	2	3	4	5	6	7	8	9	A	B	C	D	E	F
A00	2560	2561	2562	2563	2564	2565	2566	2567	2568	2569	2570	2571	2572	2573	2574	2575
A10	2576	2577	2578	2579	2580	2581	2582	2583	2584	2585	2586	2587	2588	2589	2590	2591
A20	2592	2593	2594	2595	2596	2597	2598	2599	2600	2601	2602	2603	2604	2605	2606	2607
A30	2608	2609	2610	2611	2612	2613	2614	2615	2616	2617	2618	2619	2620	2621	2622	2623
A40	2624	2625	2626	2627	2628	2629	2630	2631	2632	2633	2634	2635	2636	2637	2638	2639
A50	2640	2641	2642	2643	2644	2645	2646	2647	2648	2649	2650	2651	2652	2653	2654	2655
A60	2656	2657	2658	2659	2660	2661	2662	2663	2664	2665	2666	2667	2668	2669	2670	2671
A70	2672	2673	2674	2675	2676	2677	2678	2679	2680	2681	2682	2683	2684	2685	2686	2687
A80	2688	2689	2690	2691	2692	2693	2694	2695	2696	2697	2698	2699	2700	2701	2702	2703
A90	2704	2705	2706	2707	2708	2709	2710	2711	2712	2713	2714	2715	2716	2717	2718	2719
AA0	2720	2721	2722	2723	2724	2725	2726	2727	2728	2729	2730	2731	2732	2733	2734	2735
AB0	2736	2737	2738	2739	2740	2741	2742	2743	2744	2745	2746	2747	2748	2749	2750	2751
AC0	2752	2753	2754	2755	2756	2757	2758	2759	2760	2761	2762	2763	2764	2765	2766	2767
AD0	2768	2769	2770	2771	2772	2773	2774	2775	2776	2777	2778	2779	2780	2781	2782	2783
AE0	2784	2785	2786	2787	2788	2789	2790	2791	2792	2793	2794	2795	2796	2797	2798	2799
AF0	2800	2801	2802	2803	2804	2805	2806	2807	2808	2809	2810	2811	2812	2813	2814	2815
B00	2816	2817	2818	2819	2820	2821	2822	2823	2824	2825	2826	2827	2828	2829	2830	2831
B10	2832	2833	2834	2835	2836	2837	2838	2839	2840	2841	2842	2843	2844	2845	2846	2847
B20	2848	2849	2850	2851	2852	2853	2854	2855	2856	2857	2858	2859	2860	2861	2862	2863
B30	2864	2865	2866	2867	2868	2869	2870	2871	2872	2873	2874	2875	2876	2877	2878	2879
B40	2880	2881	2882	2883	2884	2885	2886	2887	2888	2889	2890	2891	2892	2893	2894	2895
B50	2896	2897	2898	2899	2900	2901	2902	2903	2904	2905	2906	2907	2908	2909	2910	2911
B60	2912	2913	2914	2915	2916	2917	2918	2919	2920	2921	2922	2923	2924	2925	2926	2927

	2944	2945	2946	2947	2948	2949	2950	2951	2952	2953	2954	2955	2956	2957	2958	2959
B80	2944	2945	2946	2947	2948	2949	2950	2951	2952	2953	2954	2955	2956	2957	2958	2959
B90	2960	2961	2962	2963	2964	2965	2966	2967	2968	2969	2970	2971	2972	2973	2974	2975
BA0	2976	2977	2978	2979	2980	2981	2982	2983	2984	2985	2986	2987	2988	2989	2990	2991
BB0	2992	2993	2994	2995	2996	2997	2998	2999	3000	3001	3002	3003	3004	3005	3006	3007
BC0	3008	3009	3010	3011	3012	3013	3014	3015	3016	3017	3018	3019	3020	3021	3022	3023
BD0	3024	3025	3026	3027	3028	3029	3030	3031	3032	3033	3034	3035	3036	3037	3038	3039
BE0	3040	3041	3042	3043	3044	3045	3046	3047	3048	3049	3050	3051	3052	3053	3054	3055
BF0	3056	3057	3058	3059	3060	3061	3062	3063	3064	3065	3066	3067	3068	3069	3070	3071
C00	3072	3073	3074	3075	3076	3077	3078	3079	3080	3081	3082	3083	3084	3085	3086	3087
C10	3088	3089	3090	3091	3092	3093	3094	3095	3096	3097	3098	3099	3100	3101	3102	3103
C20	3104	3105	3106	3107	3108	3109	3110	3111	3112	3113	3114	3115	3116	3117	3118	3119
C30	3120	3121	3122	3123	3124	3125	3126	3127	3128	3129	3130	3131	3132	3133	3134	3135
C40	3136	3137	3138	3139	3140	3141	3142	3143	3144	3145	3146	3147	3148	3149	3150	3151
C50	3152	3153	3154	3155	3156	3157	3158	3159	3160	3161	3162	3163	3164	3165	3166	3167
C60	3168	3169	3170	3171	3172	3173	3174	3175	3176	3177	3178	3179	3180	3181	3182	3183
C70	3184	3185	3186	3187	3188	3189	3190	3191	3192	3193	3194	3195	3196	3197	3198	3199
C80	3200	3201	3202	3203	3204	3205	3206	3207	3208	3209	3210	3211	3212	3213	3214	3215
C90	3216	3217	3218	3219	3220	3221	3222	3223	3224	3225	3226	3227	3228	3229	3230	3231
CA0	3232	3233	3234	3235	3236	3237	3238	3239	3240	3241	3242	3243	3244	3245	3246	3247
CB0	3248	3249	3250	3251	3252	3253	3254	3255	3256	3257	3258	3259	3260	3261	3262	3263
CC0	3264	3265	3266	3267	3268	3269	3270	3271	3272	3273	3274	3275	3276	3277	3278	3279
CD0	3280	3281	3282	3283	3284	3285	3286	3287	3288	3289	3290	3291	3292	3293	3294	3295
CE0	3296	3297	3298	3299	3300	3301	3302	3303	3304	3305	3306	3307	3308	3309	3310	3311
CF0	3312	3313	3314	3315	3316	3317	3318	3319	3320	3321	3322	3323	3324	3325	3326	3327

HEXADECIMAL-DECIMAL INTEGER CONVERSION (continued)

	0	1	2	3	4	5	6	7	8	9	A	B	C	D	E	F
D00	3328	3329	3330	3331	3332	3333	3334	3335	3336	3337	3338	3339	3340	3341	3342	3343
D10	3344	3345	3346	3347	3348	3349	3350	3351	3352	3353	3354	3355	3356	3357	3358	3359
D20	3360	3361	3362	3363	3364	3365	3366	3367	3368	3369	3370	3371	3372	3373	3374	3375
D30	3376	3377	3378	3379	3380	3381	3382	3383	3384	3385	3386	3387	3388	3389	3390	3391
D40	3392	3393	3394	3395	3396	3397	3398	3399	3400	3401	3402	3403	3404	3405	3406	3407
D50	3408	3409	3410	3411	3412	3413	3414	3415	3416	3417	3418	3419	3420	3421	3422	3423
D60	3424	3425	3426	3427	3428	3429	3430	3431	3432	3433	3434	3435	3436	3437	3438	3439
D70	3440	3441	3442	3443	3444	3445	3446	3447	3448	3449	3450	3451	3452	3453	3454	3455
D80	3456	3457	3458	3459	3460	3461	3462	3463	3464	3465	3466	3467	3468	3469	3470	3471
D90	3472	3473	3474	3475	3476	3477	3478	3479	3480	3481	3482	3483	3484	3485	3486	3487
DA0	3488	3489	3490	3491	3492	3493	3494	3495	3496	3497	3498	3499	3500	3501	3502	3503
DB0	3504	3505	3506	3507	3508	3509	3510	3511	3512	3513	3514	3515	3516	3517	3518	3519
DC0	3520	3521	3522	3523	3524	3525	3526	3527	3528	3529	3530	3531	3532	3533	3534	3535
DD0	3536	3537	3538	3539	3540	3541	3542	3543	3544	3545	3546	3547	3548	3549	3550	3551
DE0	3552	3553	3554	3555	3556	3557	3558	3559	3560	3561	3562	3563	3564	3565	3566	3567
DF0	3568	3569	3570	3571	3572	3573	3574	3575	3576	3577	3578	3579	3580	3581	3582	3583
E00	3584	3585	3586	3587	3588	3589	3590	3591	3592	3593	3594	3595	3596	3597	3598	3599
E10	3600	3601	3602	3603	3604	3605	3606	3607	3608	3609	3610	3611	3612	3613	3614	3615
E20	3616	3617	3618	3619	3620	3621	3622	3623	3624	3625	3626	3627	3628	3629	3630	3631
E30	3632	3633	3634	3635	3636	3637	3638	3639	3640	3641	3642	3643	3644	3645	3646	3647
E40	3648	3649	3650	3651	3652	3653	3654	3655	3656	3657	3658	3659	3660	3661	3662	3663
E50	3664	3665	3666	3667	3668	3669	3670	3671	3672	3673	3674	3675	3676	3677	3678	3679

	0	1	2	3	4	5	6	7	8	9	A	B	C	D	E	F
E80	3712	3713	3714	3715	3716	3717	3718	3719	3720	3721	3722	3723	3724	3725	3726	3727
E90	3728	3729	3730	3731	3732	3733	3734	3735	3736	3737	3738	3739	3740	3741	3742	3743
EA0	3744	3745	3746	3747	3748	3749	3750	3751	3752	3753	3754	3755	3756	3757	3758	3759
EB0	3760	3761	3762	3763	3764	3765	3766	3767	3768	3769	3770	3771	3772	3773	3774	3775
EC0	3776	3777	3778	3779	3780	3781	3782	3783	3784	3785	3786	3787	3788	3789	3790	3791
ED0	3792	3793	3794	3795	3796	3797	3798	3799	3800	3801	3802	3803	3804	3805	3806	3807
EE0	3808	3809	3810	3811	3812	3813	3814	3815	3816	3817	3818	3819	3820	3821	3822	3823
EF0	3824	3825	3826	3827	3828	3829	3830	3831	3832	3833	3834	3835	3836	3837	3838	3839
F00	3840	3841	3842	3843	3844	3845	3846	3847	3848	3849	3850	3851	3852	3853	3854	3855
F10	3856	3857	3858	3859	3860	3861	3862	3863	3864	3865	3866	3867	3868	3869	3870	3871
F20	3872	3873	3874	3875	3876	3877	3878	3879	3880	3881	3882	3883	3884	3885	3886	3887
F30	3888	3889	3890	3891	3892	3893	3894	3895	3896	3897	3898	3899	3900	3901	3902	3903
F40	3904	3905	3906	3907	3908	3909	3910	3911	3912	3913	3914	3915	3916	3917	3918	3919
F50	3920	3921	3922	3923	3924	3925	3926	3927	3928	3929	3930	3931	3932	3933	3934	3935
F60	3936	3937	3938	3939	3940	3941	3942	3943	3944	3945	3946	3947	3948	3949	3950	3951
F70	3952	3953	3954	3955	3956	3957	3958	3959	3960	3961	3962	3963	3964	3965	3966	3967
F80	3968	3969	3970	3971	3972	3973	3974	3975	3976	3977	3978	3979	3980	3981	3982	3983
F90	3984	3985	3986	3987	3988	3989	3990	3991	3992	3993	3994	3995	3996	3997	3998	3999
FA0	4000	4001	4002	4003	4004	4005	4006	4007	4008	4009	4010	4011	4012	4013	4014	4015
FB0	4016	4017	4018	4019	4020	4021	4022	4023	4024	4025	4026	4027	4028	4029	4030	4031
FC0	4032	4033	4034	4035	4036	4037	4038	4039	4040	4041	4042	4043	4044	4045	4046	4047
FD0	4048	4049	4050	4051	4052	4053	4054	4055	4056	4057	4058	4059	4060	4061	4062	4063
FE0	4064	4065	4066	4067	4068	4069	4070	4071	4072	4073	4074	4075	4076	4077	4078	4079
FF0	4080	4081	4082	4083	4084	4085	4086	4087	4088	4089	4090	4091	4092	4093	4094	4095

Appendix D
Minimum Binary Scales

DECIMAL NUMBER RANGE				BINARY SCALE
549	755	813	888.	
				+39
274	877	906	944	
				+38
137	438	953	472	
				+37
68	719	476	736	
				+36
34	359	738	368	
				+35
17	179	869	184	
				+34
8	589	934	592	
				+33
4	294	967	296	
				+32
2	147	483	648	
				+31
1	073	741	824	
				+30
	536	870	912	
				+29
	268	435	456	
				+28
	134	217	728	
				+27
	67	108	864	
				+26
	33	554	432	
				+25
	16	777	216	

DECIMAL NUMBER RANGE			BINARY SCALE
			+24
8	388	608	
			+23
4	194	304	
			+22
2	097	152	
			+21
1	048	576	
			+20
	524	288	
			+19
	262	144	
			+18
	131	072	
			+17
	65	536	
			+16
	32	768	
			+15
	16	384	
			+14
	8	192	
			+13
	4	096	
			+12
	2	048	
			+11
	1	024	
			+10
		512	
			+9
		256	

DECIMAL NUMBER RANGE								BINARY SCALE
256.								+8
128.								+7
64.								±6
32.								+5
16.								+4
8.								+3
4.								+2
2.								+1
1.								0
0.5								−1
0.25								−2
0.125								−3
0.062	5							−4
0.031	25							−5
0.015	625							−6
0.007	812	5						−7
0.003	906	25						−8
0.001	953	125						−9
0.000	976	562	5					−10
0.000	488	281	25					−11
0.000	244	140	625					−12
0.000	122	070	312	5				−13
0.000	061	035	156	25				−14
0.000	030	517	578	125				−15
0.000	015	258	789	062	5			−16
0.000	007	629	394	531	25			−17
0.000	003	814	697	265	625			−18
0.000	001	907	348	632	812	5		−19
0.000	000	953	674	316	406	25		−20
0.000	000	476	837	158	203	125		−21
0.000	000	238	418	579	101	562	5	−22
0.000	000	119	209	289	550	781	25	

Appendix E
AMP Instruction Set

ARITHMETIC & LOGIC GROUP

OPERATION NAME & (MNEMONIC)	DESCRIPTION	MACHINE FORMAT (HEX)	TIMING (CYCLES)
ADD (A)	$|M| + |A| \rightarrow A \& C$	0B	1
ADD WITH CARRY (ADC)	$|C| + |M| + |A| \rightarrow A \& C$	0A	1
ADD AND SKIP IF CARRY IS SET (ADSK)	$|M| + |A| \rightarrow A \& C$ If reeulting C = 1. skip one instruction in sequence.	09	1
ADD WITH CARRY	$|C| + |M| + |A| \rightarrow A \& C$	08	1
AND SKIP IF CARRY IS SET (ACSK)	If resulting C = 1. skip one instruction in sequence.	6D	1
DECIMAL CORRECT 1 (DC)	$66_{16} + |A| \rightarrow A$ Intermediate Carry $\rightarrow Q$ (C is not changed)	6E	1
DECIMAL CORRECT 2 (DCC)	$|$ Table 2-11$| + |A| \rightarrow A$ Depending upon states of C & Q	6C. XX	

266

ARITHMETIC & LOGIC GROUP (continued)

OPERATION NAME & (MNEMONIC)	DESCRIPTION	MACHINE FORMAT (HEX)	TIMING (CYCLES)
ADD IMMEDIATE AND SKIP ON CARRY OUT (ADI)	Add the 8-bit byte obtained in the next instruction location to A. Intermediate Carry→Q. C is neither used nor changed. If the carry-out is a 1, the next ROM word is skipped		
LOGIC AND (AND)	|A| AND |M|→A	0D	1
LOGIC OR (OR)	|A| OR |M|→A	0F	1
LOGIC EXCLUSIVE OR (EOR)	|A| $\oplus$ |M|→A	0C	1
COMPLEMENT (COMP)	One's complement of |A|→A	0E	1
SET CARRY FLIP FLOP (SC)	1→C	20	1
RESET CARRY FLIP FLOP (RC)	0→C	24	1
ACCUMULATOR RIGHT SHIFT (ARS)	|A| is shifted 1 bit right, the LSB→C, original |C|→MSB of A	22	1

OPERATION NAME & (MNEMONIC)	DESCRIPTION	MACHINE FORMAT (HEX)	TIMING (CYCLES)
DATA ADDRESS MODIFICATION GROUP			
*LOAD B INDIRECT (LB) (Occupies only 1 ROM word)	The content of the word in location OCO–OCF (page 3, ROM-0) specified by the instruction will be loaded into the least significant 8 bits of the B Register. BU (the 4 most significant bits) will be set to 0. $|SB|$ is destroyed.	CO-CF	2
*LOAD B LONG (LBL) (Occupies 2 ROM words)	The second of the two ROM words will be loaded into the 8 least significant bits of the B Register. BU will be set to 0.	00	2
INCREMENT BL AND SKIP (INCB)	$|BL| + 1 \rightarrow BL$ If the new content of $BL = 0000$, the next ROM word is ignored.	17	1
DECREMENT BL AND SKIP (DECB)	$|BL| - 1 \rightarrow BL$ If the new content of $BL = 1111$, the next ROM word will be ignored.	1F	1
LOAD BM AND BL WITH A (LBA)	$|A| \rightarrow BL$ & BM The content of the currently addressed RAM location $\rightarrow A$	04	1
LOAD BM AND BL WITH X (LBX)	$|X| \rightarrow BL$ & BM	10	1
EXCHANGE BL, BM, AND A (XBA)	$|A| \leftrightarrow |BL, BM|$	19	1
EXCHANGE BL, BM, AND X (XBX)	$|BL, BM| \leftrightarrow |X|$	18	1
SPECIAL ADDRESS (SAG)	The 8 most significant bits of the RAM address output are set to zero for the next cycle only. (The content of B is not affected.)		

OPERATION NAME & (MNEMONIC)	DESCRIPTION	MACHINE FORMAT (HEX)	TIMING (CYCLES)
LOAD A* (LD)	$|M|\rightarrow A$	30-37	1
EXCHANGE* ACCUMULATOR AND MEMORY (EX)	$|M|\rightarrow A$ $|A|\rightarrow M$	38-3F	2
EXCHANGE** AND DECREMENT B (EXD)	$|M|\rightarrow A$ $|A|\rightarrow M$ $|BL-1|\rightarrow BL$ Skip on BL = 1111	28-2F	2
LOAD ACCUMULATOR IMMEDIATE (LDI)	The 8-bit byte contained in the next instruction location$\rightarrow A$	70	2
LOAD A FROM X (LAX)	$|X|\rightarrow A$	12	1
LOAD X FROM A (LXA)	$|A|\rightarrow X$	1B	1
EXCHANGE X AND A (XAX)	$|A|\leftrightarrow|X|$	1A	1
EXCHANGE SA AND SB (XS)	$|SA|\leftrightarrow|SB|$ (All 12 bits)	06	1
CYCLE SA AND A (CYS)	An 8-bit right shift of the SA Register occurs with the 8 least significant bits of SA replacing the content of A. The content of A replaces the most significant 8 bits of SA.	6F	1

*In addition to the primary functions of these instructions, the BM portion of B Register is also modified by the result of an exclusive-OR of the least significant 3 bits of BM and 3 bits of the Instruction Immediate Field. Example: LD (35) is executed: the |B| prior to the execution is 0A3 (BM = A or 1010): upon execution of LD the modification of BM is (010) $\oplus$ (101)$\rightarrow$the least significant three bits of BM.

**Same as LD and EX with respect to BM modification, except that B is further modified by decrementing BL by 1.

CONTROL TRANSFER GROUP

OPERATION NAME & (MNEMONIC)	DESCRIPTION	MACHINE FORMAT (HEX)	TIMING (CYCLES)
TRANSFER CONTROL (TT)	Control is transferred to a ROM word on the current page. The least significant 6 bits of P are replaced by the 6-bit Immediate Field.	80 – BF	1
TRANSFER AND MARK (TM)	The address of the next ROM word is saved in SA. $|SA| \to SB$. Control is transferred to one of the subroutine entry addresses (ROM-0, pages 4 through 7). TM occupies only 1 ROM word, with the entry address information coming from page 3 of ROM-0.	D0 – FF	2
TRANSFER LONG (TL)	Control is transferred to any ROM word on any page. The first byte causes bits 9–12 of P to be modified. The second byte→bits 1–8 of P.	50 – 5F	2
RETURN (RTN)	Executes a return from a subroutine by causing $|SA| \to P$. Also $|SA| \leftarrow |SB|$.	05	1
RETURN AND SKIP (RTSK)	Same as RTN. but skips the first ROM word after subroutine return.	07	1
SKIP ON CARRY FLIP-FLOP (SKC)	Skips the next ROM word if C = 1.	15	1

CONTROL TRANSFER GROUP (continued)

OPERATION NAME & (MNEMONIC)	DESCRIPTION	MACHINE FORMAT (HEX)	TIMING (CYCLES)
SKIP ON A = 0 (SKZ)	Skips the next ROM word if A = 0.	1E	1
SKIP IF BL = INSTRUCTION IMMEDIATE FIELD (SKBI)	Skips the next ROM word if BL = bits 1—4 of the instruction.	40—4F	1
INPUT-OUTPUT GROUP			
OUTPUT LONG (OL) (2 ROM words)	The first ROM word causes the CPU to set I0 Enable. The second ROM word is received by the IOC and decoded for address and command. The content of A is placed on the Data Bus.	21—XX	2
INPUT LONG (IL) (2 ROM words)	IL functions similarly to OL, with the exception that the information held on the Data Bus replaces the content of the Accumulator.	25—XX	2
DISCRETE INPUT (DIA)	Data in the 4-bit Discrete Input Register is transferred to the least significant 4 bits of A. The most significant 4 bits are unaffected.	27	1
DISCRETE OUTPUT (DOA)	The least significant 4 bits of |A| are transferred to the Discrete Output Register. |A| is unchanged.	1D	1

271

Appendix F

RAM Work Sheet

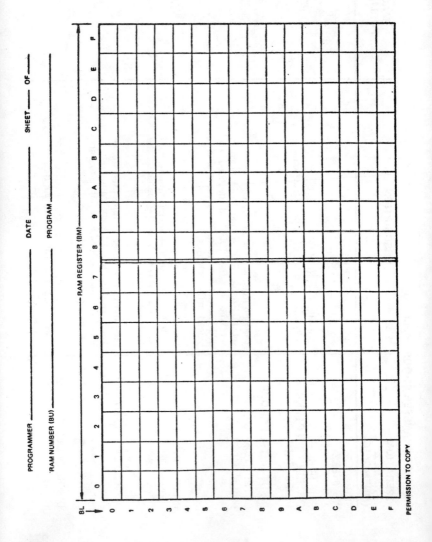

PROGRAMMER ————— DATE ————— SHEET ——— OF ———

RAM NUMBER (BU) ————— PROGRAM —————

RAM REGISTER (BM)

PERMISSION TO COPY

Index

Index

278